Treasuring the Goods of Marriage in a Throwaway Society

Written or edited by the same author:

Wisdom's Apprentice

On Love and Charity

Sacred Choral Works

Resurgent in the Midst of Crisis

Noble Beauty, Transcendent Holiness

A Reader in Catholic Social Teaching

Tradition and Sanity

John Henry Newman on Worship, Reverence, and Ritual

And Rightly So: Selected Letters and Articles of Neil McCaffrey

Reclaiming Our Roman Catholic Birthright

The Holy Bread of Eternal Life

The Ecstasy of Love in the Thought of Thomas Aquinas

Are Canonizations Infallible? Revisiting a Disputed Question

Ministers of Christ

True Obedience in the Church

From Benedict's Peace to Francis's War

Integralism and the Common Good, vol. 1: *Family, City, and State*

The Road from Hyperpapalism to Catholicism

The Once and Future Roman Rite

Sixty Years After: Catholic Writers Assess the Legacy of Vatican II

Praise for *Treasuring the Goods of Marriage in a Throwaway Society*

"In this powerful work, combining theological insight, cultural analysis, and spiritual counsel, Dr. Kwasniewski unfolds the ascetical-mystical dimensions of marriage, family, consecrated virginity, and celibate priesthood, while exposing the demonic forces of the sexual revolution that undermine these wondrous gifts of God. He speaks along the way of true mercy, the virtue of modesty, vigilance in the use of media, the unique role of fatherhood, the dignity of the body, the calling to spiritualize the flesh, the co-perfecting of spouses in common life, and much more. A book to ponder prayerfully!"

— **Bishop Athanasius Schneider**
Auxiliary Bishop of Astana in Kazakhstan

"Our contemporary disputes about the relationship between men and women — and their relationship to God — desperately require a return to fundamental principles, together with a talent for communicating them. Peter Kwasniewski has both to offer in this book, a collection of his writings on life and love, chastity and marriage. With his depth of knowledge of the theology of St. Thomas Aquinas and an awareness of current trends of thought and practice that vitiate Christian morality, he provides solid encouragement to virtue."

— **Leila M. Lawler**
Author of *The Summa Domestica: Order and Wonder in Family Life*

"Has there ever been an age less hospitable to the Church's teaching on sex, love, and life? With wisdom, good sense, and a deeply Catholic spirit, Dr. Kwasniewski helps us to see how true and good and beautiful this teaching is."

— **Dr. Regis Martin**
Professor of Theology, Franciscan University of Steubenville

"*Treasuring the Goods of Marriage in a Throwaway Society* is a comprehensive survey of the sources of divine revelation and the intellectual tradition of the Church regarding the goods of marriage. Through extensive research, Dr. Kwasniewski draws from a wide range of disciplines, including theology, liturgy, jurisprudence, and philosophy, to form an in-depth understanding of the profound truths about marriage and family that have been all but lost in today's throwaway culture. This book is a treasure."

— **Fr. Sebastian Walshe, O.Praem.**
Author of *Understanding Marriage and Family: A Catholic Perspective*

"For some time now, human beings have basically forgotten how to reason. We refuse to recognize that an intelligible reality exists and that when we fail to live in accord with it, we can expect misery. That misery becomes a gift when it opens us to supernatural truths, such as the truths revealed in Scripture. We see, for example, Jordan Peterson beautifully working his way to grasping and defending the Christian view of marriage — one that requires the spouses to ceaselessly 'work' at their marriages and in particular to work at forming and loving their children. Peter Kwasniewski is so much further down the road than Peterson. Through this incisive book, we are blessed with a glimpse of how to reap the unsurpassable joy of the loving union of spouses where not only bodies but souls become one."

— Dr. Janet E. Smith
Former Father McGivney Chair of Life Ethics
at Sacred Heart Major Seminary in Detroit
and author of *Humanae Vitae: A Generation Later*

"Marriage is the state in life entered by the vast majority of Catholics, and yet, in today's world, this 'holy estate' is treated as having little eternal significance, as merely part of the apparatus of a 'throwaway society,' to be indulged in according to our whims — and if we're ever unhappy, an annulment or a divorce is at hand. In this wide-ranging book, a mixture of the Church's bimillennial wisdom and the author's reflections arising from his own experience, Peter Kwasniewski deals masterfully with a variety of topics concerning marriage and family, priesthood and religious life. Here for the pondering is an abundance of ideas and suggestions that cannot but enliven our own thinking about a subject of both great interest and great importance."

— Thomas Storck
Author of *Seeing the World with Catholic Eyes, An Economics of Justice and Charity,* and *Foundations of a Catholic Political Order*

Peter A. Kwasniewski

Treasuring the Goods of Marriage in a Throwaway Society

SOPHIA INSTITUTE PRESS
Manchester, New Hampshire

Cover design by Updatefordesign Studio.

On the cover: Raphael's *The Marriage of the Virgin*, 1504
(WWWM34) © incamerastock / Alamy Stock Photo.

Sophia Institute Press
Box 5284, Manchester, NH 03108
1-800-888-9344
www.SophiaInstitute.com

Sophia Institute Press is a registered trademark of Sophia Institute.

paperback ISBN 978-1-64413-854-0

ebook ISBN 978-1-64413-855-7

Library of Congress Control Number: 2022947792

First printing

To the Father from whom all fatherhood is named,
the Son in whom we are made adopted sons,
the Holy Spirit, Lord and Giver of Life,
and Our Lady, Mother of Mercy,
with profound gratitude
for my wife and
children

Desecration is a kind of defense against the sacred, an attempt to destroy its claims. In the presence of sacred things our lives are judged, and to escape that judgment, we destroy the thing that seems to accuse us.

— Roger Scruton

If a man is not steadfast and zealous in the fear of the Lord, his house will be quickly overthrown.

— Sirach 27:3

Up in the heights of the tradition, protected in grandeur and difficulty, are life-giving waters that descend with surprising force into a world thirsty for courage.

— Glenn Arbery

Contents

III. Virginity and Celibacy

IV. Contraception and Abortion

Preface

Traditional marriage — that is, an indissoluble and exclusive vowed relationship between one man and one woman, ordered to the begetting, nurturing, and education of children both for the common good of earthly society and for the kingdom of heaven — has found many insightful defenders in our times, which are characterized by unrelenting attack on Christian and natural-law morality. One might recall only a few of the many shining lights whom God has raised up: Fulton Sheen, Karol Wojtyła, Cardinal Caffarra, Cardinal Burke, Paul Quay, Janet Smith, William May, Michael Waldstein, Paul Vitz, Mary Eberstadt, Carl Trueman — and the list could go on. I have enjoyed and benefited from reading their works over the decades. Why, then, another book that takes up these themes?

As an Aristotelian philosopher, a liturgical theologian, a composer, and a Benedictine oblate (after many years, I am still trying to figure out how all of those fit together!), I approach classic marriage and family issues from specific angles. For example, many books talk about the humanity of the unborn as known through science and sound ethical reasoning, the moral evil of the act of killing the unborn, the societal and cultural effects of a widespread acceptance of such killing, and so forth. All of this is perfectly true and features in these pages as well. But in my opinion, more attention needs to be given to the philosophical and theological meaning or implications of abortion, its underlying spiritual causes, and its relationship to the Church as kingdom of the God who is Lord and Giver of life.

What is the "sacramental" or sacral-symbolic significance of receiving and giving life, as opposed to the anti-sacramental, anti-sacral symbolism of refusing or eliminating life? How is contraception reflective of a certain epistemology and ontology — that is, a way of thinking about self and other and God and world, their being and their value? Just as marriage presents to us a template or pattern of the Christian life and the life of the world to come, so, too, abortion crystallizes the opposition to life here and hereafter: it is the evil fruit, or rather anti-fruit, that reveals the nature of the tree from which it springs — namely, the contraceptive mentality, which undermines or repudiates chaste and fruitful matrimony and is rooted in rebellion against the law of God.

The human body is also a liturgical vessel, an instrument of divine worship, a "place" where God wishes to meet man and where man can yield himself to God. When it is abused by being turned away from its doxological purpose, it becomes a broken, tuneless instrument, a grating and discordant music, a place of confusion, shame, self-hatred, and despair. The Church's traditional forms of worship are meant to impress upon us the primacy of our immortal soul, temple of the indwelling Trinity, as well as the glory to which our body is destined in the wedding feast of heaven. Christian life as it radiates outward from worship habituates us to thinking in both a more rooted way and a more "unearthly" or "heavenly" way about ourselves and how we love. A Russian theologian gives sublime expression to this truth:

> *In wisdom Thou hast made them all* (Ps 104:24). Lovely is Your world, Lord, and everything is lovely within it. And — strange for me to say it — lovely too is my own bodily nature, lovely because You created it. How often we lose heart on account of our sinfulness, which obscures from our very selves our true image! Satan is a slanderer, and he slanders both us and — to do us harm — God's creation as well; he implants confusion and faintheartedness within us, and as a result faintheartedness and laziness grow in our souls. We lose ourselves, we refuse to wage battle against ourselves for the sake of our very selves; but God, who created all things in wisdom, by the same wisdom created each of us as well. God's Wisdom was an artist before His face (Prov 8:30), and she artistically formed our image as well, which we, like spiritual artists, must also form.[1]

The dignity of marriage and family as well as the evils ranged against it, most prominently pornography, self-abuse, premarital promiscuity, divorce, contraception, and abortion, can and should be seen from a sacramental-mystical vantage — that is, not only in terms of what they are but also in terms of what they *signify* spiritually and cosmically. Just as there is a mysticism of the Christian life that embraces all its dimensions, including the bodily and the sexual,

1 Sergius Bulgakov, *Spiritual Diary*, trans. Mark Roosien and Roberto J. De La Noval (Brooklyn: Angelico Press, 2022), 103.

so there is an anti-mysticism, often draped in the borrowed splendors of its true counterpart, that distorts and inverts the bodily and the sexual, reconfiguring them as rivals to the divine, blinders of the inner eye, poisons of love, and sappers of society. This anti-mysticism presents its crudest form in the pseudoscientific materialism that drives both Marxism and Western liberalism. If we do not keep searching for the deepest roots both of our errors and of our salvation, we may be like those who would try to fix a building with rotten foundations by giving it a new coat of paint and a bit of landscaping. All the more necessary is this deep digging and rebuilding of foundations now that *Roe v. Wade* has been overturned by the Supreme Court of the United States of America, exacerbating already pronounced divisions and bringing into ever-greater public visibility the cosmic clash between heavenly and infernal spirits that stands behind the political battles of our time.

In these pages, I endeavor to make a distinctive contribution to the vindication of marriage and family — and indeed, of consecrated virginity and priestly celibacy as well — in the midst of a growing totalitarianism that seems hell-bent on relativizing, diluting, penalizing, and ultimately obliterating them.

In this book, I cite a wide variety of sources, secular and sacred, philosophical and theological. A favorable citation should not be taken to imply that I have no difficulties with that source in other respects. If I quote the Second Vatican Council, John Paul II, and the *Catechism of the Catholic Church*, it is simply because they have formulated a certain truth particularly well. As we see in the writings of the Angelic Doctor, a properly Catholic attitude welcomes the truth wherever it is found, even as it may respectfully register disagreements or indicate difficulties.

I have written extensively about the question of the distinction of the sexes and the diverse and complementary roles of men and women in the Church — above all, as concerns participation in the sacred liturgy — in my book *Ministers of Christ: Recovering the Roles of Clergy and Laity in an Age of Confusion* (Crisis Publications, 2021). The traditional Catholic understanding unfolded and defended in that work is taken here as a given. I have also, in my two-volume work *The Road from Hyperpapalism to Catholicism: Rethinking the Papacy in a Time of Ecclesial Disintegration* (Arouca Press, 2022), addressed certain vexing issues of the pontificate of Pope Francis, such as *Amoris Laetitia*, the shift on capital punishment, and larger questions on papal authority and governance.

The chapters of this book were developed out of articles published at *New Liturgical Movement*, *OnePeterFive*, *Rorate Caeli*, *LifeSiteNews*, *Crisis Magazine*,

The Catholic Faith, Second Spring, Truth & Charity Forum, Homiletic & Pastoral Review, and *Social Justice Review,* as well as previously unpublished material. Part of chapter 27 also appears in "A Theological Review of the Amazon Synod" in volume 2 of *Road from Hyperpapalism* (see pp. 203–5). I should note that chapter 11 mounts a rather dense philosophical argument to give the deepest possible foundation to points made in earlier chapters. Readers who fear they would get bogged down in the metaphysics should feel free to skip over it and continue with chapter 12.

Psalms are cited by their Septuagint/Vulgate numbering.

I would like to express my gratitude to a saint whose intercession, I believe, had something to do with moving me to concentrate on this book at this time. As I mentioned in the preface to *The Holy Bread of Eternal Life* (Sophia Institute Press, 2020), my family has the custom, as do many families, of picking out "saints for the year" on the first of January. In recent years, the saints have been picked for us by friends at a monastery to which we have close ties. My saint for 2022 turned out to be St. Rita of Cascia, and my daily assignment has been to ask her intercession especially for "troubled and broken families." I have a confident hunch that St. Rita was involved in the genesis of the present book, and for that, I thank both her and Our Lord.

This work bears a dedication to the Most Holy Trinity and to Our Lady. Those who turn to the Blessed Virgin Mary, confidently asking her aid, will never want for light or strength. She is the perfect teacher and exemplar — of a femininity at peace with itself and in harmony with the order of creation; of virginity open to the divine will; of motherhood filled with life and giving life; and, above all, of human nature and personality fully living its innermost mystery as fashioned, in the words of the Lord, "unto our image and likeness" (Gen. 1:26).

— Peter A. Kwasniewski
July 2, 2022
Visitation of the Blessed Virgin Mary

I

Marriage and Family

By the teaching of Sacred Scripture, we learn that there are four kinds of marriage.... The first is between a man and his lawful wife. The second is between Christ and holy Church. The third is between God and the just soul. The fourth is between the Word and human nature.... In these four kinds of marriage we discover, with admiration and veneration alike, something most dignified. Through the first, it is brought about that two be in one flesh; through the second, it is brought about that two be in one body; through the third, it is brought about that two be in one spirit; through the fourth, it is brought about that two be in one person.

— Pope Innocent III, *Liber de Quadripartita Specie Nuptiarum*

1

Love and Sacrifice

"Thou wilt be pleased with the sacrifice of justice, oblations and burnt offerings upon Thy altar, Lord" (Ps. 50:19). Here the psalmist teaches us that the Lord desires our sacrifices as long as they are *just* and are made upon *His* altar.

What else could this mean but that He wants us to sacrifice ourselves by living justly and by entering into His sacred mysteries enacted upon the holy altar of the Catholic Church? For it is by the Great Sacrament, the Holy Eucharist, that man offers himself to God through the offering of Jesus Christ, who alone is perfectly pleasing to the Father.

Since the Eucharist furnishes us with the very pattern of the Christian life, we will find here a lesson about marriage, where spouses must make sacrifices for each other's good. The sacrament of Matrimony is a holy altar upon which man and woman offer themselves up in a love that will consume their hearts as the holy fire beheld by Moses engulfed the bush without destroying it (Exod. 3:2).

This self-offering resembles the purgative stage of the spiritual life. The sacrament of Marriage has all three elements of the life of prayer: purgation, illumination, and union. Those who have been faithfully married for many years can testify that greater happiness goes hand in hand with greater sacrifice. Union is never a given, to be taken for granted; it is the fruit of suffering and perseverance.

The ancient Roman Rite has as its opening prayer for Friday after Ash Wednesday: "Watch over the fast we have undertaken, O Lord, and let this bodily penance also be a truly spiritual exercise to make us strong." This prayer summarizes Isaiah 58:1–9, where the prophet stresses that true fasting means the supplanting of our willfulness by the will of God. We are reproved: "Behold in the day of your fast your own will is found and you exact of all your debtors." The first quality noted about the willful is their preoccupation with exacting debts from debtors, a tendency to keep accounts on the behavior of others. The willful have gotten caught up in the mentality of debt and payment instead of building up the true charity that loves and does not count the cost.

Isaiah teaches here a crucial lesson for the married. To be lived worthily, marriage demands fasting from one's will — and yet this fasting must be of the right kind, not used to gain leverage on the other person, becoming an excuse for exacting debts; nor can the fasting be ostentatious and distracting, as in the case of those who "sound a trumpet before them, as hypocrites do in the synagogue and the streets, in order that they may be honored" (Matt. 5:43–48; 6:1–4).

In spite of the divine grace that never fails us, who can say that he or she has never fallen along the way, has never sinned in this vale of tears? "If we say that we have no sin, we deceive ourselves, and the truth is not in us" (1 John 1:8). "O Lord, remember not our iniquities of the past; let your mercy come quickly to us, for we are being brought very low. Help us, O God of our salvation, for the glory of thy name; deliver us, and forgive our sins, for thy name's sake!" (Ps. 78:8–9). By ourselves, we are sinners; we are brought low by our faults and our sins, and without God's mercy coming quickly to us, there is no way for us to live out the vocation to which God is calling us.

There is an aspect of man, a dark double called "the old Adam," that rebels against the good. It is clear from Isaiah, however, that the solution is not a self-despising maceration or masochism: "Deal your bread to the hungry, and bring the needy and the harborless into your house; when you shall see one naked, cover him, and despise not your own flesh" (Isa. 58:7).

What are we doing whenever we strive to make ourselves better, or to help another toward perfection? We are dealing bread to the hungry and covering the naked. Every time we forgive each other, particularly in marriage, it is like the dressing of a wound; it is like the noble compassion of the Samaritan who bent down by the side of the road to take up the neglected sufferer. It is by loving the "enemy" without and within for the love of God — loving the enemy in the only proper way to love him: namely, by leading him to embrace the gospel — that the acceptable sacrifice, the real effacement of self and the giving of self to the other, takes place and is continually taking place.

The psalmist implores us to love the Lord's house: "One thing have I asked of the LORD, this will I seek after: that I may dwell in the house of the LORD all the days of my life, to behold the beauty of the LORD, and to inquire in his temple" (Ps. 26:4). How marvelous to think about St. Joseph, the last of the Jewish patriarchs, who asked and sought after the Lord so perfectly that he was granted the singular privilege of dwelling in the very house of the Lord Jesus, or rather, of offering his own house to be the roof over the Savior's head — He who, in His public ministry, would later have nowhere to lay His head (Luke 9:58). Joseph beheld the Lord's beauty and inquired in His temple by caring for the needs of Him whose Body *was* the new temple (John 2:21).

Christian matrimony beckons a man and a woman to treasure each other in the recesses of their home, to receive with peaceful heart the consolations and trials of their common life, to place all joys and sufferings at the foot of the Cross — for from the Cross alone comes the strength and dignity of their calling (see Eph. 5:21–33). They are called to love the Lord, to whom each was originally and eternally espoused in Baptism, which makes the Christian one spirit with the Lord (see Hos. 2:19; 1 Cor. 6:17). This spiritual marriage to their heavenly benefactor endows their own marriage with the protection of the Lord's holy temple.

The poet Wordsworth beautifully expresses the need for human love to remain rooted in its divine origin and to aspire to it as the final goal:

> Unless this love by a still higher love
> Be hallowed, love that breathes not without awe;
> Love that adores, but on the knees of prayer,
> By heaven inspired; that frees from chains the soul,
> Bearing, in union with the purest, best,
> Of earth-born passions, on the wings of praise
> A mutual tribute to the Almighty's Throne.[2]

Without embracing the holy and life-giving Cross through daily prayer, self-denial, good works, and sacramental worship, marriage is left exposed to the tempests of the world, the temptations of the flesh, and the machinations of the devil. Spouses fall prey to sensuality, sloth, indifference, despair, even hatred, if they start in subtle ways, then more openly, to view and treat each other as settled enemies, opponents of real or imaginary needs and wants. The only real "pastoral program" the Church has ever had and will ever have is the Cross of Christ.

The command Jesus gives is not merely to love our enemies and pray for those who persecute us, though we might have thought this difficult enough, and work for a lifetime! No, His advice is more radical: "You are to be perfect, even as your heavenly Father is perfect" (Matt. 5:48). To be perfect means to bring everything within oneself and within one's marriage and family under

[2] William Wordsworth, "The Prelude," stanza VI, lines 97–103, in *The Oxford Book of English Mystical Verse*, ed. D. H. S. Nicholson and A. H. E. Lee (Oxford, UK: Clarendon Press, 1917), no. 68.

the yoke of love, into the kingdom of heaven. One has to learn to be humble in one's love, for it is easier for a camel to pass through the eye of a needle than for a rich man — a person in love with what he is and has — to enter into the kingdom of heaven (cf. Matt. 19:24).

We are to become *perfect* — that is what the ancient pagans missed before the coming of the Lord. They thought it enough to be virtuous, to do virtuous things, to fulfill one's duties and agreements, to be a "good citizen." That was the whole shape of a good life. The Christian aims for more: taking up his cross and dying to himself, he lives *for others*; he takes their sufferings and struggles as his own. Persevering in community life is a kind of crucifixion, as Blessed Columba Marmion said,[3] yet with an outcome not of defeat but of victory. For the worst defeat is selfishness; the greatest victory, unselfish love.

"Be ye perfect" is equivalent to saying: love in every way; do not love only when it is convenient or easy or natural to love, but cast yourself into the furnace of love, who is Christ, who died for men while all of them were still sinners and outcasts — who died to make men worthy of love by the worth His precious Blood restored to them.

The only way we can begin to love as we should is to ask God unceasingly for the grace to be transformed from within, where the old Adam, that dark double, still lurks and tries to hide under a million excuses and disguises. By making this prayer in all earnestness we are already making progress towards the goal. If these things are done, if they are persevered in, "then shall your light break forth as the morning, and your health shall speedily arise, and your justice shall go before your face, and the glory of the LORD shall gather you up" (Isa. 58:8).

[3] See Columba Marmion, *Christ the Ideal of the Monk: Spiritual Conferences on the Monastic and Religious Life*, trans. a nun of Tyburn Convent (Stamullen, Ireland: Cenacle Press, 2022): "So true it is that the common life easily becomes a continual source of friction for our weak nature.... Constant fidelity to our engagements constitutes a veritable mortification: we are, by nature, so inclined to independence, so fond of liberty and change!... Let us again look at our Divine Saviour in His Passion.... Because He remained fastened to the Cross by love, He gave His Father infinite glory, worthy of the Divine perfections. We, too, fastened ourselves to the cross on the day of our profession; we did so out of love; and if we remain faithful to our post of immolation it is still through love.... To stay a long time in a place of waiting, and there to bear monotony and annoyances, can become singularly burdensome and require a big dose of endurance. We must however remain firm and be patient till God's good time" (180–81); "the common life, that penance of penances" (185).

2

Belonging to Each Other

By the rubrics of the Solemnization of Matrimony in the Book of Common Prayer, the man is instructed to say to the woman as he places the ring upon her finger: "With this ring I thee wed, with my body I thee worship [i.e., reverence], and with all my worldly goods I thee endow: In the Name of the Father, and of the Son, and of the Holy Ghost. Amen."[4]

The spouses *give* of themselves because they *belong* to each other. Their mutual homage and lifelong union is a ratification of the covenant written that day upon their hearts by the fiery finger of the Holy Spirit, written with the word of the entire person and the absolute weight of past, present, and future as a testimony to the immortality of the human soul and the divine origin of its love. If vows like this are not possible, human beings are not rational animals or children of God.

The nuptial vow is an imitation of the Virgin Mary's faith: "Be it done *to me* according to *thy word*" (Luke 1:38). This one timeless utterance — said by Eve to Adam, Sarah to Abraham, Rebecca to Isaac, Rachel to Jacob, Mary to Joseph, Christ to His Father, the Church to Christ — is the solemn attestation of undying love, the triumph of love over death. "I am my beloved's, and my beloved is mine" (Song of Sol. 6:3).

This is why, for the Christian, divorce is not merely cruel and wrong but impossible and inconceivable. To make oneself, one's life and destiny, into a *yes* and then to say *no* is to erase the genuine freedom of the will and annihilate one's own identity as a bearer of promises. Freedom can survive only in a climate of

[4] I cite the Book of Common Prayer because of the beauty and depth of its language in this passage. The rites of marriage have always been very diverse and plentiful in Christendom, with no official Latin rite; almost every country has had (and still has) its own customs and formulations.

love, and love in a climate of exceptionless commitment, not a storm of chance or a desert of uncertainty. In marriage vows seriously intended, the man *becomes* the woman's, and the woman *becomes* the man's — in St. Paul's words, "you are not your own" (1 Cor. 6:19). Like father and child, husband and wife are *correlative*. If the father had never existed, the child, too, would vanish. Divorce of what is intrinsically united is no more possible than separating rationality from humanity. In this sense, the rejection of plighted love (divorce) is like the rejection of plighted religion (apostasy), which is itself an image of the rejection of reason (nihilism).[5]

Think of the devotion of the Virgin Mary to her Son. He asked everything of her, and she was not found wanting to His plea. When we plight faith with God, it is done *in promise of* a future beatitude we do not presently enjoy. The grandeur of faith consists in this free and unconditional surrender to a Lover whom we do not see but whose solemn word we trust.[6]

Imagine the wife of a young man gone off to war. She knows she may never see him again; she knows that nothing can give her certainty of his faithfulness overseas. But if she loves him, she will keep faith with him in expectation of reunion. Scripture says of Jacob that he "served seven years for Rachel: and they seemed but a few days, because of the greatness of his love" (Gen. 29:20). Although in human love betrayal or death may intervene, the will to love is stronger than either because it springs from the deepest spiritual core of man's heart.

In the case of our divine Lover, He longs to make Himself known to us: He has not left us orphans. Why the Incarnation? Why the parables and Passion of Jesus Christ? Why miracles? Why saints and mystics? Are these not the bouquets, the love letters, the passionate outpourings of God to man? Furthermore, if God has created the universe in a fecundative overflow of His perfect goodness, will He make it impossible for us to find Him and, when He is found, impossible for us to keep Him?

Unlike the ephemeral dreams and tragic fractures of human love, which by its very nature remains subject to change, the love of God remains everlastingly: He is faithful; He will not betray His children. They are His, and He would have them return to Him, as the father wants the prodigal son back in his arms, under his roof. We begin our mortal life in a state of alienation from God; our entire

[5] I am speaking here of *active* divorce, that is, seeking and initiating a divorce against the will of the other, not of *passive* divorce, in which a spouse is the victim of unchosen legal proceedings.

[6] See chapter 22.

life is a pilgrimage to find our way back to Him. The Father waits for us with a feast, and for our sake, He has allowed the killing not of a fatted calf but of His own beloved Son, that we might return to Him with confidence and rest our weary head on His bosom, like the poor beggar Lazarus reposing in the bosom of Abraham.

Here on earth, we can but search and follow the star: we must follow whatever light is visible to us with the unwavering faith of the Magi. Thomas Valpy French, Msgr. Ronald Knox's grandfather, wrote these words about his religious struggles: "I own I have been much perplexed.... I can but come to this, that when *full* light is not given, one must accept the best light one has, and move slowly forward with *some* hesitancy but still more *trust*."[7] That is what it looks like to abide in hope and to be faithful to one's promises, "looking for the blessed hope and coming of the glory of the great God and our Savior Jesus Christ" (Titus 2:13).

The traditional language of "rights" or "debts" in marriage was criticized a great deal before and around the time of the Second Vatican Council and has all but disappeared from Catholic discourse. Nevertheless, it bears reexamination. For it is important to recognize, particularly in our times of confusion over indissolubility, that once a marriage comes into existence, something in each spouse *belongs, by right, to the other,* and no longer simply to oneself.

Consider again the way marriage vows are formulated and spoken: "I, *N.* [the sign of my identity], give myself to you, *N.*, to be your lawfully wedded husband/wife...." The exchange is not a limited and retractable contract: it is uninhibited, irrevocable, selfless — the self is commended to the care of the *other*. I am no longer "my own business," for I *belong* to the other, I am in some sense his (or her) *possession*. The spouses can make claims on each other because each has a true and conclusive *right* over the other. That is precisely the import of *vows*, as opposed to agreements, contracts, arrangements, alliances, liaisons, trials, or flings.

A comparison with solemn religious vows may be helpful. The woman who "enters religion," as the saying goes, makes an irrevocable and unconditional vow to be spiritually wed to the Lord Jesus Christ; the man who enters religion

[7] Thomas Valpy French to Mrs. Moulson, September 12, 1890, in Rev. Herbert Birks, *The Life and Correspondence of Thomas Valpy French, First Bishop of Lahore*, vol. 2 (London: John Murray, 1895), 323.

vows to be wholly at His disposal and in His courtly service. This is no mere rainy-day fallback but the consecration of one's entire life to another.

That is why both marriage and religious life demand earnest preparation, clear-sighted intention, constant labor and prayer for perseverance, and a full willingness to accept the yoke of the other "in good times and in bad, in sickness and in health," in bright splendor and in dark nights.[8]

You are not your own — this is the resplendent cry that bursts from the mouth of the Apostle (1 Cor. 6:19). You, husband, and you, wife: you are not your own; you *belong* to each other, and you therefore owe each other *everything*.[9] This owing of the debt extends itself naturally, spontaneously, and fittingly to the children, toward whom the parents incur responsibilities and from whom they receive the blessings of joy, support, and suffering: a real participation in the paschal mystery of Christ. Every member in the family belongs, in various ways, to every other. No one is only his own.

You are not your own. We incur an eternal debt to God simply in virtue of having been created out of nothing by His wise and beneficent will. We owe Him our very being, because He makes us *to be*; He gives us the *act of being*, the flowing font of our personhood, the dynamic energy that constitutes us as real entities instead of possible ones. As if that were not enough, He saves us: "you have been redeemed at a great price" (1 Cor. 6:20).

Marriage is analogous to creation and redemption. God refashions the spouses *as* husband and wife through their freely given vows, and in a mystery of one-many, once-always, the exercise of their separate wills brings about their union of life and love. Through the vows, the relationship (by which I mean their dependence on each other) passes from possibility to reality: it becomes a *real being*, no mere idea or fancy.

The married, although they do not acquire a sacramental character in the strict sense, are truly changed: their foundation has shifted from self to other, from isolation to communion.[10] Each acquires a new relation to the other, rooted

[8] See chapter 12.

[9] Everything, that is, consistent with God's commandments — a qualification that applies to all human relationships and actions.

[10] Certain theologians argue that marriage confers a "quasi-character" because God instills in the spouses an enduring disposition and right to receive matrimonial sacramental grace, as long as the spouses are alive. For a brief account, see Francis A. P. Solá and Joseph F. Sagüés, *Sacrae Theologiae Summa* IVB: *On Holy Orders and Matrimony, On the Last Things*, trans. Kenneth Baker (n.p.: Keep the Faith, 2016), nos. 269–70.

in reason and will, by which they are newly constituted in the kingdom of God and in the domain of this world. So intimate is this relation that only death, the literal dissolution of one of the spouses, can put a *temporal* period to it. Yet inasmuch as the beatified soul of man bears within itself all that it has done within its vocation for the glory of God, the bond between spouses can continue in heaven — not as it exists on earth (see Mark 12:25) but in a transfigured higher state of perfect union that was only imperfectly realized in this life.

The foregoing helps to show why the physical union of man and woman makes sense only in the context of marriage. It is traditionally called the "marital (or nuptial) act" precisely because it is that act whereby the spiritual debt of the vows is symbolically and actually paid; it is the transient image of an enduring commitment, the momentary evidence of an ever-present intention to love and serve.

Without a vowed communion of souls, this act forfeits its meaning. Outside of marriage, the act undermines itself: it defeats its own higher purpose and becomes either an empty exercise, of which the more intelligent and artistic are bound to grow tired, or a bestial indulgence without personal value. For there cannot be a uniting of bodies worthy of human persons unless there is a prior union of souls in the plighting of solemn vows, whereby man and woman bestow upon each other the exclusive right to each other — whereby they give *themselves* to each other. Anything else is self-contradictory, or worse, mediocre, what Nietzsche would call "half-and-half."

To paraphrase the same philosopher, the hearts of man and woman desire "deep, deep eternity."[11] Our hearts desire the Whole and will not rest until we have the Whole. Marriage is a spiritual whole, a common good, made up of intrinsic parts: the husband and the wife. Remove the whole, and the parts dissolve, just as the hand loses its very substance when severed from the body and remains a hand only equivocally. Damage the whole, take away the principle of the whole, and the parts perish, just as a human being dies when cut in half, or as the body decays when the soul departs.[12]

A nuptial vow is the binding together of two *spirits*, so that their grace, peace, joy, and charity may overflow into and be reinforced by their bodily togetherness.

[11] These two phrases come from *Thus Spake Zarathustra*. The actual words of the latter phrase are: "Doch alle Lust will Ewigkeit —, / — will tiefe, tiefe Ewigkeit!" ("But all joy seeks eternity —, / — seeks deep, deep eternity!"). See chapter 4 for a further example of Nietzsche's speaking the truth.

[12] See Aristotle, *Parts of Animals* I.1; *On the Soul* II.1.

The beauty of the inner act (two persons united by one vow) redounds upon the beauty of the outer act (two persons in one flesh). The truth of the inner act precontains and magnifies the truth of the outer act. The goodness of the inner act purifies and illumines the outer act. This is another way in which it is true to say: "What God has joined together, let no one put asunder" (Matt. 19:6).

3

For Lust or Love of Children?

It takes no special observational skills to see that the world around us is saturated with sex. But is it saturated with love? In some ways, it seems that the two are inversely proportional. The more untethered, aimless, and hyperactivated the sexual drive, the less room there is for personal love — that is, a friendship between persons for their own sakes and not for the gratification they deliver. Chastity — the virtue of controlling the sexual appetite for the sake of developing well-rounded human relationships — is valuable precisely because it protects and liberates the power of loving *persons* as they deserve.

In marriage, the persons whom chastity makes it possible to love include not only one's spouse but the children whom God will entrust to the couple — the *future* persons who are hidden within the love of the present.

In the Old Testament book of Tobit, we are given an icon of noble married love in the couple Tobias and Sara. On their wedding day, Tobias said to Sara, "We are the children of saints, and we must not be joined together like heathens that know not God." Then he prayed, "And now, Lord, Thou knowest that not for fleshly lust do I take my sister to wife, but only for the love of posterity, in which may Thy Name be blessed for ever and ever" (Tobit 8:5, 9). We can learn at least five lessons from this dense pair of verses.

First, those who belong to the People of God — for Tobias and Sara, the nation of Israel; for Christians today, the new Israel, the Body of Christ — are "children of saints" and should live guided by the law of God, which, as John Paul II reminds us in *Veritatis Splendor,* is *always* for our greater good and never for our harm. We should not, therefore, behave like heathens who are utterly ignorant of their own worth in the sight of God and of the profound respect they should receive from others.

Second, prayer to the Lord is the condition *sine qua non* for progress in friendship, especially that of marriage. Notice that Tobias does not become absorbed in Sara, as much as he loves her, but turns to God, from whom he knows that he will receive the grace he needs to love her unselfishly. It is a paradox: if we want to love another person well, we cannot become fixated on or obsessed with that person, for this always suffocates and destroys love. The relationship has to be broken open to allow in the presence of God, who brings eternity and infinity with Him.

Third, Tobias calls his wife "my sister." In speaking thus, he shows the intimate nature of his love, as between siblings at peace. His is not a consuming, possessive love that sucks dry the object and spits it out when finished but a tender, chivalrous bond that looks more to what they have in common and how they might call forth the best in each other. This phrase "my sister" also calls to mind the ardent words of the bridegroom to the bride in the Song of Songs: "Thou hast wounded my heart, my sister, my spouse, thou hast wounded my heart with one of thy eyes, and with one hair of thy neck" (4:9). This verse testifies to an *eros*, or erotic love, that is nonetheless permeated with the reserve and respect of family love.

Fourth, Tobias swears to the Lord that he is not taking Sara "for fleshly lust but only for the love of posterity." This seems like an astonishing thing for him to say — does he not love Sara *herself*? Is he only looking for children? But the contrast in his statement shows what he is thinking. For him, the contrast is between lusting after a woman's embrace, which reduces her to a means, and loving her as the total woman she is, including her mysterious power of fertility, her motherhood. When a man loves a woman with children in mind, he is loving her more, because he is loving more of her: all the fullness that she holds in promise and in desire. In short, Tobias is bearing witness to the truth, taught by *Casti Connubii* and *Humanae Vitae*, that the procreative purpose of marriage is what *defines* the union of spouses, making it distinct from every other type of human relationship. Without offspring, the very existence of the two sexes, let alone their ordering to each other, would make absolutely no sense.[13]

[13] A particularly luminous exposition of this truth, albeit not as high in authoritative status as the aforementioned encyclicals, is Pius XII's Address to Midwives on the Nature of Their Profession, October 29, 1951. The growing attacks on *Humanae Vitae* from (*horribile dictu*) the Pontifical Academy for Life — gutted of its former consistently pro-family and pro-life membership and repopulated by Pope Francis with progressives — are, in fact, attacks on the foundations of Catholic morality as authoritatively formulated and consistently reaffirmed by many popes. See my article "Fr Bryan Houghton's Crisis of Faith and the Joy

Finally, Tobias says that he and his wife seek a posterity "in which may Thy Name be blessed for ever and ever." Here, most beautifully, we see that the ultimate end of marriage is not merely bringing children into the world but bringing them into the world *for the Lord*, that they might know and love Him and give glory to His Name. For Christians, this takes on an even deeper dimension, for we bring children to natural birth in order to bring them to supernatural birth in Baptism, by which they are made over to the Father and become *His* children, living the life of His Son Jesus Christ.

Behold the unfathomable physical and spiritual fruitfulness to which Christians are given access! Yet how do so many modern-day disciples of the Master respond to His summons "Let the little children come to me, and do not hinder them" (Matt. 19:14)? They say, "No, thanks, we would rather hinder them."

This was not the Jewish way; this is not the Christian way. Everyone who is going to get married or is newly married should align their hearts with the wonderful prayer of Tobias, which has so much to teach us in so few words.

We can deepen our admiration for the exemplary couple Tobias and Sara by listening to the wise words of a Doctor of the Church, St. Robert Bellarmine. Speaking of Psalm 127:1, "Blessed are all they that fear the Lord: that walk in his ways," he writes:

> "Blessed are all they," be they men or women, great or small, nobles or plebeians, learned or unlearned, in one word, all without exception; then alone will they be truly happy, that is, fortunate, contented, joyful, in the very best possible temper, a thing so much coveted by all, when they really fear God; that is, when they dread offending him, and, under the influence of such fear, never fall from God's grace, which is the fountain of all good. Now, a sign of such fear is "to walk in his ways," because such holy fear springs from love; and the Lord says, "If you love me, keep my commandments"; and again, "He that has my commandments and keepeth them, he it is that loveth me"; and again, "He that loveth me not, keepeth not my commandments."[14]

Turning then to verse 3 of the same psalm, "Thy wife as a fruitful vine, on the sides of thy house. Thy children as olive plants, round about thy table," he notes:

---

of *Humanae Vitae*," *OnePeterFive*, July 19, 2022, https://onepeterfive.com/fr-bryan-houghtons-crisis-of-faith-and-the-joy-of-humanae-vitae/.

14 St. Robert Bellarmine, *A Commentary on the Book of Psalms*, trans. John O'Sullivan (Fitzwilliam, NH: Loreto Publications, 2003), 338.

> The second blessing enjoyed by the man "that fears God and walks in his ways" consists in his having only one wife, should he ever marry; and, in marrying, that he will be influenced more by a desire of propagating the human race than by any sinful or unworthy desires, as the angel admonished Tobias when he said: "Thou shalt take the virgin with the fear of the Lord, moved rather for love of children than for lust"; and Tobias himself truly said, "And now, Lord, thou knowest that not for fleshly lust do I take my sister to wife, but only for the love of posterity." He, therefore, says, "thy wife," not thy wives or thy concubines, "as a fruitful vine," with a large family, like a fruitful vine that sends out a number of branches, "on the sides of the house"; a domestic wife that stays at home, looking after the business indoors, while her husband cares for the business outside....
>
> The third blessing, the education of the children, is now introduced. They who fear God and walk in his ways will not only have many children, but they will be well brought up and educated, because they will be taught, from their earliest infancy, to fear God and to walk in his ways. He, therefore, says, "Thy children as olive plants, round about thy table," that, by beholding them all together, eating with them, and living with them, you may have the greater pleasure and enjoyment with them.[15]

Finally, on verse 6, "And mayest thou see thy children's children; peace upon Israel":

> Another addition to the happiness of the blessed in their country above [viz., the heavenly Jerusalem] will consist in their beholding there "the children of their children" — that is, not only those who, through them, were born to God, but also the children of those children who, to the end of the world, shall have been brought to God, and will thus have cause of rejoicing for them all as if they belonged to themselves.[16]

True wisdom from a great Jesuit saint! Well did he understand how blessed by the Lord are Catholic men and women who, fearing the Lord and walking in His ways, remain faithful in marriage and bring many children into the world and into the Church — in spite of all the hardships and sufferings this fidelity entails, even at the hands of those who should know better. The Society of

[15] Bellarmine, *A Commentary on the Book of Psalms*, 338–39.

[16] Bellarmine, *A Commentary on the Book of Psalms*, 339.

Jesus has produced two Doctors of the Church, and it would be wise for today's Jesuits, at all levels, to drink in their healthful doctrine.

One last thought. Each year, we celebrate the feast (or feasts, depending on which calendar you might be following) of Sts. Anne and Joachim.[17] In Byzantine icons, Anne and Joachim are shown greeting one another at the city gate, tenderly embracing and kissing. Their love was pure but totally human: they, too, had longed for children and had been afflicted with barrenness. The Lord intervened marvelously in bestowing on them the gift of the greatest human person in the history of the world: the Ever-Virgin Mother of God, Mary Most Holy.[18] The prayer of Tobias is not, therefore, inherently about having many children. It is about loving children and being open to the gift of them, whenever and however the Lord wills to send them to us, and, most of all, humbly accepting His will.

17 On the traditional Roman calendar, St. Anne is celebrated on July 26 and St. Joachim on August 16. On the modern calendar of Paul VI, they are both placed on July 26. Their Eastern feast is July 25.

18 See Xavier Perrin, *The Radiance of Her Face: A Triptych in Honor of Mary Immaculate*, trans. Sr. Laetitia Payne and Sr. Deirdre Michael Clarke (Kettering, OH: Angelico Press, 2017); on St. Anne in particular, see pp. 25–40.

4

The Surpassing Gift of Life

In spite of being notoriously anti-Christian, the German philosopher Friedrich Nietzsche has left us in his writings many insights that admit of a Christian rereading. It's like transposing a score from minor to major and changing the tempo and dynamics: you will hear a very different piece of music, though many notes on the page will look the same.

As a grad student in philosophy, I copied down in my journal the following passage from *Thus Spake Zarathustra*:

> You are young and wish for a child and marriage. But I ask you: Are you a man entitled to wish for a child? Are you the victorious one, the self-conqueror, the commander of your senses, the master of your virtues? This I ask you. Or is it the animal and need that speak out of your wish? Or loneliness? Or lack of peace with yourself? Let your victory and your freedom long for a child. You shall build living monuments to your victory and your liberation. You shall build over and beyond yourself, but first you must build yourself, perpendicular in body and soul. You shall not only reproduce yourself, but produce something higher. May the garden of marriage help you in that![19]

Surely there are problems with Nietzsche's perspective in this passage. But what would happen if we reread it in a Christian light?

The fundamental reason for marriage is the procreation and education of offspring, in the absence of which one cannot explain why male and female sexes even exist to begin with. Christian parents strive to generate, educate, and leave behind worthy Christian sons and daughters who will surpass their

[19] Friedrich Nietzsche, "Child and Marriage," chap. 20 in *Thus Spake Zarathustra*, trans. Thomas Common (Mineola, NY: Dover Publications, 1999), 44.

parents. This "will to marriage" for the sake of descendants who will climb higher and conquer more could well describe the Catholic ideal of matrimony for the sake of rearing saints.

St. Thomas Aquinas says that husband and wife should "pay the debt" to each other *both* from the virtue of justice, because they belong to each other — justice, after all, is to give what is due — *and* from the virtue of religion, to broaden the fields of the kingdom of God. There is no bourgeois fluff in this honest picture of marriage: it is a common endeavor, a labor of joy and pain, a meeting point of creation and sacrifice, done for the reign of justice and religion. Man and woman are given to each other for the sake of producing something higher than themselves: a family, God's family, the domestic church, citizens of the heavenly Jerusalem.

Nietzsche spoke of "building yourself, perpendicular in body and soul," so that from an ethically superior man would arise living monuments to a victory over mediocrity and to a liberation from the self-imposed limits of the rest of men. Whether he intends it or not, Nietzsche is describing nothing other than the supreme victory of Christ on Calvary, which unleashed into the world a power of love that can never be equaled, surpassed, exhausted, or suppressed, and with it, the liberation of mankind from our guilty pact with sin, death, and the devil.

Those words of Jesus as He was about to plunge into His hour of obedience, surrender, and conquest ring out down through the ages, swallowing Nietzsche in their grandeur: "Now is the judgment of this world, now shall the ruler of this world be cast out; and I, when I am lifted up from the earth, will draw all men to myself" (John 12:31–32). In the "hour" when He is glorified, the hour when the Son of Man is lifted up on the Cross, drawing to Himself everyone who believes in Him, *now* is the judgment of this world — not the world as God created it, but the world of fallen man who exalts himself; the world of darkness, hatred, egoism, which the Son of Man exposes as a darkness unworthy of man. Now shall the ruler of this world, the ringleader of hatred, lies, and self-aggrandizement, be cast out, driven out — by what? By the Cross of Jesus. Wherever *His* Cross is, there is love, love that gives all of itself to the final drop of blood; and this is absolutely incompatible with selfishness.

Hence, the devil cannot function, cannot act, wherever this love is present and active. The devil is driven out, or exorcised, from the hearts of believers who are "possessed" by the Spirit of Truth, "dispossessed" of the lying spirit.[20]

[20] This is why the traditional rites of Baptism in East and West have always contained multiple exorcisms. See, e.g., *The Roman Ritual*, vol. 1, *The Sacraments*

Whoever clings to the Cross of Christ is freed from the reign of the devil and ushered into the light — that is, eternal life, which is to know the Father and the Son, the glory of an infinite love. This love is *the truth of reality*. "God is love, and he who abides in love abides in God, and God abides in him" (1 John 4:16).

It is the unexpected arrival in our world of Jesus's testimony to *the* truth of reality — the one nonnegotiable truth — that leads to *krisis*, that is, to the *separation* between light and darkness and to *judgment* as well as *condemnation* (all of these being possible meanings of the Greek *krisis/krino*). The Son of God is sent for this purpose, to testify to the truth and to win over souls who are searching for the truth — "Socratic souls," we might call them, souls hungry for meaning and hope.

In Jesus Christ, we have the origin, the model, and the full realization of man: not the Übermensch or "superman" hypothesized by Nietzsche, but the God-Man, the King of kings and Lord of lords. No one was ever more "perpendicular in body and soul" than the sinless Son of God, who was lifted up on the Cross and who stood up in the Resurrection. He drank the cup of bitterness and transformed it into the blood of love. He gave Himself to His immaculate Bride forever, and she, in turn, gives herself forever, one flesh, one spirit. From His victory in freedom, from her ardent surrender, proceed innumerable children in this fertile garden of marriage. How blessed, how privileged we are to be taken up into *His* fertility, into "the power of an indestructible life" (Heb. 7:16), into that cloud of witnesses who conquered the accuser by the blood of the Lamb (Rev. 12:10–11)!

Christians must reject contraception, therefore, not merely because practicing this vice leads to evil consequences, such as selfishness in relationships, unbridled lust, treating children as objects and possessions, and demeaning the personal dignity of the body by turning it into an object. No, the deepest reason is that human fertility is a sublime gift, an imitation of God Himself, a way in which we participate in His act of creation and providence.

The greatest pagan philosophers already recognized this truth. Plato saw fertility as the expression sought by beauty: beautiful things naturally seek to multiply themselves. Proclus saw fertility as the metaphysical property of goodness: anything truly good spreads itself. Aristotle saw it as the way in which all

---

and Processions, trans. and ed. Rev. Philip T. Weller (Boonville, NY: Preserving Christian Publications, 2005), 39–51, 85–111.

things strive to partake of the divine fullness of life: if one cannot exist eternally, like God, one can echo that eternity through offspring.[21]

It is no accident that ancient religions were characterized by cults, rites, and offerings focused on fertility. The central theme of wedding ceremonies was always fertility, begetting and bearing new life. Traditional initiation rites centered on the new and mysterious power of generation — boys became men, and girls women, because they could now exercise paternity or maternity, in common with their elders in society. And *always*, there was seen to be something godlike in this power of procreation because it reflected the power of creation hidden in the depths of nature or in the heart of the creative God. Just as man was called upon to exercise "providence" or foresight in imitation of God, so, too, he was called upon to participate in the work of creation. This is what *pagans* already perceived, still groping in the shadows of a world without revelation — unenlightened by the splendor of the Christian truth that God Himself lives a life of infinite "fruitfulness" in the relations of the Most Holy Trinity!

There is a certain aura of holiness about the power of sexuality, one rung on the ladder that is supposed to lead us to God, as Anthony Esolen points out:

> When you are in the presence of something holy, the right response is to submit to it, to be taught by it, to take your direction from it, to regard it with awe, honor, reverence, and gratitude. The human body is holy: it was fashioned by the hand of God. Its being-male and being-female is holy. The sexual powers are sacred because they are aimed toward bringing into being a new human person, a being endowed with a soul that can find its fulfillment only in God. It is a tremendous power, to shelter in your body the capacity to engender that new person, the power of fatherhood, the power of motherhood. How do we treat this power? With a shrug, with contempt. Tools for pleasure, that's all. Now try, just try, getting someone contemptuous of the holiness marked upon his body to sense the holiness of the God he cannot see.[22]

21 "For the most natural of works for living things which are complete and not disabled or spontaneously generated is the making of another like themselves (an animal an animal, a plant a plant), so that they might always share, insofar as they are able, in what always exists and in the divine. For all things have an appetite for this and do whatever they do according to nature for the sake of this." Aristotle, *On the Soul* II.4, 415a28–b2.

22 Anthony Esolen, "A Conciliar Church on a Path to Schism with the Council Itself," *Crisis Magazine*, July 20, 2022, www.crisismagazine.com/2022/a-conciliar-church-on-a-path-to-schism-with-the-council-itself.

When man can dominate his ability to have children and uses that dominion to prevent children from coming into existence, this abusive power already shows a divorce between his life (a parcel of particular desires, ambitions, anxieties, and so forth) and the goodness of life itself, which is endlessly sharable, as in the Blessed Trinity. In other words, even if a man or a woman finds his or her own existence a good, *being itself* is not felt to be a good to be multiplied. Existence is either neutral or negative; one brings a child into the world calculating the net profits and losses.[23]

Life is the first and most basic good, the one prior to and foundational of all others. We are talking here about an unconscious, pre-voluntary attitude: the love of life simply speaking, and the innate desire to share it, produce it, foster it, rejoice in it. If ever children are *not* included within a young man's or young woman's desires in thinking ahead to marriage, both the individual and the society must be profoundly diseased. There has been an atrophying of the will to live; the most elemental love of all, *love of being,* has waned almost to the point of vanishing. Contraception points to spiritual death, the death of the natural "love affair" with life.[24]

Hence, what Pius XI was reaffirming in *Casti Connubii,* what Paul VI was upholding with *Humanae Vitae,* is not some kind of arbitrary "rule," an enforced mortification of human desire. The Church is upholding the goodness of being, the beauty of creation, the godlike gift of procreation, the call to go beyond ourselves in love.

What moderns have lost sight of the most — and this extends to many Catholics as well — is the beauty of the primary end of marriage: children. Marriage is a partnership *for life,* in both senses: it is for always, and it is fruitful, for *new* life. God's love is never without fruit. Any love that imitates Him will not be without fruit either. So to think about marriage is to think about more than oneself and one's partner; it is to think about the gift of children God wishes to bring into the world and into the Church through the spouses' love and stable commitment, in which He will call forth all they have to give — and this will bring them to their full stature as He intended it.

The child, an immortal soul created by God with a body fashioned of the parents' own flesh, the singular fruit of their mutual love and of His eternal love, destined for heaven through Baptism and a life of faith — this child is the reason

[23] See Marc Barnes, "Abortion Is Eugenics," *New Polity,* May 11, 2022, https://newpolity.com/blog/abortion-is-eugenics.

[24] See chapter 29.

God brings a Christian man and woman together. It is not the *only* reason He brings them together, but without it, marriage would not exist at all. Nothing, nothing in the whole of creation, can compare with the value and worth of a single child, a son of man, a son of God. One human person is more valuable than the entire universe of nonhuman creatures — every bit of land, sea, sky, and space, all the animals and plants, all of it. And yet so many people live as if just about anything else takes precedence over the fruit of the womb, the person into whom God has breathed the breath of earthly life, into whom He breathes eternal life by the sacraments. If we fully understood this mystery of life, we would die for sheer wonder; and if we understand it just a little, we will never again make the mistake of devaluing marriage or denigrating its primary end.

5

Fatherhood and the Being of the Home

In a letter of sympathy to Evan Charteris, whose father had just died, Hilaire Belloc wrote:

> Now what has come upon you is as hard a thing as any man can have to bear. The inanimate friends, which are the truest and which never betray, the walls and scents of home, when we lose these we lose, as it were, ourselves. It is a sharp foretaste of death.... To lose one's home, Evan, is to lose one's bones and one's skin. I know it. To lose unique and mutual affection is almost (in a mad metaphor) to lose one's soul.[25]

What is left if *the home* vanishes? Little more than an incoherent mess of sensual data rushing at us from the vast world, with no possibility of resting among those to whom we know we belong. If a man seeks to find meaning while refusing to belong to his family, he will find nothing more than transient distractions to stimulate and occupy him for the present moment, until his thoughts bring him back to the emptiness of his rootless situation.

The French Catholic philosopher Gabriel Marcel (1889–1973) echoes Blaise Pascal and Søren Kierkegaard when he writes:

> I am inclined to think that those people are becoming ever more numerous whose existence coagulates round a few satisfactions which from outside seem almost incredibly petty: the daily bridge party, the football match, some recreation connected either with love or food. They would not miss these pleasures *for anything in the world*. If for some reason or another they have to do without them, existence itself becomes a desert,

[25] *Letters from Hilaire Belloc*, ed. Robert Speaight (London: Hollis & Carter, 1958), 62–63.

> a blank night of gloom. There is, of course, the most direct relation between the exaggerated value which is given to them and the insipidity which characterizes the general substance of life — an insipidity which can in an instant become nauseating. In every department the passage from what is insipid to what is unendurable is imperceptible.[26]

The lack of normalcy during the COVID pandemic forced millions of people to rethink their priorities, their work, their recreation, their family time, their children. It forced the question: What is the personal value of my home to me? Do I even *have* a home? Or have I been so drawn away in other directions that I have failed to do what it takes to remain connected with or to establish with others such a mysterious place?

When the heart of the rootless man tries to make a nest in the desperate vacuity of his whirlwind life and predictably fails, he will only redouble the search for temporary distractions, until his life becomes a fleeing from, not a movement toward, reality. The home is the first and lasting context of the fullness we can speak of as "welcome," "familiarity," "belonging." Strip it down or take it away, and eventually the only thing remaining is a frivolous masquerade. Behind the mask is nothing, yet the elaborate process of masking we see going on around us in the world — a masquerade that may be said already to have developed its own protocol, values, and lifestyle, especially in the virtual world created by social media — enables rootless men and women to bear for a time the emptiness of their existence, the inversion of being, and the nausea that would result from staring into it.

The "outer world," the world outside of us, has meaning only in terms of a stable reference point from which we gain our sense of belonging, of rootedness. When we speak of "going away," we imply that there is something central and fixed from which we depart: we go away from *home*. What does it mean to travel, if not to leave behind something familiar and to return to it afterward? The concepts "domestic" and "foreign," "near" and "far," "local" and "foreign" would have no meaning if we did not intuitively understand, as the basis of all such concepts, "home" and "away from home."

Each of us approaches the world from within a place where we are already welcome, *not* strangers — or at least where we feel we ought to be and could be

[26] Gabriel Marcel, "The Creative Vow as Essence of Fatherhood," in *Homo Viator: Introduction to a Metaphysic of Hope,* trans. Emma Craufurd (Chicago: Henry Regnery, 1951), 116.

welcome, whatever the strains and difficulties may be due to a history of human failings. This feeling of welcome, which fits like a glove and warms like hot cocoa, is hidden within the meaning of the word "familiar." If there is no home — no household, no hearth, no mother and father, no family — then the world loses its intelligibility, its benevolence, its promise; it becomes a place of emptiness and alienation, the echo chamber of the ego. We can no longer compare what we encounter along the way with that which is first and better known to us. Our center of gravity, our language and our sentiments, are so tightly bound up with our homes that we cannot even realize the extent of our indebtedness unless something goes tragically wrong.

Home is a locus of activities, memories, undefinable experiences, a shared dialect, a household way of doing things one doesn't exactly find anywhere else in the world — all circling around the mother and the father. There is no home without a man and a woman who, under God's causality, give life to their children, and thus bring into being a complete (if diminutive) community of reciprocal love, care, sacrifice, authority, dependency, education, and transmission of culture.

This home is the soil where life — physical, spiritual, cultural — is rooted, and whence it draws sustenance from day to day, year to year. For these reasons, it is an elementary *given* of human life. The home, ensouled by the family, is the beginning of the person — the beginning of our life, our consciousness, our development, our ability to engage the world, our adaptation to the demands accompanying maturity, our success in meeting others and loving them. In a real sense, home is a person's greatest natural (i.e., nonsupernatural) treasure in this world. The present times, as strange and strained as they are, push us inevitably toward these truths, or at least nudge us to awaken to them and become more appreciative of goods we may have taken for granted or failed to invest in.

Through the home of one's childhood as well as the home one may later establish with a husband or a wife, one learns to receive and reciprocate love; one makes oneself *available* to others. In our own homes, by working for and with our families, we fulfill our fundamental vocation to name and cultivate, rule and serve, carry the Cross and extend the kingdom of God.

A divine origin and a sacred purpose

When we speak of *family*, we are dealing with a rich and subtle reality that can be grasped only by reflecting on many experiences and aspects of life. We cannot give a cut-and-dried definition without in some way ignoring the ambiguity and depth of the mystery of what it means to be "kin," to share blood and culture and love, to live as one in many. Marcel writes:

> Contrary to the persistent humanistic illusion, we have good reason to assert that family relationships, like human matters in general, afford no consistency, no guarantee of solidity. It is only when they are referred back to a superhuman order, which here below we cannot grasp apart from its signs and indications, that their truly sacred character becomes apparent.[27]

In other words, they afford no consistency or solidity if they are severed from the superhuman order that endows them with their sacredness.

In its race to be as liberated as possible, the modern age has forgotten that the most important things in human life are complex and duty-bound. Fatherhood may be the most perfect example. If we were to reduce paternity to a mere biological episode with a genetic aftermath, it would have very little moral, religious, or transcendent meaning. Calling God "our Father" would be absurd if we limited ourselves to speaking in a physiological way.

To understand what "fatherhood" means, we must move out of the limited spheres of thought marked off by the world. Intimately bound up with human fatherhood are the irreducible realities of *domus,* the home or household, and *munus regale,* the kingly office that the man receives from the Almighty Father to rule and govern, protect and provide, love and serve.

What exactly *is* the reality of fatherhood? When considering a uniquely human reality, we must not limit ourselves to the external manifestations, hoping to define it in terms of what it does or how it usually appears. For a man is not simply what he *does,* but rather, he acts according to what he *is.* "Out of the abundance of the heart the mouth speaketh" (Luke 6:45). Anything can be stamped and sent along with a definition, if we are content with a bundle of items tied together by ephemeral circumstances. Knowing the *being* of a thing requires more than knowing its "look" and operation, all the havings and doings that belong to it. The man who happens to be a railway conductor is not defined in his being as a ticket puncher. Personhood transcends functionality. "The word 'tabulation' or 'repertory' is the best word for describing what the self is *not.*"[28]

[27] Marcel, *Homo Viator,* 96.

[28] Gabriel Marcel, *Metaphysical Journal,* trans. Bernard Wall (Chicago: Henry Regnery, 1952), 177.

Fatherhood is not, first and foremost, a physiological, psychological, legal, or social phenomenon. To stuff it into any one of those boxes would be either to reduce it to a hard fact — like the betrayal of personality seen in statistics and anatomy lessons — or to drape it in sentimentality and convention.

> If we try to define fatherhood in strictly biological terms, we are really not talking of it at all, but of procreation. If we introduce considerations of a judicial or sociological order, we expose ourselves to no less a danger; it is that of allowing fatherhood to be absorbed in a conception which is relative, for, from this point of view, it could only be defined in relation to a given historical civilization whose religious and judicial institutions are transitory.[29]

The reality of being a father cannot be whittled down to biology or legal obligation. It is not a bodily transaction, a contract or a code, a temporary interruption of one's life, a subjective state of seeing oneself as related by ties to which one must remain "faithful" out of a sense of obligation.

Rather, of its nature, fatherhood has a divine origin and a sacred purpose. "For this cause I bow my knees to the Father of our Lord Jesus Christ, of whom all paternity in heaven and earth is named, that he would grant you, according to the riches of his glory, to be strengthened by his Spirit with might unto the inward man" (Eph. 3:14–16).

"A conquest over difficult country"

Because he is not related to his children with emotional or physiological ties of the same intensity as a mother's, the father of a family is in an extremely precarious position.[30] Either he can run away from his responsibilities as ruler and teacher of his children, or he can all the better fulfill them due to his inherent manly authority. His position is one of danger and promise. One might say that the qualities that render a man fit to be a good ruler and teacher — his natural distance from much of what constitutes the bearing and rearing of children, his ability to look upon his own offspring as *other* than himself, present to him more *through* their mother — these and other aspects of male psychology open up the possibility of failure, even of treachery. Marcel — as we have seen, a perceptive writer on this subject — strikingly states: "Fatherhood nearly always presents

[29] Marcel, "Creative Vow," 99.

[30] See Keith Lemna, *The Apocalypse of Wisdom: Louis Bouyer's Theological Recovery of the Cosmos* (Brooklyn: Angelico Press, 2019), 389ff.

the character of a more or less hazardous conquest, which is achieved step by step over difficult country full of ambushes."[31]

The father has a pivotal, nontransferable part to play in the founding and preserving of the home. Fatherhood rightly lived involves continuous presence to others, living *for* others, being "on call." Because living out this commitment does not come as naturally to men as it does to women, it proves to be all the more crucial for the stability of the family as a community. If a man does not live up to his vocation to found a family, a permanent community of love, as the legendary Aeneas is said to have founded Rome by plunging his sword into the ground where the city would stand, then a woman will have no one to turn to as pillar and foundation. In a world of broken or nonexistent homes, the lifeblood of love, *promises kept,* which should permeate the family like an unspoken shared secret, is replaced with a psychological *promiscuity,* a haphazard shifting of allegiance that manifests itself as fragmentation and dissipation. Childbearing, child-rearing, and the countless cares that make the house a *home* will increasingly appear to the woman as intolerable burdens, affronts to her freedom, instead of expressions of loving commitment.

Fatherhood thus verifies, in a twofold way, the paradox spoken by Christ: "He that shall lose his life for my sake, shall find it" (Matt. 16:25). To bring *life,* that is, purposefulness and inner joy, to his family, a man must learn to *lose* himself, against his fallen tendency to overrate his own achievements and advancement. This is another way of saying that responsibility and suffering are inseparable in the living out of any love worthy of the name. "It behooves the man to place himself at life's disposal and not to dispose of life for his own purposes."[32] In losing himself for the sake of his wife and children, he wins back, over time and not without steady struggle, a self purified of egotism and false liberty. In this way, the divine principle of creation — God's love, guaranteed by His promise of love — is engrafted onto the family, or even better, becomes its lifeblood. Marcel again:

> We can state without hesitation that the limitations and deformations to which the fatherly feeling is liable tend to disappear in large families, and one might say that this is like the reward, the immanent sanction, of the act of prodigality by which a man generously sows the seeds of life.... By the multiplicity, the unpredictable variety of the relationships

31 Marcel, "Creative Vow," 110.

32 Marcel, "Creative Vow," 114.

> which it embraces, the large family really presents the character of a creation; there is a direct relation between the persevering and often literally heroic effort by which it is built up, and the new wealth, the wealth of life, which it receives.[33]

The connection between man's identity as father to his children and God's identity as Father to His people is not coincidental. From the beginning, the Creator revealed Himself under the image of the spousal covenant. The Almighty is both Bridegroom and Father. He chooses the Church as His bride; with her He begets spiritual children. The relation we call being a father is rooted in the deepest ground of who a man is, and from there it reaches out to embrace wife, children, and home. In this dynamic correlation between one's being and the outpouring of love to another, we catch a faint glimpse of the heavenly Father eternally giving rise to the Son, with the Holy Ghost proceeding from both like a breath or flame of love.[34]

Every time a Christian man succeeds in "founding the church" within the bounds of his home, he has furthered in a definite way the continual establishment of the Church of Christ, oriented to the consummation of the kingdom of God. Thus, it is of the essence of fatherhood to advance the work of God, the continual and arduous effort of "making all things new" (2 Cor. 5:17) in Jesus Christ, who declared: "And I, if I be lifted up from the earth, will draw all things to myself" (John 12:32). The Incarnation of the Word reveals the final purpose of God's intervention in human history: the reclaiming of the fallen universe, the re-creation of all in the image of the Father.

These profound truths do not leave human fatherhood unaffected. The man who rules and serves the family should especially strive to imitate the providential, gratuitous, unstinting love of the heavenly Father for His creation and for His espoused people. In so doing, the father secures himself from the danger of aloofness and tepidity, secures his wife from the loneliness and monotony of duty, secures his children from the temptation of revolt and ingratitude. Thanks to Our Lord's teaching, example, and gifts of grace, a husband and father learns to perceive the distant but all-important end for the sake of which he supports new life in the bosom of his family: to make present anew the supreme mystery of Love, the Love that God *is*. The husband and father extends the dominion of God's Fatherhood, the empire of Christ, the King and Bridegroom.

33 Marcel, "Creative Vow," 113.

34 See Peter Kwasniewski, "This, Too, Reveals God: The Body and Sexuality in Catholic Theology," in *Ministers of Christ: Recovering the Roles of Clergy and Laity in an Age of Confusion* (Manchester, NH: Crisis Publications, 2021), 3–12.

True Christian chivalry

The role of father is linked to the vocation of Adam in the plan of creation: naming the creatures of God through knowledge and tending the garden of the world through art. Human knowledge, however, can sour into "the pride of life" (1 John 2:16), and technology wielded as an instrument of exploitation can transform itself into the rape of nature. Fighting each of these primal temptations, the man (*vir*, male) is meant to trust humbly in God, to seek His superior wisdom and aid, to exercise chastity of life, and to mortify domineering instincts. His abilities find their best use when they are placed at the feet of another.

Addressing the themes of knowledge and technics, Pope John Paul II expressed much the same thought:

> Man is the priest of all creation. Christ conferred upon him this dignity and vocation. Creation completes its *opus gloriae* [work of glory] both by being what it is and by its duty to become what it should be. In a certain sense science and technology also contribute to this goal. But at the same time, since they are human works, they can lead away from this goal. In our civilization in particular there is such a risk, making it difficult for our civilization to be one of life and love. Missing is precisely the *opus gloriae*, which is the fundamental destiny of every creature, and above all of man, who was created in order to become, in Christ, the priest, prophet, and king of all earthly creatures.[35]

Chivalry, a tradition imbued with Christian honor, is characterized by selfless dedication to the good of others, especially those more vulnerable. "Fundamentally, chivalry is about people with strength and power using whatever gifts they have acquired from nature or education to help those weaker than themselves," writes Tracey Rowland. "It is the complete antithesis of the survival of the fittest principles which govern life among the lower primates.... The Christian idea of chivalry simultaneously affirms talent and ability while holding that such talents are best put to use in the one-to-one service of those less able."[36] The truly chivalrous person places the "lives and love" of others above his own life and self-love.

[35] John Paul II, *Crossing the Threshold of Hope*, ed. Vittorio Messori, trans. Jenny McPhee and Martha McPhee (New York: Alfred A. Knopf, 1994), 18.

[36] Tracey Rowland, *Portraits of Spiritual Nobility: Chivalry, Christendom, and Catholic Culture* (Brooklyn: Angelico Press, 2019), 3. See also chapter 33 below.

The vocation of the father is one form of the universal calling to holiness, a calling that takes flesh primarily in deeds of love. Holiness is no abstraction: it means to be faithful to one's duties in life, to make sacrifices for loved ones, to open up room for other souls to blossom, to help where help is needed. In this way, the father is present to his wife and children as the saint is present to the world — each re-presents Christ before others. In a family where Christian love is the measure and the goal, the possibility of despair is for all practical intents unthinkable. We still suffer; the Christian faith offers no panacea. But our suffering is part of the life we willingly embrace out of love for God, who turns hardship into a source of merit and glory.

Fatherhood is a saving reality to the degree that a man fulfills his role as "savior" of the mutable world of daily life; the one who, united with Christ, redeems the humdrum and exalts the lowly. If, by the grace of God, such single-minded devotion becomes as real, as tangible, as the union by which man and woman possess each other, as real as the conception and birth of the fruit of their embrace, then the family will escape the inner poverty to which it lies perilously open, especially in an age in which falsehood has usurped the place of truth and worldly compromises have tainted human hearts.

What, in the end, should a man strive to save? He must save or restore life in community, life as gift. He rescues life from passivity, protects it as well as he can from the battering of misfortune, endows it with direction, habituates himself and his children to the practice of religion. Fatherhood, Marcel explains,

> only exists as the carrying out of a responsibility, shouldered and sustained.... It is probably in contrast with inertia and blindness that we can best understand what the pure act of fatherhood should be. By that I mean a self-spending which can be compared to a gift, because it prepares and requires an engagement and because without this it is nullified.[37]

At the root of fatherhood we find *the creative vow*, capturing in a simple phrase the whole character of this vocation:

> We can see clearly enough that the *vœu créateur* implies the combination of a deep personal humility and an unshaken confidence in life, conceived of not as a natural force but as an unfathomable order, divine in its principle.[38]

[37] Marcel, "Creative Vow," 116–17.

[38] Marcel, "Creative Vow," 121.

When it is seriously undertaken and sanctioned by self-giving, fatherhood makes God *more present in the world,* so to speak, by bringing something of His justice, mercy, and love to bear upon the natural and social spheres in which we move. The Apostle Paul instructs Christians to "redeem the time" (see Eph. 5:15–16). What is fatherhood, if not a way, perhaps the chief way, for a man to root his temporal love in immortality, leaving behind him a testament of sacrifice and bearing witness to an interior wealth that cannot be priced? Generosity, love without price, is the legacy of Our Lord to His followers. A man who devotes himself to the family is learning — and at the same time teaching — the wisdom of Christ.

Because the contemporary world is bedazzled by the spell of technology, the ruse of convenience, the bustle of gratification, and, at the root of these, the repudiation of the sacred, we should not be surprised to find all around us the phenomena of moral irresponsibility, weariness of life, skepticism down to the bones, loneliness, and betrayal. We are happily startled and thankful when we meet men and women who have somehow withdrawn themselves, unscarred, from the chaos. "The life of man upon earth is a warfare" (Job 7:1). Indeed, now more than ever, Catholic fathers are called to be soldiers for Christ, protecting their families and defending the truths of our Faith in season and out of season.[39]

Seen in its nature and supreme importance, fatherhood is an expression of piety toward creation and an exaltation of the Holy Cross. It is, in Marcel's suggestive phrase, "the hallowing of the real." To make the world holy is at once a *cross,* because our hearts and the hearts of others resist God's love, and a *resurrection,* for God's grace triumphs in those who persevere. Now we are in a better position to appreciate a phrase of Charles Péguy: "the fathers of families, those great adventurers of the modern world"![40]

The family engendered and nurtured by husband and wife is an irreplaceable community, one for which no substitute or imitation can ever suffice. In spite of a diversity of customs and practices in different societies, the roles of father and mother are stable in their nature and necessary in their purpose. Even as the essence of human nature remains *one,* regardless of the immense variety of man's thoughts, passions, and inventions, so, too, the nature of fundamental realities cannot be changed or buried by any degree of effort.

39 See Peter Kwasniewski, "Christian Militancy in the Prayer of the Church," *OnePeterFive,* March 16, 2022, https://onepeterfive.com/christian-militancy-in-the-prayer-of-the-church/.

40 Quoted in Marcel, "Creative Vow," 113.

Despite their intrinsic and complementary differences, the vocations of man and woman unite in the love that results in self-denial, self-overcoming, and self-gift. "Leading the kind of life in which a Christian conquers the 'rule of sin' in himself by means of self-denial," wrote Karol Wojtyła as Cardinal of Krakow,

> is thus clearly a question of sanctity in the moral sense, of dominion over evil, in which, in a sense, man's own kingliness is displayed.... Every Christian who conquers sin by imitating Christ achieves the royal self-dominion that is proper to human beings; by so doing he shares in the *munus regale* of Christ and helps to bring about Christ's kingdom.[41]

The circle is closed: every time a man rightly exercises his paternity, in begetting and educating, chastising and rewarding, modeling endurance in labor and strength in principles; every time a woman rightly lives from within her maternity, bearing and nursing, training and instructing; every time husband and wife join efforts to rear the fruit of their love, they are sharing in the kingly office of Christ, His *munus regale,* which is a gift from "the Father of lights" (James 1:17) to the faithful Christian. It is only through the prophetic and royal priesthood of Jesus Christ that the countless sacrifices and labors of life make any sense in the end. It is only in Him that human love, so often obscured and tarnished, becomes aware of its own immortal dignity and beauty. The father and the mother share in the redemptive mission of the Lord. If they have "redeemed the time" (Eph. 5:16), they will share in His salvation.

[41] Karol Wojtyła, *Sources of Renewal,* trans. Paul Stephen Falla (San Francisco: Harper and Row, 1980), 263.

6

The Reasonableness of Marriage

The sharpest irony of the everyday feminism that has trickled down to all levels of society is simply that *men* — and certainly not the best men — stand to profit most from the so-called liberation of women. Indeed, as a moment's reflection can show, it is no exaggeration to say that the feminist movement from its inception has played into the manipulative hands of pleasure-hungry males.

To see why this is so, we need merely consider what things used to be like before the heralds of "equal rights" and "sexual liberation" came on the scene announcing a new code of behavior. In the past, when a woman's "honesty" or "virtue" (as the state of premarital and marital chastity came to be called) was guarded by social convention, firm moral codes, parental supervision, religious belief, and a deeply rooted sense that love quite naturally leads to marriage and children, the man (always in the position of *suitor,* one who must suit himself to the woman he wishes to woo) was expected, and usually obliged, to *honor* his would-be bride, promising her the fidelity of his body and the integrity of his intentions.

Now, however, nearly any man can arrange to keep a woman (whom a more forthright age would have called a mistress) for his entertainment at a minimal cost to himself, with little need for vows, forethought, or responsibility. Since women brainwashed by feminism take offense at the idea of *dependency,* they will bring in extra money; since they are equally horrified at the prospect of offspring (who might curtail their "liberated" desires), a man need not worry himself about the natural result of coition and is therefore free to indulge his own bodily wants with relative impunity. If a man gets what his libido wants without any effort or sacrifice, chances are he will never stop to ask what his soul needs — or for that matter, what his mistress's soul needs. And if a pregnancy should unexpectedly darken the horizon, liberal Western society provides the "perfect out": a quick procedure for removing the "product of conception."

In *Crossing the Threshold of Hope*, John Paul II wrote:

> I think that a certain contemporary feminism finds its roots in the absence of true respect for woman. Revealed truth teaches us something different. Respect for woman, amazement at the mystery of womanhood, and finally the nuptial love of God Himself and of Christ, as expressed in the Redemption, are all elements that have never been completely absent in the faith and life of the Church. This can be seen in a rich tradition of customs and practices that, regrettably, is nowadays being eroded. In our civilization woman has become, before all else, an object of pleasure.[42]

Traditions of courtship and engagement have precisely this deeper purpose: to lay the foundations for a lasting friendship and affection rooted in the common good of man and woman together, teaching them to rise above the limitations of their private goods. That is why continence is required throughout the years prior to consummating the marriage vows. The consummation is meant to be the sacred seal on a pledge *already inscribed* in the hearts of bride and bridegroom. When they have made their solemn vows to each other, the marriage of wills has already taken place because of their prior devotion and sacrifices. Seen in this light, the privileges of marriage are always secondary to the demands of committed love, although nuptial love receives its most intense and fitting expression through those privileges.

In like manner, the Church counsels couples to be *chaste* (i.e., temperate) in their use of marital privileges for the same reason she counsels continence in courtship: that the spiritual goods of a friendship of virtue — the only real friendship, founded upon truly common possessions — may take precedence over, and ultimately spiritualize, the goods of sensual pleasure, which are beautiful and perfective only to the extent that they solidify the deeper foundations of charity and illuminate the image of God in the souls of husband and wife.[43]

As St. Augustine teaches, the virtuous man is he who can transform the water of earthly pleasure into the wine of heavenly joy, without scorning the genuine goods of this world. Christ does not say to the steward, "Get rid of that ordinary water and bring something better." He says, "Fill your jars with water and bring them to me," whereupon He miraculously transmutes one substance into another, a drink of necessity into a draught of delight. So, too, God calls upon the husband and wife to elevate and purify their fleshly union, *not* so that it

[42] John Paul II, *Crossing the Threshold of Hope*, 217.

[43] See chapter 11.

may cease to be fleshly but, rather, that its very fleshliness may become holy and beautiful — a constant renewal of the nuptial promises, a song of praise to the Creator, a worthy symbol of the union of Christ and His Church. The union of husband and wife on all its levels — physical, psychological, spiritual — should be a sacrament of presence, a redemption from selfishness, a banquet where each is offered to and for the other, a celebration of the solemn vows spoken months, years, decades before. And, it seems almost superfluous to add, if such a love is truly present and active in the lives of the spouses, it will bear fruit in children whose advent is eagerly sought and generously welcomed.

The wisdom of this approach becomes evident when we consider one of the basic reasons why the Church, listening to the voice of nature, must forbid contraception. It is wrong for couples to indulge their sensual appetites whenever they please for the simple reason that each appetite of the human being needs to be kept in due proportion or balance with the other activities of a fully human life. When all aspects of a man's or a woman's life are properly measured, with nothing too prominent or submerged, we then speak of a person of *integrity*, someone who "has it all together."

A consequence immediately follows: as the ancient philosopher Democritus said, "If you exceed the measure, what is most enjoyable becomes least enjoyable."[44] Food is naturally good, and eating is an operation according to a natural inclination for sustenance; but one can eat to excess, thereby perverting the goodness of the act. By so exceeding the mark, one brings upon oneself numerous other defects of body and soul. Gluttony is thus an instance of the kind of habit of indulgence that is capable of upsetting a person's inner peace and outward behavior; it is impossible to cultivate the presence of Christ if the parts of the soul are out of order and cannot harmonize with one another.

Likewise with the act of marriage: allowing unrestrained indulgence out of a mistaken "realism" is nothing other than approving the malformation of character and the disordering of wills, which is contrary to human dignity and fulfillment. Such a lax and permissive attitude, in fact, leads to the carnalization or cheapening of authentic love, which, of its proper essence, is a spiritual good having union with God as its final goal. Put otherwise, the Church forbids sensual vice not because she has a problem with pleasure but because too much pleasure causes problems. It is the *nature* of man as created by God that lays down the laws by which ordinary conduct is to be governed. An ethical code or a magisterial

[44] *Early Greek Philosophy*, trans. and ed. Jonathan Barnes (New York: Penguin, 1987), 274.

pronouncement is only meant to *help* us find the right measure, without having to ruin ourselves by the regrettable mishaps of ill-advised experimentation.

The most poignant irony of our times is that self-consciously "liberated" women have all but invited men — already inclined by fallen nature to promiscuity and, as a result, in dire need of a woman's good example and discipline — to persevere stubbornly in their own worst vices: arbitrariness of physical passion and the constant temptation to run after the next beautiful girl. Josef Pieper aptly describes the acidic effects of depersonalized sex, or sex severed from *eros* (desiring love) and *philia* (friendship love):

> Precisely this is what is so bad and so inhuman about sexual activity separated from eros: it frustrates the very experience that constitutes the meaning of the erotic encounter within the whole of existence. That experience is the escape from one's own limitations and egotism by union with another person. The mere sex partner does not come into focus as a personal being, that is, as a living self with an individually cast human countenance. An American has put the matter very wittily, remarking that where the "playboy" is concerned, the fig leaf has merely been moved to another place; it now covers the human face.... The encounter that is sheer sex and nothing else has rightly been called deceptive in character. For the moment, an illusion of union arises; but without love this apparent union of two strangers leaves them more remote from one another than they were before. Thus it should cause little surprise that "in a society that makes sexuality the prerequisite for love and not love the condition for the gift of physical union," sex paradoxically "rather separates than unites man and woman, leaving them alone and lonely precisely where they thought they would surely find each other." As such sex consumption increases, this effect is intensified and the sexual encounter becomes increasingly disappointing.... Ricoeur points out, "Everything that makes the sexual encounter easy simultaneously speeds its collapse into insignificance." At bottom that is hardly surprising. It might be called an iron law. What can be had on demand and almost gratis, and almost at once as well (Americans use the robust expression "short-order sex"), necessarily loses both its value and its attractiveness.[45]

[45] Josef Pieper, *Faith, Hope, Love*, trans. Richard and Clara Winston and Sr. Mary Frances McCarthy (San Francisco: Ignatius Press, 1997), 264–66, citing (prior to Paul Ricoeur) Rollo May, Erich Fromm, and Joachim Bodamer.

The behavior (not to mention dress) of many modern women has the result of frankly encouraging men to satisfy their desires in a bestial way, destroying at its roots the foundation for constancy and fidelity in marriage. On the assumption that such women actually want their present or future husbands to remain faithful to them, to love them *as persons,* one can only marvel at their nearsightedness. I am not saying that they are always or even generally culpable for having and acting on erroneous views, nor that men, for their part, are not guilty of even worse vices, such as the viewing of pornography, which brings about the worst interior corruption of purity, chastity, and modesty. At this point in time, most inhabitants of the Western world are pickled in evil and brined in falsehood from the moment they walk through the doors of the public school system, if not earlier, when they are suckled on screen time.

According to current standards of dating and engagement, a man and a woman are free to parade their concupiscence and feed it wantonly. In modern times, there is nothing *holy* or *dignified* about the way people approach the real union of lover and beloved, an act ennobled in healthier ages by the sacrament ("sacred pledge") of Matrimony. Is it any surprise that a vast number of marriages end in divorce, when a vast number of relationships begin in lust?

Now as before, there is but one way to conquer the blindness of the world and the folly of man: living out the Christian ideal of marriage. "Your body is the temple of the Holy Spirit," writes St. Paul (1 Cor. 6:19); again, "Let marriage be honorable in all things, and the bed undefiled" (Heb. 13:4). We must strenuously avoid, or penitently overcome, the many ways of defiling that marriage bed — be it through impurity and unchastity prior to or during marriage; by pornography, which is a form of infidelity to one's present or future spouse or vocation; by listening to raunchy music with offensive lyrics or watching distasteful movies, which populate the memory and imagination with vicious images that contradict the righteousness of the Gospel. To avoid these things is not to live a confined or boring life but to live free of slavery and with eyes fully open to the beauty of the souls whom God gives us to love. For God Himself is the source and end of marriage, the One who effects the bond and perfects its blessings: "What *God* has joined together, let no man put asunder" (Matt. 19:6). Love that is rooted in God, a union nourished by faith and purified through suffering — this love alone will prosper and bear fruit in time and in eternity.

7

Holy Matrimony, Sanctified Bodies, and Sacramental Grace

In our times, we have seen the important work of Pope John Paul II on the "theology of the body" misunderstood and applied in a superficial and, at times, morally problematic way.[46] One example is a claim I once heard that the very bodies of spouses are causes of grace, such that when they come together in the marital act — and assuming no moral impediment, such as contraception — an increase of sanctifying grace is bestowed on each or both spouses. This claim, as it stands, is false — although something *like* it is true.

The only signs that *effect*, or bring about, the sanctifying grace they signify are the seven sacraments of the New Law. In this sense, it is impossible that the spouses' bodies, as such, should be causes of grace in a proper sense, such that when the cause (bodily action) is posited, the effect (increase of grace) follows. Rather, the bodily mutual self-giving, open to new life, is the outward sign of the sacrament of Matrimony itself, which, present and operative in a mysterious way in the *souls* of the spouses, is the cause of an increase in sanctifying grace. Put more simply, the efficacious sign is not the bodily action but the sacramental union and state, which is represented and furthered by the bodily action.

On the other hand, *any* bodily act done out of charity is a cause of grace in the sense of being a moral cause of meriting an increase of such grace. In this way, the nuptial act is like an act of almsgiving, or clothing the poor, or instructing the ignorant: all of these are acts of a will animated by charity, performed with the help of the body and meriting an increase of grace.

We find many profound passages in the writings of John Paul II on these matters, such as the following passage from *Evangelium Vitae*:

> Within this same [contemporary] cultural climate, the body is no longer perceived as a properly personal reality, a sign and place of relations with

[46] See chapter 10 for further discussion of the "theology of the body."

others, with God, and with the world. It is reduced to pure materiality: it is simply a complex of organs, functions, and energies to be used according to the sole criteria of pleasure and efficiency. Consequently, sexuality too is depersonalized and exploited: from being the sign, place, and language of love, that is, of the gift of self and acceptance of another, in all the other's richness as a person, it increasingly becomes the occasion and instrument for self-assertion and the selfish satisfaction of personal desires and instincts.

Thus the original import of human sexuality is distorted and falsified, and the two meanings, unitive and procreative, inherent in the very nature of the conjugal act, are artificially separated: in this way the marriage union is betrayed and its fruitfulness is subjected to the caprice of the couple. Procreation then becomes the "enemy" to be avoided in sexual activity: if it is welcomed, this is only because it expresses a desire, or indeed the intention, to have a child "at all costs," and not because it signifies the complete acceptance of the other and therefore an openness to the richness of life which the child represents.[47]

The pope chooses his words with care: the body is a "sign" — a sign of self-giving — a "place," and a "language," but, in and of itself, it does not expressly signify sanctifying grace or directly confer it. This is what the sacrament of Marriage, or Matrimony, is and does. If the spouse's body were a cause of grace just by being what it is — namely, a sign of self-giving — it would follow that the body or the nuptial act is an eighth sacrament, a claim certainly contrary to the dogma of the Faith. I know a priest (he was married as an Anglican curate and was later ordained a Catholic priest) who refers to this kind of loose talk as "gamolatry," that is, a sort of worship of things pertaining to marriage.

In our times, so given to vapid pseudomysticism, we do well to remember that Our Lord instituted the seven sacraments as the ordinary means of conferring His supernatural life and charity upon us. It is through the sacraments that we become "sons in the Son" and receive all that we need to grow in our sonship until the day of glory.[48] Thus, even that which theologians have taken to

[47] John Paul II, Encyclical Letter *Evangelium Vitae* (March 25, 1995), no. 23.

[48] I do not engage here the centuries-old debate over what precisely it means to say that Jesus Himself instituted each and every one of the seven sacraments; various more or less convincing hypotheses have been proffered. In any case, Catholics are obliged to believe that which the Council of Trent defined as *de fide* dogma — namely, that Christ Himself instituted the seven sacraments of

calling the "primordial sacrament," the humanity of Christ, is effective among us in this world precisely *through* the seven sacraments of the Church and not somehow over and above and apart from them, as if it were an eighth sacrament that could be numbered alongside the other seven. The Church, too, may be called a "sacrament" analogously, a sign and cause of communion with God by grace — for she, too, is built up from the seven sacraments, from which she derives her existence and activity. The Eucharist, especially, is the root and the constant origin of the Church in this world. Without the Eucharistic Body, there would be no Mystical Body. This is why St. Thomas Aquinas teaches that the "reality" of the sacrament of the Eucharist is nothing other than the unity, in charity, of the Mystical Body itself.[49]

How beautiful it is that spouses receive in marriage a new participation in the love of God and the Passion of Christ, as well as a new power to participate in creation and redemption by begetting children and offering them to God in Baptism! The quasi-character imprinted on their souls by the marriage vows remains throughout their life as a constant claim before God of all the graces each needs to fulfill the duties of his or her state in life; it is a permanent mark of their mutual surrender to and "ownership" of each other; it is a likeness of the relationship that unites Christ to His Bride and unites the Church, in turn, to her Bridegroom, in an unbreakable union of eternal fecundity.[50]

The comparative nobility of the sacraments

Marriage, as one of the seven sacraments of the New Law, is a metaphysical and supernatural reality of immense power and beauty in the Christian scheme of things. It inaugurates and sustains a noble state of life, within which spouses who follow the law of Christ and His Church receive all the graces they need to achieve personal holiness and to bring one another and their family to heaven.

The nobility of marriage derives chiefly from four things: (1) its institution by the Creator, in the beginning, as the highest form of friendship between man and woman; (2) its fertility in providing citizens of the heavenly Jerusalem — a

---

the New Law. See Session 7, Canon 1: "If anyone says that the sacraments of the New Law were not all instituted by our Lord Jesus Christ, or that there are more or less than seven, namely, baptism, confirmation, Eucharist, penance, extreme unction, order, and matrimony, or that any of these seven is not truly and intrinsically a sacrament, let him be anathema." *The Canons and Decrees of the Council of Trent*, trans. H. J. Schroeder (Rockford, IL: TAN Books, 1978), 51.

49 See *Summa Theologiae* [*ST*] III, Q. 61, art. 2.

50 See note 10.

fertility blessed by God and beloved to Him because it is the echo, in the material world, of His own infinite and eternal processions and the overflowing of His goodness in creating the universe; (3) its use by Divine Providence as an instrument by which the race of Israel gave to Christ His human flesh and blood; (4) its elevation by Our Lord to be a sacred sign of His indissoluble union with His immaculate Bride, the Church.

The attack on marriage today — whether by the world and its prince or by modernist clergy and their lackeys — is therefore nothing less than an attack on the Creator and the order of creation, on the supreme mystery of the Blessed Trinity, on the people of Israel and the life and teaching of Jesus Christ, and on the innermost nature of His Bride, the Church. Put simply, if you attack marriage, you attack all of reality, front to back, top to bottom.

The Church's teaching about marriage and the family is, therefore, an integral and central part of the glorious heritage of our Faith. Nevertheless, I sometimes wonder if moderns do not fall into the tendency of viewing the sacraments individually, in isolation from one another (and largely depending on which of the sacraments might be getting neglected or attacked at any given time), rather than taking care to ponder and appreciate the entire sacramental system. If we do this, we might come to see, with St. Thomas Aquinas, that while Marriage is truly a "great sacrament" (see Eph. 5:32), it is, absolutely speaking, the *least* of the seven sacraments. Rather than denigrating Marriage, this ranking serves only to magnify the underappreciated greatness of the other six. It is like a building in which the first room you enter is already magnificently decked out, but each successive room, as you walk toward the throne room, is more resplendent still; or like a chest of wondrous medicines in which the least is already more potent than any natural remedy known to man.

Let us, in any case, consider the reasoning of St. Thomas. In his *Commentary on the Sentences*, Marriage is relegated to last place among the seven sacraments because, while it has "the greatest signification [*habet maximam significationem*]," it *works* a lesser effect as regards the spiritual life than the other six sacraments do.

> One sacrament may be said to be nobler than another in five ways. In one way, as regards the reality of the sacrament, or its effect; and thus *baptism*, which wipes away all guilt and takes away all punishment, is the greatest sacrament. In another way, as regards that which is contained in the sacrament; and thus the *Eucharist* is the noblest, in which is contained Christ himself. In a third way, as regards the grade of dignity in which it consists; and thus *holy orders* is the noblest sacrament. In a

> fourth way, as regards the minister; and thus *confirmation*, and *holy orders* too, are the noblest, because they are administered only by a bishop. In a fifth way, as regards what is signified and not contained therein, and thus *marriage* is the noblest, because it signifies the conjunction of the two natures in the person of Christ.
>
> Nevertheless if we compare these dignities with one another, that dignity is found to be foremost that a sacrament has from its content, because that is more essential. And so the sacrament of the *Eucharist* is simply the most noble, and to it, in a certain way, all the sacraments are ordered. However, the dignity that consists in bringing about some effect prevails over that which consists in the signifying [of some reality]; and that which consists in bringing about some effect with respect to good, simply speaking, prevails over that which consists in the removal of evil.
>
> And so, simply speaking, after the Eucharist the noblest sacrament is *holy orders*, through which a man is established both in grace and in a grade of [special] dignity; and after this, *confirmation*, through which the perfection of grace is conferred; and after this, *baptism*, through which is accomplished a full remission of guilt and punishment; and after this, *marriage*, which has the greatest signification [i.e., it signifies the greatest of mysteries].
>
> But *penance* and *extreme unction* are placed between baptism and marriage, because they are directly ordered to the removal of evil, although in this regard penance has less efficacy than baptism, because it is ordered against actual guilt alone, and does not totally take away punishment; and still less has extreme unction, which is ordered against the remnants [*reliquias*] of sin.[51]

The conclusions at which St. Thomas arrives can ring true only to one who holds, as he does, a robust view of the effects produced by Confirmation, Holy Orders, Penance, and Extreme Unction. This poses a question for the Church today and for her leaders: Do *we* have a robust view of Confirmation and Extreme Unction? I think it would be fair to say that believing and practicing Catholics have a pretty clear idea of the unique power of Holy Orders (it makes

[51] Response of *In IV Sent.*, Dist. 7, Q. 1, art. 1, qa. 3. Like other Scholastic authors, Thomas talks simply of *ordo* or "order" rather than "Holy Orders," as we do in English. I have nevertheless used the phrase more familiar to us.

a man a priest) and Penance (it takes away the guilt of sin), but it's harder to say whether we appreciate the mysteries of Confirmation and (as we tend to call it nowadays) Anointing of the Sick. And yet, Aquinas is claiming that, as good as sacramental Marriage is, Confirmation and Anointing are superior in their effects. We remember and celebrate the anniversary of our Marriage, but do we remember and celebrate the anniversary of our Confirmation? And do we pray and prepare for a holy death — one in which "the consolation of the sacraments" (especially Extreme Unction) is made available to us by the mercy of God and the ministry of the Church?

Another intriguing point to consider in the above text is where Aquinas says that "the sacrament of the Eucharist is *simply* the most noble, and to it, in a certain way, *all* the sacraments are ordered." He must mean that marriage, too — not just the individual Christian who happens to be married — is ordered to the Eucharist. As far as I know, he never works out exactly how this is so or the implications of it, beyond the observations that, first, "marriage, at least in its signification, touches this sacrament, in so far as it signifies the conjoining of Christ and the Church, whose unity is represented (*figuratur*) by the sacrament of the Eucharist; hence the Apostle says: 'This is a great sacrament, but I speak in Christ and in the Church' (Eph 5:32)," and, second, that the celebration of the Eucharist is the point of arrival in the celebration of the other sacraments.[52]

In the Tertia Pars of the *Summa Theologiae*, written at the other end of his career, St. Thomas describes the "excellence" of marriage as follows, in answer to an objection that tries to make Baptism a greater sacrament than the Eucharist:

> For in that way [i.e., from the vantage of necessity], *baptism*, since it is of greatest necessity, is the most powerful of the sacraments — just as *holy orders* and *confirmation* have a certain excellence by reason of their administration [because they are given by a successor of the Apostles], and *marriage* by reason of its signification. For there is no reason why a thing should not be worthier from a certain point of view which is not worthier absolutely speaking.[53]

This, then, is the greatness of marriage: it is the enduring physical and spiritual sign, the signature as it were, of the one and only union for which the world was created in the beginning, the union for which souls and bodies were

[52] For both observations, see *ST* III, Q. 65, art. 3. The latter was also made in the *Sentences* text just quoted.

[53] *ST* III, Q. 65, art. 3, ad 4.

brought into being, the union for which the Son of God became man and in which He makes men sons of God. Even if the other sacraments are greater in their effects (and even though the Eucharist is infinitely greater in its content), no sacrament is greater in the message it declares, the promise it makes, the fullness it symbolizes, the ultimate fruition to which it gestures. It announces, without itself being able to secure, the ultimate purpose of our lives: to love and be loved perfectly, with a love that opens outward to embrace all whom the Lord gives us.[54]

[54] For a thorough study of St. Thomas's theology of the sacrament of Matrimony, see Peter Kwasniewski, "St. Thomas on the Grandeur and Limitations of Marriage," *Nova et Vetera* (English ed.) vol. 10, no. 2 (2012): 415–36, https://stpaulcenter.com/05-nv-10-2-kwasniewski/.

8

How to Elevate the Dignity of Weddings

The Catholic Church has been known throughout the ages for the strong, unambiguous stand she takes on the sanctity and indissolubility of marriage and on the naturalness, goodness, and social priority of the family that emerges, by God's blessing, from the union of man and woman.

There is, nevertheless, a monumental disconnect between this exalted doctrine and the disgraceful, if not sacrilegious, manner in which weddings are often conducted.[55] Experience, records, and anecdotal evidence suggest that far too many Catholic weddings are not conducted as befits a holy or sacred occasion, but rather, are turned into carnivals, with the officiant acting as ringmaster. At times, the giddy banter in the church before or after Mass is so loud that an organist playing at full volume can still hear it. Sermons become the priest's

[55] There is a similar disconnect between Catholic eschatology and modern-day Catholic funerals, which have degenerated into maudlin wakes of the Protestant "low church" kind. The primary purpose of the Mass for the Dead is to pray for the soul of the departed, that it may be saved and, if in need of purification (as the vast majority of *saved* souls will be), may be delivered soon from the fires of purgatory. Hence the traditional Requiem Mass focuses *all* of its attention on the faithful departed: there is no homily; gone are blessings of certain objects or of the people; a special Agnus Dei begs for the repose of souls; the Propers are a continuous tapestry of prayers for the dead; and so forth. The way that modern funerals have been turned toward the emotional relief of the living and the "celebration" of the mortal life of the deceased is, in reality, a double act of uncharity: first, it deprives Christians of the opportunity to go out of themselves in love by praying for the salvation of the soul of a loved one, thus exercising a great act of spiritual mercy, rather than being passive recipients of an act of spiritual mercy; second, it deprives the departed soul of the power and consolation of collective prayer on its behalf. Of course, all of this presupposes an orthodox understanding of the Four Last Things.

own version of a wedding-reception toast or a sentimental fireside chat with the couple, complete with reminiscences, chestnuts, and down-home advice. The kissing of the bride can be a real performance, complete with whistling and clapping; needless to say, everyone goes to Communion! A beautiful and sacred space is turned into a sports arena and a fashion show. One thinks, in this connection, of Ratzinger's rebuke:

> Wherever applause breaks out in the liturgy because of some human achievement, it is a sure sign that the essence of liturgy has totally disappeared and been replaced by a kind of religious entertainment. Such attraction fades quickly — it cannot compete in the market of leisure pursuits, incorporating as it increasingly does various forms of religious titillation.[56]

If we *believe* in the sanctity of marriage, this kind of Hollywood travesty has to be stopped, and if we do not do all in our power to stop it, we are effectively endorsing a secular redefinition of marriage and allowing the faithful to be formed by it and in it. Clergy should take as a model the Lord Jesus in His expelling the money changers from the temple: "My house shall be called the house of prayer; but you have made it a den of thieves" (Matt. 21:13). He didn't set up a Pontifical Committee for Relations with Thieves or make a public apology for the bad treatment of thieves over the centuries; He simply drew a line between sacred and profane and threw them out. God's house is, first and foremost, a house of prayer. The prophet Isaiah says: "The Lord of hosts, Him you shall honor as holy. Let him be your fear, and let him be your dread" (Isa. 8:13). The prophet Malachi likewise: "The son honoreth the father, and the servant his master: if then I be a father, where is my honor? and if I be a master, where is my fear? saith the LORD of hosts" (Mal. 1:6).[57]

Connected with the fear of the Lord and respect for His temple is the evangelistic opportunity presented by a beautiful liturgy. I do not mean, of course, that the liturgy should be turned into an occasion for catechesis or apologetics

[56] Joseph Ratzinger, *The Spirit of the Liturgy*, trans. John Saward (San Francisco: Ignatius Press, 2000), 198–99; Joseph Ratzinger, *Collected Works*, vol. 11: *Theology of the Liturgy: The Sacramental Foundation of Christian Existence*, ed. Michael J. Miller (San Francisco: Ignatius Press, 2014), 125.

[57] See Peter Kwasniewski, "Consecrated Buildings and Their Officially Sponsored Profanation" in *The Road from Hyperpapalism to Catholicism: Rethinking the Papacy in a Time of Ecclesial Disintegration* (Waterloo, ON: Arouca Press, 2022), vol. 2: *Chronological Responses to an Unfolding Pontificate*, 98–106.

but, rather, that simply by being as it *should* be — dignified, expressive, and noble — it will touch the hearts and minds of at least some of the nonpracticing Catholics and unbelievers present. To quote Ratzinger again:

> If the Liturgy appears first of all as the workshop for our activity, then what is essential is being forgotten: God. For the Liturgy is not about us, but about God. Forgetting about God is the most imminent danger of our age. As against this, the Liturgy should be setting up a sign of God's presence. Yet what happens if the habit of forgetting about God makes itself at home in the Liturgy itself and if in the Liturgy we are thinking only of ourselves? In any and every liturgical reform, and every liturgical celebration, the primacy of God should be kept in view first and foremost.[58]

A priest in Ireland told me that when, on one occasion, he offered a Novus Ordo funeral Mass in English and merely prayed slowly, chanted the texts, and kept silence at appropriate points, generally acting as if he were earnestly praying for the deceased and as if he believed in what he was doing, a number of people said to him afterward: "My goodness, Father, if *every* Mass was like that one, I'd start coming to church again."

Has there not been an incredible failure to face the obvious fact that treating the most sacred mysteries casually and horizontally necessarily leads to the eclipse of God? I speak of the eclipse of His transcendent Fatherhood and His right to our total homage, intellectual and moral, as well as the eclipse of man's own nature, his need for redemption, his capacity for the infinite and the eternal, and his heavenly destiny, with all the self-denial and self-mastery it demands of us here and now. The use of such completely foreign imports as "the unity candle" or jars of sand to signify the uniting of two families or two lives exemplifies the stress on horizontality that, together with ritual made from whole cloth, is one of the worst legacies of the general agitation for liturgical reform that afflicted all the Christian churches and ecclesial communities in the twentieth century.

There will never be a renewed acceptance of the full truth about marriage and family, an adherence to divine and natural law, if there is not a renewed

[58] Joseph Ratzinger, foreword to Alcuin Reid, *The Organic Development of the Liturgy: The Principles of Liturgical Reform and Their Relation to the Twentieth-Century Liturgical Movement Prior to the Second Vatican Council* (San Francisco: Ignatius Press, 2005), 13; also in Ratzinger, *Theology of the Liturgy*, 593–94.

acceptance of the full truth about the sacred liturgy: an adherence to the natural law of religious homage (the obligation of creature to Creator) and to the divine law of Christian worship (the sacrifice of the Cross).

Here are a few ways in which weddings could be improved in the context of the Novus Ordo. (Some of these suggestions would also apply, *mutatis mutandis,* to weddings in the traditional Roman Rite.)

1. The most important precondition for resacralizing weddings is that those who are to be married understand ahead of time *something* of the beauty, holiness, and lofty demands of the sacrament, not as described in some wishy-washy pamphlet, but by reading and discussing together, in segments, a robust treatment of the subject. In all my years of teaching, the best document I have yet found is Pope Pius XI's Encyclical *Casti Connubii,* which has the benefit of being relatively short, frank, and challenging.[59] I imagine that some couples would never do the reading at all, but some others would, and it could at least spark honest, difficult conversations that need to happen, such as the reasons behind the Church's teaching on the good of abstention before marriage and chastity during it, the corrosive evil of contraception, the inherent ordering of married life to the begetting and educating of children, and the distinct but complementary roles of husband and wife in the family.

2. The ceremony of betrothal should be restored as a *sacred* way of marking the period of engagement and preparation. Lest this suggestion be viewed as a form of romantic medievalism, it is worthy of mention that one sees betrothals happening quite regularly at the more traditional colleges listed in The Newman Guide. My wife and I were betrothed in a ceremony led by the priest who married us about six months later, and the idea occurred to us in the first place because we had seen so many others doing it. The rite is still not as well known as it should be, however, and the publication by the USCCB of a rather lackluster "blessing of engagement" could throw some people off the scent. The traditional rite of betrothal is readily available online and in print.[60]

59 A particularly valuable tool has been provided in Leila Marie Lawler's little book *God Has No Grandchildren: A Guided Reading of Pius XI's Encyclical* Casti Connubii, *On Chaste Marriage,* second ed. (Waterloo, ON: Arouca Press, 2021).

60 See *Solemn Rite of Betrothal and Publishing of the Banns, Laudate Dominum,* http://laudatedominum.net/files/bet.pdf; Chester Wrzaszczak, "Engagements — In Church," *American Ecclesiastical Review* (October 1962): 243–54, *Catholic Culture,* www.catholicculture.org/culture/library/view.cfm?recnum=2978; "Rite of Betrothal," *Latin Mass Wedding,* www.latinmasswedding.com/rite-of-betrothal; and Society of Saint Pius X, *The Rite of Betrothal* (Angelus Press), https://

3. The pastor or celebrant should insist on worthy music being utilized for the wedding: the Ordinary of the Mass and the Propers of the Nuptial Mass (perhaps in simple English psalm tones, if the choir cannot handle more) and additional pieces chosen from a list of suitable hymns and instrumentals.[61] A priest friend of mine told a delightful story. One day, he was meeting with a lady to go over the plans for her wedding Mass. She listed a number of popular songs she wanted to have performed at the Mass. The priest smiled and said: "I'll let you have those songs, as long as you agree to one request of mine." "What's that, Father?" "That you play Gregorian chant at your reception." "But, *Father*, that's not appropriate for the occasion!" "Right. Neither are these songs appropriate for the occasion of divine worship. Now let's rethink the music for the Mass. Here's what I propose ..."

4. If one is working with Catholics who have a modicum of faith and open-mindedness, one could suggest holding a Holy Hour after the wedding rehearsal while the priest hears confessions, particularly those of the bride, the bridegroom, and the wedding party. Among other benefits, this practice would greatly increase the possibility of the bride and bridegroom marrying in a state of grace so that they receive the fruits of the sacrament of Matrimony, rather than being vowed to one another in a graceless state of mortal sin. (Theologians teach that when marriage is contracted in a state of sin, the parties are indeed indissolubly wed, but the *grace* of the sacrament is not actually received by the sinful party until he or she is restored, through absolution or perfect contrition, to a state of grace, and then the sacramental grace is said to be "revived.")

5. For the ceremony itself, the priest should use the most beautiful vestments and vessels he has access to, chant his own parts of the Mass, avoid the pitfalls of showmanship, and see to it that the service is conducted with solemnity. If possible, the traditional readings for a Nuptial Mass should be chosen.[62] Such an *ars celebrandi*, together with the aforementioned music and the Holy Hour and confessions of the evening before, would accentuate the sacredness of the great mystery being celebrated.

---

angeluspress.org/products/rite-of-betrothal. The rite is also found in Weller, *The Roman Ritual*, vol. 1, 588–94.

61 Samuel Weber's book *The Proper of the Mass for Sundays and Solemnities* (San Francisco: Ignatius Press, 2015) has several settings of the Nuptial Mass Propers, ranging from psalm-tone to melismatic.

62 For details, see my article "The New Lectionary and the Catholic Wedding," *OnePeterFive*, May 22, 2019, https://onepeterfive.com/lectionary-wedding/.

When I discuss these matters with priests, I generally get two reactions (and usually from the same people): "You're right" and "It's impossible." I think there is a lot of discouragement out there about weddings and funerals, because these occasions, more than any others, bring home to the clergy just how horribly lacking in basic Christian faith and morals most baptized Catholics are. Nowhere is the postconciliar collapse of the Church and the destruction of the liturgy more apparent.

Nevertheless, with St. Thérèse, I maintain that discouragement is a form of pride and that Christ is looking for "a few good men" to make the strenuous efforts needed, "brick by brick," to elevate the seriousness and beauty of all of our sacramental life — be it Baptisms, Confirmations, weddings, and funerals, or daily and Sunday Mass. This is obviously a long-term project, but it begins with making whatever improvements we can, here and now. With all the care and goodwill in the world, we will sometimes offend people who do not know better, but let us strive to explain, clearly and patiently, as circumstances allow, the rationale behind all that we do or propose to do. During the Mass itself, such explanations should be kept to a minimum, lest they detract and distract from the mystery being celebrated; it is generally best to make any announcements (e.g., about who may or may not come forward to receive Holy Communion) either before the ceremony begins or at the start of the homily.

9

What Makes a Family Holy?

If the goal of the individual Christian is to become a saint, the goal of a married Christian couple is to become saints together, with each other's aid, and the goal of a Christian family is to strive to be a *holy* family, in imitation of the model of Jesus, Mary, and Joseph. Thus, it behooves us to think carefully about how to define family holiness.

In order to do so, we need to identify the *causes* of family holiness, lest we be arbitrary about the effects we should be looking for or prioritizing. One might, after all, skew in this or that direction because one is not holding oneself responsible to the root causes. It's like defining man as risible, tool-using, linguistic, social, and religious, without saying that he is *rational,* which is the root of all of these things.

The teaching of the authentic Magisterium is of great help to us because it shows again and again the primacy of prayer, the sacramental life, and the Holy Eucharist for the holiness of all Christians, whether single, married, religious, or clergy.

> The liturgy is the summit toward which the activity of the Church is directed; at the same time it is the font from which all her power flows.... The renewal in the Eucharist of the covenant between the Lord and man draws the faithful into the compelling love of Christ and sets them on fire. From the liturgy, therefore, and especially from the Eucharist, as from a font, grace is poured forth upon us; and the sanctification of men in Christ and the glorification of God, to which all other activities of the Church are directed as toward their end, is achieved in the most efficacious possible way.[63]

[63] Vatican II, Constitution on the Sacred Liturgy *Sacrosanctum Concilium* (December 4, 1963), no. 10.

> Participating in the Eucharistic sacrifice, the source and culmination of the whole Christian life, they [the faithful] offer the Divine Victim to God, and offer themselves along with It.[64]

Confirming this doctrine by their lives, all of the saints prioritize prayer over action, the interior life over the exterior apostolate, the Holy Eucharist over any other work of devotion or charity. They are simply taking Our Lord at His word: "Abide in me, and I in you. As the branch cannot bear fruit of itself, unless it abide in the vine, so neither can you, unless you abide in me. I am the vine: you the branches: he that abideth in me, and I in him, the same beareth much fruit: for without me you can do nothing" (John 15:4–5). In an age preoccupied with activism, engagement, and "results," there is no truth as frequently neglected or even denied as this one tends to be.[65]

It should come as no surprise, then, that the Magisterium stresses the intimate bond between marriage, the family, and the life of prayer, which has its font and apex in the Eucharistic sacrifice. One might say that the Most Blessed Sacrament is the pulsing heart of a most blessed sacramental marriage and a holy family. Of these connections, Pope John Paul II is the most authoritative exponent:

> The sacrament of marriage is the specific source and original means of sanctification for Christian married couples and families.... The gift of Jesus Christ is not exhausted in the actual celebration of the sacrament of marriage, but rather accompanies the married couple throughout their lives.... Christian marriage, like the other sacraments, "whose purpose is to sanctify the people, to build up the body of Christ, and finally, to give worship to God," is in itself a liturgical action glorifying God in Jesus Christ and in the Church.... Just as husbands and wives receive from the sacrament the gift and responsibility of translating into daily living the sanctification bestowed on them, so the same sacrament confers on them the grace and moral obligation of transforming their whole lives into a "spiritual sacrifice."[66]

64 Vatican II, Dogmatic Constitution on the Church *Lumen Gentium* (November 21, 1964), no. 11.

65 The perfect remedy is Dom Chautard's book *The Soul of the Apostolate*. See "Confronting the Heresy of Activism with the Primacy of Prayer," in Kwasniewski, *Ministers of Christ*, 203–17.

66 John Paul II, Post-Synodal Apostolic Exhortation *Familiaris Consortio* (November 22, 1981), no. 56. The internal quotation is from *Sacrosanctum Concilium* 59.

The Church prays for the Christian family and educates the family to live in generous accord with the priestly gift and role received from Christ the High Priest. In effect, the baptismal priesthood of the faithful, exercised in the sacrament of marriage, constitutes the basis of a priestly vocation and mission for the spouses and family by which their daily lives are transformed into "spiritual sacrifices acceptable to God through Jesus Christ" (1 Pet 2:5). This transformation is achieved not only by celebrating the Eucharist and the other sacraments and through offering themselves to the glory of God, but also through a life of prayer, through prayerful dialogue with the Father, through Jesus Christ, in the Holy Spirit.[67]

Far from being a form of escapism from everyday commitments, prayer constitutes the strongest incentive for the Christian family to assume and comply fully with all its responsibilities as the primary and fundamental cell of human society. Thus the Christian family's actual participation in the Church's life and mission is in direct proportion to the fidelity and intensity of the prayer with which it is united with the fruitful vine that is Christ the Lord.[68]

"Fairest love" is learned above all in prayer. Prayer, in fact, always brings with it, to use an expression of Saint Paul, a type of interior hiddenness with Christ in God; "your life is hid with Christ in God" (Col 3:3).[69]

[67] *Familiaris Consortio* 59.

[68] *Familiaris Consortio* 62. An especially important way of keeping the branches united to the vine is to bring the liturgy into the home through devotions relating to and nourished by the Church's liturgical worship and calendar. The domestic echoes of the Church year were a pervasive part of Catholic life in all cultures, even up to the eve of the star-crossed liturgical reform of the 1960s. The reform killed most of these devotional instincts and customs due to its anti-devotional rationalism and its downplaying of the goodness of past traditions in general. Happily, they have begun to return in enclaves surrounding the traditional Latin Mass. See, among other excellent resources, the Illustrated Liturgical Year Calendar published by Sophia Institute Press; Leila Marie Lawler's *Summa Domestica*; Mary Reed Newland's *We and Our Children: How to Make a Catholic Home* and *The Year and Our Children: Planning the Family Activities for Christian Feasts and Seasons*; Maria Augusta von Trapp's *Around the Year with the Von Trapp Family*; and David Clayton and Leila Marie Lawler's *The Little Oratory: A Beginner's Guide to Praying in the Home.*

[69] John Paul II, Letter to Families *Gratissimam Sane* (February 2, 1994), no. 20.

Benedict XVI reaffirms the same connection:

> The Eucharist inexhaustibly strengthens the indissoluble unity and love of every Christian marriage. By the power of the sacrament, the marriage bond is intrinsically linked to the Eucharistic unity of Christ the Bridegroom and his Bride, the Church (cf. Eph 5:31–32). The mutual consent that the husband and wife exchange in Christ, which establishes them as a community of life and love, also has a Eucharistic dimension. Indeed, in the theology of Saint Paul, conjugal love is a sacramental sign of Christ's love for his Church, a love culminating in the Cross, the expression of his "marriage" with humanity and at the same time the origin and heart of the Eucharist.[70]

This "community of life and love" extends outward in works of charity (including the spiritual and corporal works of mercy), beginning with one's children and radiating to one's parish, town, and larger society, according to the proper order of charity. Yet everything we do as Christians flows from and leads back to the sacrifice of Our Lord Jesus Christ, of which the Holy Mass is the supernatural re-presentation, and of which the Holy Eucharist is the supreme sign and mystical reality. We are pilgrims who live from and for the Bread of Life, until we gaze upon His divine and human face in the Beatific Vision.

We are living in dark times, when fidelity to the integral teaching of Scripture, the witness of Tradition, and the fullness of the Church's Magisterium is met with increasing incomprehension, incredulity, mockery, ostracism, and penalties and will eventually be met with outright persecution. We must do our utmost not to lose sight of these authoritative guideposts, by which we can confidently walk, with God's grace, along the path of holiness — as men and women, as husbands and wives, as parents and children, as priests and religious. Nor can we accept any substitutes, dilutions, or subterfuges. Christ and His Church have spoken clearly about who we are and what we are to do if we would remain in the truth of Christ and live the truth in love.

[70] Benedict XVI, Post-Synodal Apostolic Exhortation *Sacramentum Caritatis* (February 22, 2007), no. 27.

10

Is the Human Body Part of the "Image of God"?

Over the past twenty years, I have noticed an interesting trend in regard to the ecclesial reception of Pope John Paul II's "theology of the body." At first, among Catholics seeking to be faithful to *Humanae Vitae* — an encyclical for which, in fact, Wojtyła's general audiences from 1979 to 1984 were intended to provide a deeper foundation — there was a sense of wild enthusiasm: here, at last, was the definitive answer to the critics of the Church's teaching. A veritable industry arose around the promotion of the "theology of the body": books, articles, pamphlets, workshops, conferences, diocesan programs. And I think it is beyond doubt that much of this material did help to bring Catholics in the grips of a materialistic, reductionistic, or dualistic mindset to a perspective more in keeping with Christian moral principles and the natural law.

On the other hand, there were the critics who wondered (1) if the popularizers were paving the way to a more subtle form of sensuality or *luxuria*, the vice of lust, by placing a Catholic veneer over the modern West's preoccupation with all things sexual; (2) if the response of John Paul II was adequate to the hydra-like nature of the problems facing modern Catholics, which are not just moral, but also doctrinal and liturgical — such that the state of Catholic belief and worship is constantly undermining efforts at moral probity;[71] (3) whether there even *is* such a thing as a "theology" of the body, considering that theology deals primarily with God, who is spirit, and secondarily with man because (like the angels) he is "made to God's image" according to his spiritual nature and has God for his final end. The other animals that live on the earth, which are bodily, sexual beings, are nevertheless not made to God's image; they are neither like Him in personhood nor capable of attaining the knowledge and

[71] See chapter 8, as well as Kwasniewski, *Ministers of Christ*, 31–40 et passim.

love of Him. Such, at any rate, is the teaching of the Church's Common Doctor, St. Thomas Aquinas.

I sympathize with both sides. When I read John Paul II's audiences in Michael Waldstein's accurate translation together with his introduction and notes — as opposed to online soundbites or the hyped-up materials of popularizers — I find there much profound content, informed by Aristotelian philosophy and Thomistic theology. It is worth studying and taking seriously, not so much because it is by a pope (since it has little magisterial authority) as because of its insightfulness.[72] At the same time, I believe that what married Catholics stand to gain from the most is a regular routine of prayer and penance, reading the Bible and spiritual masters, and assisting at solemn and beautiful liturgies. I remember reading an article in which a married couple explained that their marital troubles eventually went away when they both made an effort to stop focusing on their problems and instead made a decision (in spite of any feelings to the contrary) to go to Mass and pray together regularly. I know of the healing in my own life and in the lives of others that has come through prolonged Eucharistic adoration. This is not to say that we must ignore the right solution to particular issues; it is simply to reiterate that there is a proper hierarchy to all that we are and do: God first, the soul second, the neighbor third, the body last. This is the classic "order of charity."

All this being said, we should not be too quick to say that the notion of a "theology of the body" is utterly absent from or antithetical to the thought of St. Thomas. There are a few suggestive texts in the first part of the *Summa Theologiae*, question 93, that point toward a relationship of the body to the image:

> We may speak of God's image in two ways. First, we may consider in it that in which the image chiefly consists, that is, the intellectual nature. Thus the image of God is more perfect in the angels than in man, because their intellectual nature is more perfect, as is clear from what has been said (I, Q. 58, art. 3; I, Q. 79, art. 8).
>
> Secondly, we may consider the image of God in man as regards its accidental qualities, so far as to observe in man a certain imitation of God, consisting in the fact that man proceeds from man, as God from God; and also in the fact that the whole human soul is in the whole body,

[72] See, for two extensive treatments, Michael Maria Waldstein, *Glory of the Logos in the Flesh* (Ave Maria, FL: Sapientia Press, 2021) and David C. Hajduk, *Healing the Culture and the Family According to John Paul II* (Waterloo, ON: Arouca Press, 2022).

> and again, in every part, as God is in regard to the whole world. In these and the like things, the image of God is more perfect in man than it is in the angels. But these do not of themselves belong to the nature of the divine image in man, unless we presuppose the first likeness, which is in the intellectual nature; otherwise even brute animals would be to God's image. Therefore, as in their intellectual nature, the angels are more to the image of God than man is, we must grant that, absolutely speaking, the angels are more to the image of God than man is, but that in some respects man is more like to God.[73]

St. Thomas is saying that, absolutely and properly, the image, which is in the intellect, is found more perfectly in angels because they are higher intellectual beings; but in certain respects, man as a body-soul hylomorphic composite imitates things that are true about God in ways that angels cannot do. It is striking that when a human father begets a child, he is imitating God the Father in a particular way — something foreign to the bodiless, nongenerative angels. The human *person* in his bodily nature imitates God in this way, not due to bodiliness as such but due to the body's being informed by and, so to speak, permeated with, the rational soul. This at least suggests that one may give a theological account of how our bodiliness, distinctively *human* due to its animation by a rational soul, is pertinent to and included within the image in the intellect and the will. After all, in the metaphysics of Aquinas, man is not so much "embodied intellect" (an expression with Origenistic overtones) as he is "intellectualized body" (a more Aristotelian way of putting it).

Thus, we may expect man's body to reveal something about his spiritual soul, as indeed Aquinas admits:

> Although the image of God in man is not to be found in his bodily shape, yet because "the body of man alone among terrestrial animals is not inclined prone to the ground, but is adapted to look upward to heaven, for this reason we may rightly say that it is made to God's image and likeness, rather than the bodies of other animals," as Augustine remarks. But this is not to be understood as though the image of God were in man's body; but in the sense that the very shape of the human body represents the image of God in the soul by way of a trace.[74]

[73] *ST* I, Q. 93, art. 3.

[74] *ST* I, Q. 93, art. 6, ad 3, citing Augustine's *Eighty-Three Questions*, Q. 51.

While a "trace" (*vestigium*) is not an image or specific likeness, it is nevertheless a pertinent consideration when looking at how man, as a body-soul composite, reflects God in a way that other living organisms cannot do. Strikingly, St. Thomas teaches in his *Sentences* commentary: "Man is a partaker in beatitude to the extent that he exists in the image of God. Now, the image of God consists first and principally in the mind, but through a kind of derivation a representation of the image is found also in man's body, insofar as the body must be proportioned to the soul."[75] Or, in the words of a modern Russian theologian, Sergius Bulgakov: "The [human] body is not flesh that suppresses and shuts off the light of the spirit. On the contrary, the body is the image and self-revelation of the spirit."[76] This subtle interplay is well expressed in the *Catechism of the Catholic Church*:

> The human body shares in the dignity of "the image of God": it is a human body precisely because it is animated by a spiritual soul, and it is the whole human person that is intended to become, in the body of Christ, a temple of the Spirit: "Man, though made of body and soul, is a unity. Through his very bodily condition he sums up in himself the elements of the material world. Through him they are thus brought to their highest perfection and can raise their voice in praise freely given to the Creator. For this reason man may not despise his bodily life. Rather he is obliged to regard his body as good and to hold it in honor since God has created it and will raise it up on the last day."[77]

The ultimate "corporate promotion" of the dignity of the human body and its ability to reflect the divine occurs in the Incarnation: due to the hypostatic union, the body of Christ can now be said to be "the body of God"; hence, this human flesh is not merely an instrument of the rational soul but an instrument and manifestation of a Divine Person. Since Christ is the exemplar cause of our spiritual regeneration in Baptism and ultimately of our bodily resurrection at the end of time, it is reasonable to maintain that the image of the Son of God is newly present in and through our bodies, inasmuch as they are conformed to the body of His lowliness and of His glory. Drawing on the Fathers of the Church, William Daniel suggests that there are two ways of seeing, one that is of earth and earthly, another that is of heaven and heavenly (cf. 1 Cor. 15:47–49):

75 *In IV Sent.*, Dist. 49, Q. 4, art. 5.

76 Quoted in the introduction to Bulgakov, *Spiritual Diary*, 32.

77 *Catechism of the Catholic Church* [CCC] 364 (citing *Gaudium et Spes* 14.1).

> The contrast between the tree of life and the tree of the knowledge of good and evil is nearly identical in the accounts of Athanasius, Gregory of Nyssa, Gregory of Nazianzen, Basil, and John of Damascus. The tree of life is the tree of obedience — Christ's cross. The tree of the knowledge of good and evil is disobedience, whereby the human understands his or her relation to creation only in terms of his or her aligned or misaligned passions and desires. To eat the fruit of the tree of knowledge is to phenomenologize the world, a kind of Kantian, reasoned tastefulness. That is, to notice the other as naked is to see only the body — to see only matter, which is not to truly see the body in its relation to the soul and its co-mingling with divine light. It is to construe the object of one's gaze in a kind of radical subjectivity, permitting no reciprocal identification, only projection.... The tree of life does not see through the bodily passions where all objects are objects of desire. The tree of death — the tree of knowledge of good and evil — is the tree of non-being or privation of good. The two trees are two distinct forms of perceiving. The first is through active participation in the good, the co-mingling of lights; the second denies the penetrating light of divinity, which is the result of an absence of virtue in action — privation of good.[78]

Did not Our Lord Himself speak these mysterious words: "If your whole body is full of light, having no part dark, it will be wholly bright" (Luke 11:36)?[79]

As we have seen, then, the roots of a theological treatment of the body (even if one prefers to avoid the expression "*theology of* the body") are clearly found in several texts of the Angelic Doctor. John Paul II's audiences delving into the meaning of these roots are surely a worthy endeavor, though we must also be cautious about exaggerating their message or forgetting what is prior and more fundamental.

78 William Daniel, *Christ the Liturgy* (Brooklyn: Angelico Press, 2020), 55–56.

79 These words find their initial fulfillment in graceful Eucharistic Communion and their ultimate fulfillment in the resurrection of that body in which the Body of Christ has been sown. See Peter Kwasniewski, *The Holy Bread of Eternal Life: Restoring Eucharistic Reverence in an Age of Impiety* (Manchester, NH: Sophia Institute Press, 2020), 5–11, 61–64.

11

The Ideal Basis and Fruition of Marriage

As mentioned in the preface, this chapter is a metaphysical demonstration of some truths taken for granted elsewhere in the book, and, as such, has a denser texture. Some readers may prefer to skip ahead to chapter 12.

"Spiritual goods are more communicable than bodily goods," according to St. Thomas Aquinas. Drawing upon this axiom as well as similar insights from the ancient Neoplatonist Plotinus, I want to make an argument that the ideal basis of marriage is the union of minds or spirits through goods that are truly common, communicable, and inexhaustible.[80] "Ideal" here is to be taken in the Platonic sense of the essential, definitive identity that invests a particular instantiation with its recognizable character. The union of marriage will be contrasted with one that attempts to base itself on material goods, which are inherently private (sharable only by predication), divisible, exhaustible, and potentially divisive. It will become apparent that, when marriage is founded on the former goods, it has the potential for a continual inner growth and fruition that is limited, humanly speaking, only by the death of a spouse.[81]

[80] *ST*, Supplementum, Q. 56, art. 4. A common good (*bonum commune*) is not something over and above what is "good for me" personally; it is precisely what is best for and most perfective of me, simply speaking. That which is most commonly sharable is, in being shared, the most beneficial to all who partake of it. For a compact treatment, see Peter Kwasniewski, *True Obedience in the Church: A Guide to Discernment in Challenging Times* (Manchester, NH: Sophia Institute Press, 2021), 19–22; for a fuller treatment, see Edmund Waldstein and Peter Kwasniewski, eds., *Integralism and the Common Good: Selected Essays from* The Josias, vol. 1: *Family, City, and State* (Brooklyn: Angelico Press, 2021), 22–30; 39–45.

[81] If the spouses are reunited as fellow citizens in the heavenly Jerusalem, they will enjoy an eternity of fruition in love, which will achieve its maximum amplitude. Although hypothesizing about the relationship of spouses in the world to come falls outside the scope of this chapter, all that is said here bears on that topic.

If the thesis is true, it follows that the very possibility of an indissoluble commitment in marriage — the possibility of a lifelong relationship that remains free, alive, and life-giving — is based on the conscious pursuit of spiritual goods and a continual effort to place material goods at their service. This conclusion flies in the face of modern Western culture, preoccupied as it is with amassing and enjoying material goods, laboring under a social-contract mentality, and vainly seeking in physical beauty, health, and pleasure not only a sense of personal worth but even salvation from nauseating boredom and meaninglessness.[82]

Spiritual union contrasted with bodily union

The intellect, an immaterial power neither rooted in nor bounded by the body or any bodily organ, is the ultimate source of all properly human activity. St. Thomas teaches that man's final happiness, his beatitude, consists in the perfect operation of the intellect.[83] From this, of course, loving is in no way excluded, for whatever reason apprehends as good, the will is naturally apt to love; and thus, the greater the good perceived, the stronger is the will in tending toward it or resting in it.

The union of bodies is not the chief model or earthly end of marriage. Passing beyond the earthly goods that naturally pertain to matrimony, the union of spouses is meant to culminate in a union of *minds*, a union of intellects in the true, and of wills in the lovable. As God is the fullness of truth and goodness, so the supreme unifying reality, the point of convergence, is in God. Thus, to the extent that the spouses know and love God, they will be drawing nearer to perfect union with each other. How otherwise can Scripture be understood? Eve is called the "helper," one who helps in such a profound way that Adam acknowledges her as the completion of his very self, the one who makes him no longer alone in his humanity (Gen. 2:18–25); and St. Paul teaches that spouses are to imitate the union of Christ and the Church, an eternal spiritual union (Eph. 5:21–33). The union of souls is the higher and proper end of matrimony as regards the persons of the spouses.[84]

82 See Luke Bell, *The Mystery of Identity* (Brooklyn: Angelico Press, 2022).

83 See my article "On Intellectualism and the Beatific Vision," *Aquinas Review* 23 (2019–2020): 189–203, https://www.thomasaquinas.edu/sites/default/files/media/file/aquinas-review-2019-20.pdf.

84 Nothing said in this chapter should be construed as denying or relativizing the natural primacy of procreation as definitive of the species of friendship known as marriage. This primacy, without which marriage would not even exist, is here taken for granted (see chapters 3–4). Cf. Pius XI, *Casti Connubii*, no. 24: "This mutual molding of husband and wife, this determined effort to perfect

By definition, bodies are such that they exclude one another's co-presence. This, in fact, is the experiential origin of the principle of noncontradiction. The reason we know that *y* cannot be both *x* and not-*x* at the same time in the same respect, or that *y* cannot be not-*y*, is that two bodies cannot be in the same place at the same time in the same respect. This is evidently true of the union of spouses in the nuptial act. Although it is a wonder of creation and a taste of the profoundest union, this act is an experience more of *psychological* than of *spiritual* unification. The subjective apprehension of total unity is made possible by the cessation, during the act, of discursive thought, whose work is to distinguish and separate.[85] The *phenomenological* reality is of psychical unity and physical presence, while the *ontological* reality is the contact of bodies that mingle but remain distinct and separate. In its very bodiliness, the nuptial act is fleeting and returns its participants to a state of felt separation that corresponds to their ineluctable bodily identity. It cannot be the summit of spousal union, for bodiliness is not what is highest in man; the body is not the purest expression of a person's spiritual uniqueness or capacity for giving and receiving.[86]

If we look to the nature of mind, however, we shall see that a perfect union of minds *is* possible: two minds *can* be "in the same place," apprehending one and the same undivided truth, without contradiction. The same is true of the will with respect to spiritual goods. Because the intellect is never *somewhere*, properly speaking, it is capable of being everywhere within the range of its created possibilities. And because the presence of mind is not extended or dense in the way matter is, and therefore not subject to the strictures of bodily exclusivity, two intellects can be wholly "within" the same truth, and two wills can be wholly within or "toward" the same good. Therefore, the union of spouses is complete and perfect only when their incorporeal souls, acting in and through the body, have learned how to *be* in the same mental place by *thinking* and *willing* the same truths and goods, grounded in the one sovereign Truth and Good.

---

each other [in order to imitate that most perfect example of holiness placed before man by God, namely Christ, and by God's grace to arrive at the summit of perfection], can in a very real sense, as the Roman Catechism teaches, be said to be the chief reason and purpose of matrimony, provided matrimony be looked at not in the restricted sense as instituted for the proper conception and education of the child, but more widely as the blending of life as a whole and the mutual interchange and sharing thereof."

85 See *ST* I-II, Q. 34, art. 1.

86 See *ST* I-II, Q. 31, art. 5, on why spiritual pleasures are greater than bodily pleasures.

This is a necessary condition for the possibility of their "interinanimation," as the poet John Donne calls it.[87]

A stirring passage from Plotinus describes the relationship of liberated soul to Intellect in words exactly capturing what I wish to say about husband and wife:

> When it is in that region [of the intelligible], it must come to unity with Intellect, by the fact that it has turned to it, for when it is turned, it has nothing between, but comes to intellect and accords itself to it, and by that accord is united to it without being destroyed, but both of them are one and also two. When therefore it is in this state it could not change but would be unalterably disposed to intelligence while at the same time having a concurrent awareness of itself, as having become one and the same thing with its intelligible object.[88]

In context, Plotinus is speaking of the higher soul rising up to the realm of Pure Intellect, inferior coming to superior; I do not give the text with that aspect in mind but simply for its beautiful description of perfect union on the level of intellect—that is, on the level of spirit. This union I believe to be the highest form of togetherness attainable by spouses: *total unity in duality,* where even one's substantial individuality is meaningful only as referred to the beloved's.

The experience of rapture is found in such a union of mind and heart, despite the fact that our closeness to body as wayfarers in time makes the phenomenal union of the nuptial act more evident as a form of togetherness. It feels much more intense *to us,* although it is not more intense *in itself.*[89] We must learn to

87 John Donne, "The Extasie," in *The Complete English Poems,* ed. A. J. Smith (Harmondsworth, UK: Penguin, 1971), 56–57.

88 *Ennead* IV.4.2, in Armstrong, 143. All Plotinus citations are from A. H. Armstrong's translation of the *Enneads* for the Loeb Classical Library (Cambridge, MA: Harvard University Press, 1966–1988).

89 "Conscious awareness, in fact, is likely to enfeeble the very activities of which there is consciousness; only when they are alone are they pure and more genuinely active and living; and when good men are in this state their life is increased, when it is not spilt out into perception, but gathered together in one in itself" (*Ennead* I.4.10, in Armstrong, 201). This statement of Plotinus emphasizes the primacy of intellectual unity over perceptual or phenomenal union, as well as the importance of *habitual* surrender to the good instead of the labored efforts of self-consciousness (which sense-perception and bodily union have the general effect of *heightening* rather than purging). The closer one approaches to pure intellect, the less attention one pays to one's limited and lower self. The highest purity attainable parallels the highest self-forgetfulness.

use it as a rung of the ladder stretching up to the divine unity and the unity of all souls in God, especially those privileged souls (I refer to faithful spouses) who have labored together in the common enterprise of co-redemption.

Bodily goods image forth and yield to spiritual goods

Five truths flow from this principle that spiritual goods are more communicable than bodily goods.

First, in the divine plan, bodily goods have the purpose of introducing us to, or schooling us in, spiritual goods. As we have seen, the nuptial privilege of copulation is ordered by its very nature to a union of what is metaphysically nobler than and prior to the body—namely, the part of each spouse that is capable of being *communicated without contradiction* to the other by a mode of participation in the things of the spirit. As Plotinus keenly observes:

> For bodies are hindered from communion with each other by bodies, but incorporeal things are not kept apart by bodies; nor are they separated in place, but by otherness and difference; when therefore there is no otherness, the things which are not other are present to each other.[90]

The body cannot without contradiction be communicated to another or made to be in another, for there is always a residuum of privately possessed organic space from which we cannot step out or which we cannot translate into a common intelligible language—we cannot divest ourselves of our body and give it to another *in lieu of* that other's body. But something very much akin to this translation and communication *can* be done on the level of spirit or intellective soul.[91] The spouses give each other the privilege of being with one another bodily in a very intimate way, but they cannot, except imperfectly (and perhaps metaphorically), be *within* each other's bodies in a way that would bring about the full interpenetration called for by love's mutual indwelling and ecstasy.[92] *Qua* animals distinct in space and time, man and woman cannot overcome their

[90] Plotinus, *Ennead* VI.9.8, in Armstrong, 333.

[91] A private good is always bodily or tied to the body (e.g., wealth and property, health, peace as absence of violence, traffic laws, and the most important example, one's own body *qua* possession), whereas the common good, properly understood, is spiritual (e.g., knowledge, moral virtue, divine grace, peace as tranquility of order).

[92] On *mutua inhaesio* and *extasis* as effects of love, see *ST* I-II, Q. 28 and the commentary in Peter Kwasniewski, *The Ecstasy of Love in the Thought of Thomas Aquinas* (Steubenville, OH: Emmaus Academic, 2021), 194–249.

independence or separateness — not even through marriage. The attempt to resolve this *aporia* at a sensual level is doomed to end in frustration.

The body is exclusive because its first accident (speaking of the Aristotelian categories rather than in terms of everyday life) is quantity in the sense of extension, each part being outside of other parts. In contrast, their rational nature beckons the spouses to give to each other the privilege of *suneinai*: of existing together in the same intellectual and volitional space or sphere of reality. Because spirit is not *extensive,* spread out in a spatial sense, but rather *intensive,* or wholly self-contained as an immaterial activity, the wife's spirit can co-intend what the husband's spirit intends, and vice versa; their sphere can be totally one, because truth and goodness are perfectly and integrally sharable without diminishment of their unicity. Plotinus sketches out this oneness in paradoxical language:

> So then the seer does not see and does not distinguish and does not imagine two, but it is as if he had become someone else and he is not himself and does not count as his own there, but has come to belong to that and so is one, having joined, as it were, centre to centre. For here too when the centres have come together they are one, but there is duality when they are separate. This also is how we now speak of 'another.' For this reason the vision is hard to put into words. For how could one announce that as another when he did not see, there when he had the vision, another, but one with himself?[93]

Truth is not a private good in such a way that your taking a part deprives me of a part. It is a common good in the strict sense of being infinitely partakable by mind as such: every mind, according to its degree, can encompass all truth.[94]

We can unfold this proposition in another way. Where there is unity in a thing that is not entirely simple, there must be a cause of that unity. A whole is not merely the sum of its parts, but *qua* whole brings something *to* the parts that they would not otherwise have or be. The parts are parts in virtue of belonging to some whole that encompasses them and establishes them in a certain order. This is no less true of the "whole" (the "one flesh") constituted by spouses. There must be a cause of their unity, a holistic principle greater than either, which accounts for their being ordered to each other and encompassed by each other. In order to cause the *unity* of the *whole,* this principle must be immaterial, for

93 Plotinus, *Ennead* VI.9.10, in Armstrong, 341.

94 See the references in note 80.

the corporeal as such is incapable of acting as a common ground between two materially distinct individuals.

Matter makes human things separate and private, whereas the life-giving form of man, the rational soul, tends toward unification and communication. Thus, intellect and will are again seen to be the essential principle of unity in human love in its highest form, inasmuch as the mind and heart of both spouses are focused on the same truth, concentrated on the same good, enamored of the same beauty, aspiring to the same nobility.

A corollary follows. Husband and wife can inhabit each other's sphere of truth and goodness — their centers of being can coincide — because spiritual reality emanates from the selfsame divine infinity. Thus, husband and wife are capable of rising to a perfect union, of which the bodily union is a shadow, foretaste, and promise. It is tragic when the opportunity to attain this glorious unification of the highest part of each spouse's being — their spiritual communion, which is more real than their sensual tangency — is ignored, denied, or undermined by distortions or perversions of the nuptial act. As Plotinus again observes: "We are concerned with its [the body's] pains and pleasures, more in proportion as we are weaker and do not separate ourselves, but consider the body the most honorable part of ourselves and the real man, and, so to speak, sink ourselves in it."[95]

All human relationships seem to have some share in the spiritual dimension. How could it be otherwise, if human beings are incapable of becoming *essentially* irrational, and so always act within the scope of the inclinations of will and the reach of intellect, even if particular acts or habits be vicious? Properly human love has an intrinsic orientation toward the divine, although man can neglect to cultivate that orientation or even attempt to destroy it.

Marriage vows are spiritual in essence

Second, we must look to the spiritual plane for the ultimate fulfillment of the marriage vows, wherein each spouse declares that he or she belongs to the other. The only way this total self-giving and ego-dissolution can take place is through intellection and volition, which are, taken in themselves, unconfined to place and time.

Speaking of time, Plotinus writes: "It is preserved, up to a point, by eternity ... but destroyed if it passes altogether into temporal dispersion."[96] Complete

[95] Plotinus, *Ennead* IV.4.18, in Armstrong, 183.

[96] Plotinus, *Ennead* I.5.7, in Armstrong, 223.

temporality (dispersion) would be equivalent to nonbeing. Thus, to immerse oneself in time or matter is to tend increasingly toward nonbeing. This folly is the opposite of the wisdom loved by the philosopher, who strives, in a way, to rise above time and matter, reaching for the divine ideas in their primal source. A similar "dialectic of ascension" would apply to the lifelong convergence of spouses toward each other and up to their first beginning and last end, the Good from whence their love streams forth. This simultaneously horizontal (husband-wife) and vertical (man-God) convergence is a rising above time and matter so as to rest, forever united, in the Beatific Vision of the Triune God.

Self-giving and ego-dissolution cannot finally be achieved by bodily contact. While the body is truly (part of) myself and expresses who I am, still it is not communicable, it cannot be *given* except symbolically or iconically, as a symbol of a greater and nobler giving. St. Thomas, however, in contrast to many of his contemporaries, insists that Matrimony is more than a mere *symbol* of the union of Christ and the Church; it is a grace-conferring *reality* through which the power of that prior mystical union emanates into the laity and the world they shape. For Aquinas, the sacrament of Marriage originates and (when no resistance is offered) perfects a profound union of hearts and minds patterned after the union of Christ and the Church. In its own proper way, this graced human relationship is capable of bearing fruit that will last for eternity.

St. Thomas is aware of the importance of granting the sacramental reality its legitimate due. Often medieval thinkers did not adequately ponder the implications of the grace present in and merited by the union of man and woman in the state of charity. St. Thomas does not waver on the primacy of the spiritual even in that most "worldly" of vocations, the vocation to conjoin two separate earthly lives and make, by God's power, one heart and mind out of two individuals. Hence, Thomas vigorously defends marriage against Manichaean objections while emphasizing that the essence of marriage does not consist in carnal relations, nor, for that matter, in the begetting of children *as such*.[97] Both of these things are implicit in marriage as effects in their cause, but that does not make

[97] To be precise, for Aquinas, marriage necessarily includes *consent* to carnal relations according to the will of God, the handing over of the *right* to bodily possession, and openness to and desire for offspring. It does not, however, *consist* in the act of sexual intercourse or bodily possession, nor (*a fortiori*) in the act of conception and birth. Rather, it is inherently *ordained* to such activities and their natural effects, which are the complement or completion of what is promised by the spouses to one another. Key distinctions emerge in St. Thomas's treatment of the marriage of St. Joseph and the Blessed Virgin Mary: see chapter 26.

the cause reducible to the effects. No, the effects must be precontained more eminently or more perfectly in the cause, if it is to be a cause in the fullest sense.

Hence, St. Thomas can defend virginity for the kingdom of God as well as the practice of continence within marriage, precisely because there is a certain union of spouses higher than the cooperation that takes place on the physical or procreative level. This higher union of will and intellect constitutes the essence of the love and the life vowed by the spouses to each other; it generates their duties and privileges, vouchsafes their fidelity and friendship, furthers their salvation, and gains eternal merit for them.

St. Thomas is speaking about spiritual goods that are communicable in the highest degree; and from these highest goods, all lower goods naturally flow to their proper places, participating in the purity and worthiness of the best mutual activity. The hierarchy of marriage goods is brought into being by the emanation of all aspects of spousal life from this first principle, *the sacred vow*, by which the married soul is disposed to receive the rich graces of God in all that it does for and with the other, in whom and by whom it has constituted itself in the nuptial state of existence.

The primacy of the spiritual dignifies old age

Third, the principle expressed by Aquinas (viz., that spiritual goods are more communicable than bodily goods) makes it possible to see in old age the fruition of the marriage vows — a thing impossible to see within a narrowly physical, that is, procreational and sensual, model of marriage. If one were to hypothesize that the nuptial act is constitutive of marriage, what could we say about spouses when they legitimately lose interest in the sexual expression of their love, or lose their bodily power to enact it? Or of the barren, in whom the act, while guiltless, does not seem to justify itself?[98] Or of spouses who choose to abstain from sexual intercourse for valid spiritual reasons? What shall we say about a woman's loss of beauty over time or a man's loss of fitness?

If one adopts in full the spiritual vision of marriage, the process of aging not only fits into the vocation without inconsistency (inasmuch as the mind and

[98] I am referring to the almost ubiquitous experience of couples who, understanding by a natural and supernatural instinct that the nuptial act is inherently procreative as well as unitive, feel a certain frustration even with the legitimate use of marriage when it consistently fails to lead to offspring. It's almost like having a vehicle that, though comfortable, is incapable of reaching the destination one has in mind.

heart will, in the best circumstances, grow better and wiser with the passage of time, permitting a richer communion) but also can be seen as *desirable* from the point of view of securing a deeper and more lasting unity of soul. For the passions of the body can, to some extent, stand in the way of the full development and sharing of the interior man, whereas the gradual recession of the physical appetites of the spouses opens the way for a purgative, illuminative, and unitive experience of each other at the level of what is most inward and unique in the person — what is most precious in this man and this woman.

Love and knowledge of the other can and ought to become more perfect over time, not in spite of but precisely as a natural result of aging together, with the crosses and graces it offers. No other understanding of marriage can explain how aging, physical decline, and loss of sensuality fit, by the Creator's design, into the organic unfolding of the inner meaning of the nuptial sacrament, and how the loss of one privilege leads to the gaining of a more sublime privilege that re-creates at a higher level what the earlier had accomplished at a lower level.

If we see the intrinsic tendency of Matrimony to be an ascension toward spiritual communion, then, far from fearing old age or death, the spouses will receive these gifts with humility and hope. They will trust that Christ, if we remain faithful to Him, can turn us into little children the older we grow, and that He who conquered death can raise us up to the splendor of beatitude, where spouses will at last perfectly know and love each other because they are united with the one who is All in All and who sustained them throughout the life they wrought together.

A consequence of the prevalent, if not always conscious, view that physical affection is the central feature of human love in its youthful stage is the sad fact that *when* marriages last (as too many sadly do not), the spouses are forced to adjust uncomfortably to the later stages of life inaugurated by children, middle age, and finally, old age. All of these subsequent stages, to one degree or another, lack the supposed raison d'être of love between a man and a woman. The Catholic, on the other hand, sees the mutual attraction of man and woman as a precursor to the state of marriage in which the full expression of love, in its physical dimension, properly and rightfully belongs, and at the same time sees marriage as ordered to the rearing of a family. The richer and fuller Catholic teaching, implied in St. Thomas and developed by the Church, reveals the continuous lifelong character of Matrimony, from honeymoon to old age and death.

By emphasizing the Augustinian blessings of faith (*fides*), sacrament (*sacramentum*), and offspring (*proles*) received and educated in the Faith, the Church gives priority to the lasting goods of intellect and will and exhorts her children to strive for the better things that purify, intensify, and sanctify the lesser goods, putting every aspect of husband and wife at the service of the communion of persons with each other and with God. Thus, instead of experiencing damaging tectonic shifts between youth and middle age, middle age and old age, the natural continuum of a common life as it is channeled through the grace of the sacraments and perfected in a union of mind and heart — which is the Catholic ideal of Holy Matrimony — can be welcomed and savored for the divine blessings it carries with it from beginning to end.

In secular (i.e., nonsacramental) marriages, and even more so in cases of cohabitation, there is an element of undignified guesswork and makeshift bandaging in the co-adaptation of the partners to each other and the gradual process of trying to make one life out of two. If the guessing falters or the bandages run out, the relationship comes to a stop and bleeds to death. The very opposite is true in a Christian marriage worthily entered into and nobly lived out from day to day: there is a higher purpose and ever-deeper roots; there is salvific truth and growing constancy.

The good of children is amplified

Fourth, if we understand Aquinas's axiom rightly, the bearing and rearing of children glows with a new urgency and dignity of meaning. The children of a marriage are not a by-product, desirable or undesirable, of some unrelated contract entered into between two adults; they are the most perfect *worldly* mirroring and blossoming of the creative fidelity pledged in the vows of marriage. They are the choice fruit produced by the physico-spiritual fecundity of love.

Love, like its object, the good, seeks to communicate itself to others (*bonum est diffusivum sui*). There is nothing it desires more than to spread out, multiply, consolidate, establish lasting works that bear witness to the truth of the vows by which man and woman agree to make themselves one. But the begetting of children is as nothing compared with their upbringing and education, for nearly anyone can do the former, indeed without even intending to do so, while the latter requires a panoply of virtues, patient dedication, unwavering commitment. St. Thomas observes that one of the motives for the nuptial act is the virtue of religion: the spouses desire to rear disciples of God; they desire to extend the kingdom of God over more souls by consecrating the fruit of their love to him who is Love in Person.

The spiritual health of the child, his maturation in knowledge and faith, is a function of the spiritual communion of his parents; he is predisposed to know and to believe what they themselves exemplify in their shared life. Agreement is the nurse of persuasion; concordance (sounding together) in the highest things forms a child who is concordant with his family, his vocation, and his destiny. For children to be worthily begotten and reared, they must be offspring of a *mutual spiritual labor*, in which is discerned the very same intellectual and volitional unification spoken of earlier.

Note the suggestive parallelism or symbiosis between the children of the flesh, which are the offspring of the nuptial act, and children of the spirit. The phrase "children of the spirit" can be meant in two ways: (1) the consonance of ideas and the beauty of communal life as a work of art; (2) the result of a spiritual paternity and spiritual maternity that husband and wife exercise through catechizing and consecrating their bodily offspring to Christ and the Church. The children, catechized and consecrated, are the ultimate flower of the nuptial vows and of the life of fidelity and striving-toward-oneness built upon them.

This relationship of physical to spiritual parenthood is directly analogous to the corporal and spiritual works of mercy: the child of flesh stands to the child of spirit as feeding the hungry to instructing the ignorant. The spiritual illuminates and perfects the corporal, and the corporal, by its very nature, leads to the spiritual, whenever man places no impediment in the way of this providential path.

The mysticism of marriage

Fifth and finally, it begins to be evident from what we have seen so far that there is a mystical or "revelational" way of looking at the relationship of the exterior to the interior, the bodily to the intellectual, the sensual to the spiritual, the particular to the universal, the exemplate to the exemplar. In other words, the principle enunciated by Aquinas suggests an abundant harvest of moral and metaphysical insight about human relationships in all their complexity and subtlety, as regards both how they fail and how they flourish.

Parts of animals, e.g., bone and muscle, grow in unison. As the healthy organism develops, each of its parts increases or matures in right proportion to all other parts. This is a good metaphor for the mutual growing together of husband and wife. In a healthy marriage, the elements of one person — his character, his thoughts, his feelings, his desires and needs, his gifts, his spiritual life — grow or evolve alongside those of the other, in harmony with and in proportion to her character, her thoughts, her feelings, her desires and needs, her gifts, her spiritual life. They are "growing together" in both senses of the phrase: the spouses grow or mature alongside each other, and their very growth is a unification, a growing to be one. We see both the maximal development of the person and the maximal communion of two persons, with, as the family grows, the welcome addition of more persons who are able to participate in that communion. As John Paul II declares in one of the general audiences on the "theology of the body":

> Love not only unites the two subjects, but allows them to interpenetrate each other, belonging spiritually to one another, to the point that the author of the letter [to the Ephesians] can affirm, "The one who loves his wife loves himself" (Eph 5:28). The 'I' becomes in some way the 'you,' and the 'you' the 'I' (in the moral sense, of course).[99]

In this ideal, we can see the reality that Plotinus calls a "one-many," a multiplicity rooted in and ordered to unity. A community is, by definition, a "one-many": for there to be a co-unity, there must be individuals who are distinct and at the same time "at one," in unison, intermingling, in those things that are more important, more lasting, more beautiful than anything each possesses by him- or herself. Spiritual goods are indeed more communicable than bodily goods — a truth of immense profundity that underlies John Paul II's "theology of the body" and must animate all the valuable efforts that are being made to utilize his programmatic catechesis for evangelizing our contemporaries.

[99] Audience of September 1, 1982, no. 7, in *Man and Woman He Created Them: A Theology of the Body*, trans. Michael Waldstein (Boston: Pauline Books & Media, 2006), 485.

12

Cross and Crown

Looking to my own experience and that of so many married friends and acquaintances, it is hard to escape the conclusion that marriage is the most difficult vocation in the world. This is not to say that it does not have its beautiful and wonderful side. It was fitting that St. Paul should compare the union of Christ and the Church to the communion of spouses, for in the world of creation, there is no greater experience of two beings becoming one — even if this oneness, in the fallen order, never achieves total perfection. And surely there are few things more amazing than holding a newborn baby in one's arms or seeing him smile for the first time; it is like Adam awakening to see the sun on the day of his creation.

What I have in mind is more subtle. Prior to marrying, it is almost impossible to fathom the selfishness latent in one's soul and in the soul of one's companion. The sacrament has a mysterious way of exorcising evil by calling it forth and compelling one to deal with it. For years and years, spouses have to work through every sort of difficulty, personal and familial, internal and external — and the difficulties, like weeds, never entirely disappear but spring up in new and unexpected places. If the couple are strong in faith, they will make progress, slowly, humbly, placing their trust in Divine Providence and begging God's help. It calls for the perseverance of saints in the making.

Let's be honest: the life couples lead before marriage often keeps them so face-to-face and emotionally absorbed in each other that they are not yet *able* to discover (and so, to begin patiently working through) their numerous faults, the hidden burdens they bear from their past, the unspoken, perhaps unconscious, and frequently unrealistic expectations they have for their future. Living in close proximity in that peculiar state of prenuptial revery, a lover or beloved can be so centered on the present moment and the presence of the other that it is hard to get sufficient perspective on past and future and oneself. This lack of perspective can make a marriage tougher later on, but it's impossible to see how one could entirely avoid a certain amount of illusion; indeed, a cynic might say that the only reason people get married is because they *don't* know what they're getting into.

Christian realism might endorse that sentiment on a global scale: the Lord, in His mercy, holds back the future from *all* of us, since, as T. S. Eliot says, "human kind / Cannot bear very much reality."[100] That is why we pray for our daily bread, not for a year's worth of bread. God reveals His will to us here and now, in the love we owe to the persons He has placed in our care. We will inevitably fumble as we carry out the task and sometimes make a mess of things. Our awareness of being mere creatures of dust, mere children, will prevent us from either exaggerating the disaster to the point of despair or downplaying the need for repentance and forgiveness.

God knew what He was doing in making the sacrament of Matrimony monogamous, lifelong, indissoluble. Humanly speaking, there are times when you may want to *kill* your spouse, or, more modestly, get as far away on the planet as possible. Hard to believe, isn't it? My betrothed and I thought we would be the Platonic ideal couple, always understanding each other, always so full of kindness and gentleness. How could it be otherwise, when this special person "means the world" to me? But, as we know from experience, there *is* such a thing as world-weariness. In hard times, which can last for days or weeks or months or even years, your selfish self (if I may so put it) insists that you stand on your rights, that the other unconditionally surrender, or even that you should *sever* a relationship so unconducive (as it may seem) to your own happiness.

Here is where blind faith comes in. You say to yourself: "I have made a solemn vow in the presence of God. If I break this relationship, I have broken faith with God. That means I am an atheist or a devil. But I am not an atheist, and I do not want to be a devil. Therefore, I will not break this relationship; in fact, I will do everything I possibly can, in spite of my feelings, to heal, to forgive, to go forward."

In the secular world, at just that point, most people say: "Okay, we have to get a divorce; we're not 'compatible.'" (As G. K. Chesterton famously said: "I have known many happy marriages, but never a compatible one. The whole aim of marriage is to fight through and survive the instant when incompatibility

[100] T. S. Eliot, *Four Quartets*, "Burnt Norton," in *Complete Poems and Plays 1909–1950* (New York: Harcourt Brace Jovanovich, 1980), 118.

becomes unquestionable. For a man and a woman, as such, are incompatible."[101])
And so they are in danger of moving on from one relationship to another, in a semipermanent state of discontentedness, because they have never radically surrendered their freedom. Catholic marriage and religious life have precisely this in common: a radical surrender of the freedom of self-determination. Both of them promise, over time, the regaining of a freedom far superior to the one that has been given up.

This, it seems to me, is the massive truth at stake in the debate over marriage and family: spousal love's inherent demand for totality, fidelity, permanence, and, yes, self-sacrifice to the very end, without which it is not love but a shadowy imitation or parody of love, something unworthy of the children of God. As Pope Benedict XVI writes:

> Corresponding to the image of a monotheistic God is monogamous marriage. Marriage based on exclusive and definitive love becomes the icon of the relationship between God and his people and vice versa. God's way of loving becomes the measure of human love.[102]

Marriage was created by God *in order to show us an image of His own total, faithful, permanent love*. In turn, God's grace makes it possible for human marriage — so weak, feeble, and fragile after the Fall — to *be* this image and to endure as an image in spite of all obstacles. The Church's defense of indissoluble marriage is nothing less than a defense of the nobility of human love, created, like man and woman, in the image of God's own love, and, when healed and elevated by His grace, capable of sharing in His indomitable power to overcome evil.

If we reject this image of God, we are rejecting God Himself; dishonor paid to the image passes to its archetype. No matter what their good intentions may be, those who are promoting the admission of the divorced and civilly remarried to the banquet of Holy Communion are promoting the cult of a false god, an idol; their religion cannot be that of the Church, the spiritual Israel. Indeed, in a diabolic reversal of Pope Benedict's statement, *human* love (or rather, its shadowy imitation) becomes the measure of *God's* love. Now *He* is expected to be unfaithful to the demands of His own covenant. Polyamorous relationality becomes the icon of an incoherent and conflicted deity. Let there be no mistake about it: even a so-called pastoral accommodation *means* the worship of a god

[101] G.K. Chesterton, *What's Wrong with the World* (New York: Sheed & Ward, 1942), pt. I, chap. 7, pp. 67–68.

[102] Benedict XVI, Encyclical Letter *Deus Caritas Est* (December 25, 2005), no. 11.

other than the Blessed Trinity. Nor are there true sacraments in this worldly religion, since the spousal bond of Jesus Christ with the Church is no longer the measure and model of all reality — including the reality of Christian man, his capacity to love and be loved, to forgive and be forgiven, to suffer and to die. The pastoral accommodation is a rejection of Christianity as such, in its deepest and most characteristic trait — namely, the revelation of a love that is both inconceivably demanding and unfathomably merciful, as it confers on its recipients the very desire and ability to live out the gospel.

I do not wish to be misinterpreted as saying that anyone whose marriage is failing or has completely fallen apart, or anyone who has taken the step of attempting remarriage while still married sacramentally to another man or woman, is a "lost cause," incapable of redemption. But the sober truth is that people in this situation have been drawn into a deeper participation in the Cross of Christ. They are being called upon to bear witness to the truth of the indissoluble union of Christ and His Church by honoring the bond that unites them in this vale of tears to another baptized soul, no matter how sinful, cruel, or negligent the other spouse may have become after marriage. If they are separated and alone, it will take the form of a "dry martyrdom" of loneliness and reparation for the many sins committed against human life and divine love. If they are separated but "remarried," the martyrdom will be a holocaust: it will necessitate giving up adulterous sexual relations and living together as brother and sister, so that Confession may be approached with sincerity of heart, and Our Lord Jesus Christ may be received in the Most Holy Eucharist with a clean conscience. We know that there are situations where a person is more sinned against than sinning, but the vocation to honor the sacrament of marriage *no matter what* cannot be evaded if one wishes to save one's soul from eternal death.

Spiritual growth is governed by a law, a sevenfold pattern, as applicable to one's relationship with God as it is to one's relationship with a spouse. Growth is often premised on passing through this furnace alive: (1) trial, offense, disaster; (2) despondency, anger, bitterness, recrimination, sulking; (3) period of struggle, angels wrestling with demons; (4) victory of the angels, by God's grace; (5) discovery of the root problem, with shame, humiliation, and contrition; (6) forgiveness, healing, consolation; (7) stronger, deeper, richer love, ready to face the next trial, offense, or disaster. Something like this cycle happens again and again in most marriages. What keeps the marriage together is, in the end, two things: total commitment to the vow and total willingness to forgive. Neither is possible without imploring and receiving God's grace, through personal prayer and liturgical prayer. God has not left us orphans, but we, by not turning to our Father, often act as if we were orphaned.

How full of supernatural common sense is St. Thomas Aquinas when he states:

> The indissolubility of the union of male and female belongs to good morals. For (1) their mutual love will be the more constant if they know that they are indissolubly united; (2) they will also be more carefully provident in the conduct of the household, when they realize that they are always to remain together in possession of the same things; (3) again, this precludes the origin of quarrels which must needs arise between the husband and his wife's relatives, if he were to put his wife away; and those who are connected through affinity have a greater regard for one another; (4) moreover, it removes the occasions of adultery that would occur were the husband free to put away his wife, or vice versa: for this would encourage the seeking of further marriage.[103]

All of these reasons are perfectly clear and right. If you know that you *must* remain with your spouse, you will seek to improve your relationship by showing signs of love and working out difficulties; you will even seek to improve yourself to please your spouse. In 1 Corinthians, St. Paul seems to think it a drawback of marriage that it compels the spouses to think constantly of each other rather than of the Lord. Even if we fully endorse his apologia for the celibate or virginal life on account of its single-minded devotion to the Lord, it is no less obviously true that a husband's or wife's constant concern with the other spouse's needs and desires is a peerless school of purification from self-centeredness. If you are not going to be a religious or a priest who has handed everything over to Christ, you will likely need to be cured of your innate egotism by the grueling school of service called marriage and family.

Continuing with St. Thomas's argument, when you know that you're "stuck for life," you are that much more inclined to be provident in your management of the goods of the household. If you could easily break with your wife, just think of the difficulties it would create with her family and friends who live in the vicinity or have other contact with you. (Admittedly, this argument carried greater force in a world of more numerous and more tightly knit social relations,

[103] St. Thomas Aquinas, *Summa contra Gentiles*, bk. III, chap. 123.

and far less relocating, than is typical of our times.) If you could easily break up, the first serious difficulties, or any lingering dissatisfaction, would become the pretext for divorce and the never-ending search for a "perfect partner," who simply does not exist in this vale of tears. You might find another who would satisfy you for a short time, and then you'd split with him or her too. This is exactly the modern pattern: rampant fornication, promiscuity, multiple divorces, and the enormous heartache caused to spouses, children, and other relatives who must live among the rubble of collapsed marriages.[104]

God's wisdom in establishing the great mystery of indissoluble marriage with its blessings of fidelity, offspring, and sacrament is evident on so many levels — but only to those who, peering with the light-filled eye of faith and the eye of reason sharpened by faith, can see that unchanging wisdom. They know that there is something better than this life, higher than human freedom, deeper than autonomy. They know the ultimate truth of the Gospel: "For whosoever will save his life shall lose it: but whosoever will lose his life for my sake, the same shall save it" (Luke 9:24, KJV). Would not the words of St. Peter fit the case? "You will do well to pay attention to this [prophetic word] as to a lamp shining in a dark place, until the day dawns and the morning star rises in your hearts" (2 Pet. 1:19). We, as the human race, as the Western world, as the Church on earth, are in a dark place; but the lamp of Christ's doctrine is still shining for us today as it was yesterday and as it will tomorrow, saving the souls who embrace it as the way to eternal communion with the Blessed Trinity. The Morning Star, Jesus Christ, is risen, and He rises anew in every faithful soul.

104 See Leila Miller, *Primal Loss: The Now-Adult Children of Divorce Speak* (Phoenix: LCB Publishing, 2017).

13

Building and Rebuilding Community

When studying classic works of Catholic theology, one might be struck by the overwhelming emphasis on unity in love as the characteristic mark of the Church. This is not a mere theological opinion. It is a truth everywhere announced in the prophets and is given its most sublime expression by Christ Himself in the discourse at the Last Supper, recorded in chapters 14 through 17 of the Gospel of St. John. Sin disunites, fragments, isolates, sets at odds; grace gathers together, builds up, heals, harmonizes. In the words of Origen:

> Where there are sins, there are multiplicity, schisms, heresies, dissensions. But where there is virtue, there is singleness and union, on the basis of which all believers are one heart and one soul. And, if I may speak more plainly, multiplicity is the source of all evils, whereas clustering together and being brought back from a crowd into singleness is the source of good things.[105]

This "singleness" is a reflection of the simplicity of God, ultimate source of all good things, while the multiplicity Origen denounces is not just any kind of multitude (for man has many spiritual powers as well as ten fingers and ten toes, and this is all to the good) but that deceitful and destructive pluralism

[105] Cited in Henri de Lubac, *Catholicism: Christ and the Common Destiny of Man*, trans. L. Sheppard and E. Englund, O.C.D. (San Francisco: Ignatius Press, 1988), 33. "Ubi peccata sunt, ibi est multitudo, ibi schismata, ibi haereses, ibi dissensiones. Ubi autem virtus, ibi singularitas, ibi unio, ex quo omnium credentium erat cor unum et anima una. Et, ut manifestius dicam, principium malorum omnium est multitudo, principium autem bonorum coangustatio et a turbis in singularitatem redactio." My citing of this work does not imply agreement with de Lubac's *nouvelle théologie*, particularly his defective theory of the relationship of nature and grace.

in which the devil specializes, which can be seen in the lack of unanimity in Catholic doctrine or the lack of stably beautiful universal rites of worship. Well in advance of the "Benedict Option," Origen is urging us to get away from crowds and to cluster into real communities where virtue can take root and bear fruit, where the many can be one heart and one soul in their common love of God and their common devotion to His unchanging truth.

Unfortunately, nowadays the anarchical crowd is all the rage, and the well-oriented parish, the united and loving family, and the flourishing monastery or convent are viewed as anachronisms. How are we to respond to the challenge of fragmentation and cynicism?

The first and most important step in bringing life to the world is an unceasing quest for personal holiness. Superficial activism has always been and will always be a great temptation for fallen human beings, inveterate "do-gooders" that we are. When there is a problem, the first thing people suggest is to interview experts, hold a conference, or create a new government office. Nobody suggests that we should retire to our local churches for prayer or undertake penances. The thought that the quickest path to sanity is sanctity occurs to very few. I should cultivate the one and only vineyard that is mine to cultivate, and in doing this, I will make a *lasting* difference in the world — lasting because it occurs at the deep level of the spirit. As St. Catherine of Siena reminds us:

> Any soul, in cultivating its vineyard, cultivates that of his neighbor as well. The two are so closely united that no one can do good or evil to himself without doing good or evil to his neighbor at the same time. Together, you form but one single, universal vineyard.[106]

[106] *Dialogue*, chap. 24, cited in de Lubac, *Catholicism*, 77. This is the antithesis of the attitude we find placed in the mouths of sinners by the prophet Isaiah: "Keep to yourself, do not come near me, for I am set apart from you" (Isa. 65:5). To the claim that "I should be able to do whatever I want as long as I'm not harming anyone else," Roger Scruton replies: "The problem with classical liberalism is that it never pauses to examine what is involved in 'not harming others.' Do I leave others unharmed when I destroy my capacity for personal relationships, through drug-taking, promiscuity, or porn addiction? Do I leave them unharmed when I stupefy myself with pop music?" ("'Cows Too … Can Easily Be Made into Ideas': An Interview with Roger Scruton," *Clarion Review*, October 9, 2009, www.clarionreview.org/2009/10/interview-roger-scruton). In like manner, Anthony Esolen observes: "They [who downplay sin] miss *the implications of the evil*, which are both logical and social. Evil dissolves its makeshift container. The evil premise of the Lonely Revolution was that whatever consenting adults,

When my vineyard begins to bear fruit, it bears an abundance of fruit that can be shared with our hungry neighbors. If I have nothing within me, I shall have nothing to give, as the old Scholastic saying recalls: *nemo dat quod non habet* — nobody can give what he doesn't have.

This being said, however, there can also be a subtle temptation to "go it alone," to create a little hermitage where one can indulge one's desires rather than submitting to that ideal school of charity: a life in common with others. Only *there* is one perfected, like stones or bits of glass tossed in the waves until they are smoothed. The eremitical life is for the perfect, not for those on the way to perfection; and even the hermit is a member of the greatest community of all, the Mystical Body of Christ. Living with other people, in a spirit of openness to life — the lives of those already known to you, as well as the lives of those who may someday be entrusted to you — is the safest and surest route to perfection if one perseveres in it, just as refusing to make the sacrifices demanded by a common life leads to egoism and sterility.

These dynamics are vividly displayed in marriage. Only a fool could promise young lovers a married life of paradise on earth. In reality, it is a hard path of reciprocal sacrifice, and the joys are not sufficient to carry the day. It takes the kind of love St. Paul describes in 1 Corinthians 13, a realistic, energetic, patient, even stubborn love that can say, "I don't feel like doing this or that, or suffering this or that, but I will do it, for the love of God and for my spouse, to whom I promised my fidelity." It is at moments like this that the sacrament — or for religious, the vow — tests the reality of one's desire to become a saint. And it is in and through moments like this *that God really sanctifies us*.

On the aims and efforts of laity in the modern world, Joseph Ratzinger offers these perceptive remarks:

> No one can be a Christian alone; being a Christian means a communion of wayfarers. Even a hermit belongs to a wayfaring community and is sustained by it. For this reason it must be the Church's concern

---

man and woman, do with their bodies is morally permissible, and so it is none of anyone else's business. It is solipsism and idiotism to the tenth power. It has not been contained. The principle of utter selfishness has infected other features of our no longer common life. Old television commercials sold goods on two grounds: they worked, or they would make you happy. New television commercials sell goods to narcissists: if you buy this, *you will express yourself*. You want what you want, and you need not consider anybody else. You are the center of your world" ("A Conciliar Church on a Path to Schism").

> to create pilgrim communities. The social culture of [today's] Europe and America no longer offers these wayfaring communities. This brings us back to the previous question about how the Church will live in this increasingly dechristianized society. It will have to form new ways of pilgrim fellowship; communities will have to shape each other more intensely by supporting each other and living in the faith.... Close association with monastic communities will certainly be one way to have an experience of the Christian reality.
>
> In other words, if society in its totality is no longer a Christian environment, just as it was not in the first four or five centuries, the Church herself must form cells in which mutual support and a common journey, and thus the great vital milieu of the Church in miniature, can be experienced and put into practice.[107]

Catholic families cannot "go it alone." Families need families: couples need couples, children need children, relatives need relatives. To the extent possible, we must form the "cells" or "pilgrim communities" about which Ratzinger is speaking. They are already organically springing up in the vicinity of traditional parishes and religious houses around the world, even as medieval towns grew up around the monasteries. This is both a natural and a supernatural process, unfolding by the design of Providence.

[107] Joseph Cardinal Ratzinger, *Salt of the Earth: Christianity and the Catholic Church at the End of the Millennium*, trans. A. Walker (San Francisco: Ignatius Press, 1997), 264–65.

II

Living Chastely

"I have a body, but I am not my body. I have feelings, but I am not my feelings. I have desires, but I am not my desires. I have a mind, but I am not my mind" (Assagioli). This is, really, the work of the desert ascetic: to avoid absolutizing any of these identifications. None of them tells us absolutely what we are: only God can do that. If we are in the desert seeking to know God, and so receive entirety of being from Him, we need to know that our mind cannot know Him: identity is not found there. If we are pilgrim souls who would be at Jerusalem, we need to struggle against the desires that want to be all that we are: we cannot be as little as that. If we are praying, we need to realize that wholeness or holiness is not in feelings: our sacred identity is deeper than that of which they can speak. Above all — and this is the core of the ascetic tradition — the body is not our confining and absolute identity. That is to say our body is not our final, immortal, eternal identity; yet it is integral to our identity in this world and who we are in this world determines what we shall be in the next.

— Dom Luke Bell, *The Mystery of Identity*

14

The Duty to Be Chaste

Whatever may be said about the theory of evolution's truth or falsehood, G. K. Chesterton aptly identifies one of its unfortunate psychosocial consequences:

> Darwinism can be used to back up two mad moralities, but it cannot be used to back up a single sane one. The kinship and competition of all living creatures can be used as a reason for being insanely cruel or insanely sentimental; but not for a healthy love of animals. On the evolutionary basis you may be inhumane, or you may be absurdly humane; but you cannot be human.[108]

Beginning with Rousseau, the world has never suffered a lack of self-consciously "modern people" who argue that the human race would be far happier if all of us could simply indulge our natural inclinations, in imitation of our ancestors and relatives, the animals of field and forest. The theory might sound plausible, and not a few have tried to put it into practice — to the extent consistent with civil laws and social conventions. But we may want to ask (as human beings distinctively do ask) whether this opinion is tenable according to what a man can hear from *within,* when he examines himself as he really is.

Emulation of animal libido is a reason for being promiscuous and heated but not for establishing and maintaining harmonious love with another person. Arguments drawn from instinct and applied to human sexual desire — concluding that the denigration of lust is nothing but a primitive taboo later turned into a hypocritical instrument for wielding power — stand on the tenuous premise that man is not meant to lead any better or qualitatively different sort of life, that is to say, a rational life of virtue within a community of friends.

[108] G. K. Chesterton, *Orthodoxy,* chap. 7, in *The Collected Works of G. K. Chesterton,* vol. 1, ed. David Dooley (San Francisco: Ignatius Press, 1986), 316–17.

The "freedom" manifested by the brute is no more than a lack of predetermined action toward any instance of a specific good. The animal can in no way choose, color, or temper its involuntary appetite for that object of attraction once it falls within its sphere. Its appetites are commanded or harnessed by no loftier end. During mating season, the animal can, stretching the word, "choose" to couple with this or that particular mate, according to immediate sense impressions, proximity, circumstance, and so forth; but it cannot *choose* to mate, for nature *compels* it to a distinct and unalterable end. The supposedly free and easy life of the animals, therefore, is obviously and dramatically the contrary. They obey an internal impulse that fixes onto whatever object the season of the year and the operation of their senses have brought before them. The animal is not only irrational but supremely unfree because it lacks that *power to choose* that is traditionally called free will.

Our ability as a race to recognize and name a host of moral vices — among them, lewdness, lechery, lust, intemperance, immodesty, gluttony — is based on the experienced truth that man is not merely a creature of instinct, provoked irresistibly by external objects over which he has no interior control, but a creature of knowledge and freedom, who can ask himself, "Why am I acting? *Should* I do this or that action? What is the best way for me to act here and now, if I am to be happy? What are the most suitable means I can choose for attaining this end?"

For man to imitate his animal kin, he must pull out the crowbar and, with considerable effort, cram his will and intellect into a little box marked "superstition" or "guilty feelings," after which he must proceed to act solely and whenever possible upon the spontaneous movements of his aroused passions. But not even the animals behave this way. Nature restrains them by appointing seasons and limits to their eating and reproducing. She has not so restrained man, who is capable of discerning for himself the virtuous mean and setting times and boundaries according to its demands. In any case, we could not act altogether like animals even if we wanted to, since, owing to our very nature, we have more going on in our souls than sensations and passions, however temporarily overwhelming these may be.

The perfectly "instinctual" man, the one who managed to ape his evolutionary relatives, would be a monster of insatiable appetites, as willful as a bratty child and as heartless as a criminal. The often specious and always sophistical arguments one hears in favor of birth control, abortion, autoeroticism, and homosexuality invariably mask what is, in the final analysis, a blanket approval of indulging animal instincts according to the individual's self-constructed system of values. These values may include the supremacy of pleasure, convenience, or whim, over indebtedness, responsibility, duty, and the health of human nature; they tend to ignore the demands of mental and even physical health and the common good of family and society. In so many cases, we are confronted with an elaborate rationalization for living the slavish life of one who has nothing more or better to live for. Chesterton, once again, puts his finger on the nub of the issue:

> Only the supernatural has taken a sane view of Nature. The essence of all pantheism, evolutionism, and modern cosmic religion is really in this proposition: that Nature is our mother. Unfortunately, if you regard Nature as a mother, you discover that she is a step-mother. The main point of Christianity was this: that Nature is not our mother: Nature is our sister. We can be proud of her beauty, since we have the same father; but she has no authority over us; we have to admire, but not to imitate.

On a stroll once in Dublin, walking from the Pearse train station to the National Gallery, I beheld a large billboard, provocatively stationed over a café at which several gallons of milk must surely be gone through each day. I really could not believe my eyes and had to take a picture of it. The billboard stated: "Dairy takes babies from their mothers." The mother cow, with bovine pride, licks her cute calf, from which she is soon to be tragically parted so that evil humans can drink the surplus milk.

Upon making inquiries, I learned that this billboard started going up around Ireland just a few months after the abortion referendum legalized abortion by a landslide majority. Apparently, abortion — the ultimate example of *taking babies away from their mothers* — should be legal, while presumably dairy farms should be illegal. Such is the twisted logic that obtains when faith and reason alike are abandoned in favor of the postmodern trinity of "me, myself, and I." (As Chesterton almost quipped: "When a man stops believing in God, he doesn't believe in nothing, he believes in anything."[109]) The billboard informs us that we can obtain a "free vegan guide" from www.goveganworld.com. A glance at that website brought up a title-page video that proclaims: "We all have the right not to be used or killed regardless of species." Alas, this "right" seems to hold only for subhuman species.

[109] I say "almost" because, while Chesterton said many similar things, he never used this formulation, in spite of its popular attribution to him. See Dale Ahlquist, "Believing in Anything," *Faith & Culture*, May 29, 2019, www.faithandculture.com/home/2019/5/29-believing-in-anything.

Chesterton's "two mad moralities" are writ large in modern Western societies: insane sentimentality toward brute animals and insane cruelty toward the most vulnerable and innocent members of the human race. Humane to the point of inventing rights where they do not exist;[110] inhumane to the point of undermining the most fundamental right that *does* exist and without which all other rights are meaningless. If we cannot even treat *one another* humanely, what does that suggest about our conception of the universe we inhabit?

We see fulfilled before our eyes this wise statement from the Second Vatican Council: "Without the Creator, the creature would disappear.... When God is forgotten, the creature itself grows unintelligible."[111] Take away God, in whose image and likeness man is created, uniquely among material beings, and you take away awareness of man's very distinctiveness and dignity. Instead of seeing *vices* as the true cause of human misery and the rape of nature, with virtues (above all, the virtue of religion) as the only cure for these diseases of fallen humanity, you begin to see human beings themselves not as blessings to be welcomed but as evils to be thwarted. This is what it means for the creature to "disappear" and "grow unintelligible." Male and female are confused; the ranks and relations of animal species are confused; *all* is confused, in a false exaltation of "Mother Nature" and a false denigration of the noblest being on the face of the earth.

A friend sardonically put it to me this way: "1500 BC: worship animals, sacrifice babies; AD 2020: worship animals, sacrifice babies." The Bible says *nihil sub sole novum*: there's nothing new under the sun. That includes the moral and metaphysical darkness from which Christianity rescued mankind and to which mankind is doomed to return when Christ, true man and true God, is rejected. Part of this darkness is the loss of awareness of what is uniquely distinctive, elevated, and precious about man, which grounds the quasi-infinite value of the human person.

[110] See Dorothy Cummings McLean, "Pope Francis Proposes Adding 'Ecological Sin' against 'Common Home' to Catechism," *LifeSiteNews*, November 15, 2019, www.lifesitenews.com/news/pope-francis-proposes-adding-ecological-sin-against-common-home-to-catechism. I would also note that this pope invents a fictitious absolute right to life for criminals, against traditional Catholic teaching on the legitimacy of the death penalty in certain circumstances. See "What Good Is a Changing Catechism? Revisiting the Purpose and Limits of a Book," in Kwasniewski, *Road from Hyperpapalism*, vol. 2, chap. 40; for a detailed study, Edward Feser and Joseph M. Bessette, *By Man Shall His Blood Be Shed: A Catholic Defense of Capital Punishment* (San Francisco: Ignatius Press, 2017).

[111] Vatican II, Pastoral Constitution on the Church in the Modern World *Gaudium et Spes* (December 7, 1965), no. 36.

With all due respect to the prince of paradoxes, it is worth acknowledging the extent to which even the pagan philosophers recognized clearly (to use a phrase of Mortimer Adler) "the difference of man and the difference it makes." As I was once preparing a reading from Aristotle for a philosophy class, I couldn't help but be struck by these words:

> Not every action or feeling admits of a mean.[112] For some have names immediately connected with depravity, such as spite, shamelessness, envy, and, among actions, adultery, theft, homicide. All these, and others like them, are so called because they themselves, and not their excesses and deficiencies, are bad. In their case, then, one can never hit the mark [of virtue], but always misses. Nor is there a good or bad way to go about such things — committing adultery, say, with the right woman, at the right time, or in the right way. Rather, doing one of them, simply speaking, is to miss the mark.[113]

Aristotle, who lived more than three hundred years before the coming of Christ and did not enjoy the benefit of divine revelation, is arguing here that certain free human actions are intrinsically evil. No circumstances or excuses can ever make them good. And he says in one of his many memorable lines: "A bad man can do ten thousand times as much evil as a brute animal."[114]

When the Apostles met for the first synod in Church history (it is not numbered among the ecumenical councils, being a sort of protocouncil or model for the rest), they debated the question of whether Gentile converts needed to observe the Mosaic law. Their conclusion? No, Gentiles need not follow the ceremonial precepts, but they *do* need to observe a couple of simple precepts — one of which was to "abstain ... from fornication [or, as other translations have it, unchastity]" (Acts 15:20). As if to say: The very *baseline*, the lowest common denominator, is to avoid sharing a bed with someone to whom you are not married. This is by no means presented as the worst sin nor its avoidance as the height of virtue. It is, however, treated as a sine qua non, a minimal adherence

[112] The "mean" of virtue is that which is neither too much nor too little but just right: e.g., not too little *thymos* or spiritedness in battle, which is cowardice, or too much, which is rashness, but holding one's ground and fighting in accord with what is reasonable for the circumstances. See Aristotle, *Nicomachean Ethics* II.2 and 6–9.

[113] *Nicomachean Ethics* II.6.

[114] See *Nicomachean Ethics* VII.6.

to the natural moral law that must be demanded of everyone who dares to call himself a Christian.

But when was the last time you heard fornication, unlawful sexual activity, preached against from the pulpit? Apart from a few brave pastors who are willing to risk their careers instead of hiding the truth, the Church, at least in the modern West, has completely and utterly lost its conviction and courage when it comes to this elementary point of biblical revelation.

What we see, then, is that the best of the pagans and the best of the Jews (that is, the early Christians) saw clearly that the virtue of self-control in sexual matters was fundamental to a good and holy life, and that those who depart from this are incapable of being counted among practicing Christians. It is no less clear that there has never been the slightest doubt in Catholic tradition on this point. Whatever we may think of his, at times, overenthusiastic popularizers, Pope John Paul II, in works such as *Love and Responsibility* and *Male and Female He Created Them*, gave eloquent expression to the moral beauty, psychological value, and theological meaning of chastity, a virtue *all* are required to live out in any state of life, be it single, married, clerical, or religious.

It is no less clear that chapter 8 of Pope Francis's *Amoris Laetitia* departs from pagan wisdom and Judeo-Christian orthodoxy by teaching that couples living in sexually active so-called second marriages (while their sacramentally married spouse is still alive) need not be considered to be living in a state of sin and may even be considered to be doing what God is asking of them, thereby allowing access to sacramental absolution and Communion. According to this warped way of speaking, they may be acting *virtuously* by cohabiting extramaritally and even pleasing God in so doing. Both pagan philosophers and Christian believers have always known better than to fall for such an error, which is contrary to both reason and faith.[115]

The view that keeping up adulterous sexual relations is the best that a certain person is capable of doing in some circumstances is seen to be fallacious when we consider it in connection with any other mortal sin. Is the abortionist who says, "The best I can do right now is to kill only ten babies a week, which is better than a hundred" ready to receive Communion? Is the one who says, "The best

[115] For a detailed analysis of the errors in *Amoris Laetitia*, see John R. T. Lamont and Claudio Pierantoni, eds., *Defending the Faith against Present Heresies* (Waterloo, ON: Arouca Press, 2021); Lukáš Novák and Marie Tejklová, eds., *Dispelling the Fog: Critical Essays on* Amoris Laetitia (Neunkirchen-Seelscheid, Germany: editiones scholasticae, 2022).

I can do is to steal candy bars, which is better than stealing handgun ammunition" or "I used to skim off a fair amount of incoming cash from my company in a clever way that no one ever noticed; but I felt bad about that, so today I just take a little now and again to pad the wallet" ready to receive absolution? What these people have in common is that they are *still attached to serious sins*; it requires no special psychological insight, no advanced degree in theology, and no hierarchical office to see this. Before anything else, they have to acknowledge their sins, do penance for them, and take counsel about overcoming their bad habits *for real*. The sacraments are not "magic," as the progressives like to say (when it suits them). Sacraments do not, cannot, substitute for practices by which vices are overcome and the soul is prepared for readmission to the communion of the Church, such as prayer, fasting, almsgiving, and other penances. So far from modern Christians being more advanced than those of past generations, we are, in fact, sorely lacking in the wisdom they possessed. As Dr. Anna Silvas explains:

> Just as to participate fully in the Eucharist was the final denouement of a process that followed catechesis, Baptism, and Confirmation, so for a penitent to be finally admitted to the Eucharist again was the denouement of a long process of training that involved verifiable repentance and sacramental absolution. To undertake penance for mortal sins committed after Baptism in the fourth-century church was like being returned to the catechumenate all over again — to pray and be prayed for, to be retrained at length in the imperatives of Baptism and the life in Christ, before being readmitted at last to the Eucharist, the sacrament of ecclesial communion. In St. Basil's day and place, the worst of mortal sins incurred a *fifteen-year* penance. Such sins included adultery, public apostasy, and murder, the last of which included also procured abortion:
>
>> A woman who has deliberately committed abortion incurs the penalty for murder [ἡ φθείρασα κατ᾽ ἐπιτήδευσιν, φόνου δίκην ὑπέχει]. And any fine distinction about its [the fetus's] being formed or unformed is not admissible among us [ἀκριβολογία δὲ ἐκμεμορφωμένου καὶ ἀνεξεικονίστου παρ᾽ ἡμῖν οὐκ ἔστιν]. (*Letter* 188)
>
> Imagine it: standing outside in the narthex for *years*, asking the prayers of those going in so that you might hold steady in repentance from your behavior.

> It is true that the administration of Penance underwent great changes over the centuries, but the core truths to which the fourth-century practice bore witness abide. Admission to the Body and Blood of Christ is in every way an *ecclesial* event. Every sin — not only mortal sin — is an act against the Body of Christ; it harms the Church. The greater the sin, the greater the damage to self and community, and the more need for sincere contrition, voluntarily accepted punishment, and the retraining of the will. How have we become so casual, so blasé, so inexorably minimalist in our morals? How have we Catholics so forgotten our own long history? It is a common warning among writers on the spiritual life that we must be on our guard lest we dismiss mortal sins as venial sins and venial sins as minor blemishes of character.[116]

The exception progressives make for adultery derives from their assumption that sexual activity is a nonnegotiable default — the same assumption that drives the liberal sanitizing or even approbation of other actions contrary to the virtue of chastity, such as masturbation, fornication, contraception, abortion, homosexual relations, pedophilia, and pornography. In truth, these actions are intrinsically evil not only by divine decree, known through supernatural revelation, but also according to natural law, which means that human beings both *can* know them to be such and *ought* to know them to be such. Put simply, any human being is culpable before God for not knowing the natural moral law and living according to it. St. Paul in Romans teaches that it is at least on *this* basis that all men will be judged at the end of time, with a reckoning of whether they have lived up to the "law written on their hearts" (Rom. 2:15).

The modern perspective, on the other hand, while paying lip service to the truth that Christ calls us to renounce every sin in our striving to be holy, treats the use of the sexual organs as if it were a special case. Actions in this sphere are viewed as either not evil at all or as evil but uncontrollable and excusable. In our hypersexualized society, some psychiatrists argue that it is not possible to be "healthy" without frequent sex, and that virginity, chastity, and continence are defects rather than perfections. This irrational "faith in Freud," so to speak, has proved remarkably resistant to mountains of contrary evidence.[117]

[116] Private correspondence with author.

[117] On how the tectonic shift in attitudes toward sexuality came about, see the extraordinary books by Carl Trueman: *The Rise and Triumph of the Modern Self: Cultural Amnesia, Expressive Individualism, and the Road to Sexual Revolution* (Wheaton, IL: Crossway, 2020); and *Strange New World: How Thinkers and*

As R. R. Reno of *First Things* argued, the debacle over chapter 8 of *Amoris Laetitia* is an unmistakable sign that the sexual revolution has finally conquered the minds of many members of the Church's hierarchy.[118] They would not dream of preaching against sex before marriage or against contraception because "that's how things are nowadays." They try to find the "positive values" in it. Would the same leaders counsel us not to preach against trashing the natural environment or setting up Third World sweatshops because "that's just how things are done nowadays"? Would they try to find the "positive values" in pollution and exploitation? Of course not. Social justice is real, but it also happens to be fashionable; it wins the applause of the world. Sexual justice is real but no longer fashionable. Indeed, it is bitterly hated, ridiculed, and suppressed by all who set themselves up as arbiters of modern culture.

Christians, however, do not take their marching orders from the world but from the Lord and His Apostles, who teach, in the luminous words of St. Paul:

> This is the will of God, your sanctification: that you abstain from unchastity; that each one of you know how to take a wife for himself in holiness and honor, not in the passion of lust like heathen who do not know God; that no man transgress, and wrong his brother in this matter, because the Lord is an avenger in all these things, as we solemnly forewarned you. For God has not called us for uncleanness, but in holiness. Therefore whoever disregards this, disregards not man but God, who gives his Holy Spirit to you. (1 Thess. 4:3–8)

Activists Redefined Identity and Sparked the Sexual Revolution (Wheaton, IL: Crossway, 2022). See also Brian Mullady, *St. Thomas Aquinas Rescues Modern Psychology* (Irondale, AL: EWTN Publishing, 2022).

[118] See the *First Things* editorial of December 2017, "Liberal Tradition, Yes; Liberal Ideology, No," www.firstthings.com/article/2017/12/liberal-tradition-yes-liberal-ideology-no. For recent confirmation of the truth of this judgment, see Luisella Scrosati, "Vatican Finds Way to Approve Contraception and Assisted Fertilisation," *Daily Compass* of *La Nuova Bussola Quotidiana*, July 5, 2022, https://newdailycompass.com/en/vatican-finds-way-to-approve-contraception-and-assisted-fertilisation.

15

The Two Greatest Mercies of God

Moses, the greatest prophet of the Old Testament and a type of Christ, the supreme Lawgiver, delivered one overarching piece of advice to the people of Israel:

> Lay to heart *all* the words which I enjoin upon you this day, that you may command them to your children, that they may be careful to do all the words of this law. For it is no trifle for you, but it is your life, and thereby you shall live long in the land which you are going over the Jordan to possess. (Deut. 32:46–47)

When Our Lord dwelt among us on the earth, He solemnly stated: "Think not that I have come to abolish the law and the prophets; I have come not to abolish but to fulfill" (Matt. 5:17). For this reason, He says: "If thou wilt enter into life, keep the commandments" (Matt. 19:17), and "If you love me, keep my commandments" (John 14:15). His beloved disciple, St. John, writes in his first epistle: "By this we know that we have known him, if we keep his commandments. He who saith that he knoweth him, and keepeth not his commandments, is a liar, and the truth is not in him" (1 John 2:3–4). And again: "For this is the charity of God, that we keep his commandments: and his commandments are not heavy" (1 John 5:3). Of St. Paul the Apostle, we read: "He went through Syria and Cilicia, confirming the churches, commanding them to keep the precepts of the apostles and the ancients" (Acts 15:41). "It is no trifle for you."

The New Testament did not abolish the Old Testament or the teaching of Moses. Far from lessening the moral standards, the New Testament removes some of the exceptions and concessions that were made to the weakness of fallen men (see Matt. 5 and 19) because we are now in the era of Christ, who has won for us the grace we need to be holy and shares it with us in His seven sacraments and in the Holy Spirit poured forth upon us. Christ brought the

Old Law to its absolute perfection in His holocaust of love on the Cross, the reality of which is made present to us in the Holy Eucharist.

The parts of the Law that merely prepared Israel for the Messiah's coming came to an end in Christ, but the moral code of the Law was incorporated into the Gospel and raised to a higher level. Thus, the emphasis on law in the Old Testament — as in the great Psalm 118, whose verses play so central a role in the Divine Office — is not superseded by a supposed "freedom from law" in the New Testament. Divine revelation remains constant and consistent with itself, as does the moral law, discernible to natural reason with God's help.

What changes, rather, is *man's ability to adhere to it,* to remain faithful to it. Christ, in His gift of sanctifying grace, in the gift of His sacraments and the power of His Holy Spirit, *makes possible for us* the living of the Law. With the finger of the Holy Spirit, the Father writes the Law not on tablets of stone but on the fleshy tablets of the heart (see 2 Cor. 3:3). This is why John Paul II in *Veritatis Splendor* says that we must rely upon (which presupposes persistently asking for) the gift of the Holy Spirit, we must use all the means Our Lord has given us, if we are to conquer our sins and grow in holiness. It will never be easy, but it is now possible and desirable, and the saints show us it can be done.

With the sweet name of mercy being so much abused today in the Church, we are in danger of forgetting the two greatest mercies that God has, in fact, given to us. The first is *the Law* — the Divine Law that enunciates and clarifies for us the natural moral law by which human persons are required to live and outside of which they cannot be either virtuous or happy, in this life or in the world to come. The second is *the grace to live according to this law.* As St. Thomas Aquinas explains, what Christ has brought us is not a new law in the sense of new content that differs from the natural moral law, but rather, the gift of the Holy Spirit, by which we fallen creatures are empowered to *live* that law, day in and day out.[119] This is the delicious fruit of the Passion and the magnificent gift of Pentecost: we who, by our own power and efforts, are doomed to fail, are lifted up by God's help to a life of fidelity to His commandments.

Why are these the two greatest mercies?

For human action, two things are required. First, we must know where we are headed so that we can choose the right path to reach it. Second, we must have the strength to follow that path, or, to put it more simply, the will, the inclination, to set out toward our goal and to persevere until we reach it. It is not enough to have knowledge if we are weak or powerless to act according to

[119] See *ST* I-II, QQ. 106–8.

it; it is not enough to have energy or willpower if we don't know what direction to go in. As a result, God, in His special care for us rational creatures made in His image and likeness, has provided both the knowledge of what we should do (and should not do) and the interior motivation to carry it out (or, in the case of evil, to refrain from carrying it out).

We may see in the Sign of the Cross a reminder of this truth. When we start, "In the Name of the Father," we place our hand on our forehead: the Father is the origin of all truth, and in His Light we see light (Ps. 35:10). Then we bring our hand to our heart, "and of the Son," as if to say: "May my heart be conformed to the Sacred Heart of Jesus; may I love what He loves, desire what He desires." Then we touch each side of our torso, from one shoulder to the other, as if to say: "May the Holy Spirit, the Lord and Giver of Life, surround me and make me *live* the truth I have seen, make me *do* the good I have desired."

Throughout the Christian centuries, heretical trends have perverted these mercies. Some, embracing antinomianism, reject the Law as an enslaving imposition and seek for a freedom or a toleration that ends up destroying itself and harming those around us who must suffer from the consequences. Others, on the contrary, hold to the Law in its externals only, making it into a loveless fixation with propriety and respectability. We see the former alive and well today in clergy and theologians who oppose the Gospel to the Ten Commandments, or who see the Christian path as one of simultaneous sinning and righteousness (as Martin Luther did). We see the latter in anyone who does not see love of God and neighbor as the very heart of law-abidingness and therefore does not see that the most crucial work for us to be doing is begging the Lord for the grace to *live* His truth, "doing the truth in charity" (Eph. 4:15). Without that grace, there is no righteousness; without that righteousness, there is no salvation.

Nowhere is our need for grace more apparent than in the battle for chastity, which concerns an especially vulnerable part of our fallen nature. Let us heed the same divine words by which St. Augustine, no stranger to the struggle, oriented himself in prayer when begging for continence, that is, sexual self-control:

> All my hope is naught save in Thy great mercy. Grant what Thou dost command, and command what Thou wilt. Thou dost command continence. And *when I knew,* as it is said, *that no one could be continent unless God gave it, even this was a point of wisdom, to know whose gift it was* (Wis 8:21). For by continence we are collected and bound up into unity

> within ourself, whereas we had been scattered abroad in multiplicity. Too little does any man love Thee, who loves some other thing together with Thee, loving it not on account of Thee, O Thou Love, who art ever burning and never extinguished! O Charity, my God, enkindle me! Thou dost command continence: grant what Thou dost command and command what Thou wilt.[120]

It is not the one who is an activist, always seeking the next great conquest in the public sphere, who has grasped the primacy of God's Law, nor is it the relaxed exponent of "anything goes" or the nonchalant trumpeter of "God is love" who has awakened to the severe mercy and the transformative grace of God. It is rather the one who is found in the temple of God, begging Him for the knowledge of His Law and the grace of His charity with which to live it out. He or she will be there, in that temple, either literally or figuratively, at the break of day, throughout the day, in the evening, at night. This is the telltale sign that one has hearkened to these two great mercies and has understood what is required if we are to know and live the law of the Lord.

Seven holy brothers, one holy law

A vivid testimony to the truth of the supremacy of God's Law is the martyrdom of the Seven Holy Maccabees, who are commemorated as saints in the traditional Roman Rite on August 1 and also on the calendars of Eastern Christians, both Catholics and Orthodox. These Jewish brothers died under horrible torture rather than break the law of the Lord in the slightest way. And what was the law for which they died? Something major, such as "Thou shalt not kill" or "Thou shalt not steal" or "Thou shalt not commit adultery"?

No — that they should not consume pork, which was forbidden by the law of Moses.

This very small detail of the law, one that was destined to pass away with the coming of Christ, was nevertheless commanded by God as something that His people were to follow unwaveringly. Yes, there were reasons for it. For example, the Jews were taught to slaughter animals that the Egyptians worshiped as divine and to avoid animals that were dirty and herded by Gentiles.

[120] St. Augustine, *Confessions*, trans. F. J. Sheed, ed. Michael P. Foley (Indianapolis: Hackett, 2006), X.19.40, 211. See Fr. John Hardon, "Prayer and Chastity," *Real Presence Association*, www.therealpresence.org/archives/Chastity/Chastity_006.htm.

Yet whether or not we fully understand the reasons behind a prohibition, what matters is obeying God's will, as He makes it known to us. The restriction on the tree of the knowledge of good and evil, the first commandment ever given, was arbitrary in the strict meaning of the word — that is, there was nothing wrong with the tree, and yet its fruit was forbidden in order to establish clearly that God is the Creator and that He is the measure of what is right and wrong for His creatures.[121] It was a pedagogy in trust: "If you accept this limitation, I will bless you for it, and in due time, I will give you more than that which I withheld." By obeying, they would signify their subordination to Him, their trust in His superior wisdom, and their willingness to be led rather than to take affairs into their own hands and pretend to be gods who are above the law.

As we know, Adam and Eve did not prove obedient. Nor, tragically, did the people of Israel, to whom the Lord had shown so many and such great acts of deliverance and mercy, above all in giving them a law more comprehensive, more just, and more rational than that of any other nation. And this brings us to the reason why the seven Jewish Maccabean brothers, to whom tradition gives the names Abim, Antonius, Gurias, Eleazar, Eusebonus, Alimus, and Marcellus, have been universally venerated by *Christians* for many centuries. They are, in fact, the only Old Testament saints to be found in the Mass of the Roman Rite.[122]

This band of brothers is venerated because in them we see the obedience, the trust, the faithfulness to God's word and will and law that Adam and Eve failed to show. We see the willingness to suffer and die even for a small matter, if it is known to be God's will, rather than the practical atheism that cares nothing for God's will and scorns Him in matters great and small. We see a model of the total dedication of the disciple to the master, the son to the father, the creature to the Creator. In short, we see a pattern for our own attitude when it comes to the commandments of God, over which *nothing* may be allowed to prevail.

[121] See, e.g., the remarks of Augustine and Aquinas at *ST* I-II, Q. 102, art. 1, obj. 2 and ad 2.

[122] At least until the reforms of the late 1960s that removed so many saints, including them — but fortunately, with the gradual return to our churches of the authentic Roman Rite (sometimes called the "Tridentine"), the Maccabees have returned as well. See Gregory DiPippo, "The Feast of the Holy Maccabees," *New Liturgical Movement*, August 1, 2021, https://www.newliturgicalmovement.org/2021/08/the-feast-of-holy-maccabees.html.

The story of the seven martyrs for the Law is told in the seventh chapter of 2 Maccabees. The eldest of the brothers says to the king: "What wouldst thou ask, or learn of us? We are ready to die rather than to transgress the laws of God, received from our fathers." The youngest of them, in like manner, says to the king, after having watched all his brothers be killed: "For whom do you wait? I will not obey the commandment of the king, but the commandment of the law, which was given us by Moses. . . . For my brethren, having now undergone a short pain, are under the covenant of eternal life: but thou by the judgment of God shalt receive just punishment for thy pride." The narrative then observes: "So this man also died undefiled, wholly trusting in the Lord."

Should we not be shocked and appalled that there are people in the Catholic Church today who maintain that not even the *Ten Commandments* must be kept inviolable by Christians? Or who do not believe that we should be prepared to suffer any hardship and even give up our lives rather than act against these Commandments?

One cannot help seeing a link — perhaps a subtle one, but real nonetheless — between the abolition of such an ancient commemoration as that of the Maccabees; the trend to avoid using the Commandments as a basis for examining one's conscience when preparing for sacramental Confession; the sharp opposition made between, on the one hand, love and mercy, and, on the other hand, obedience and law; and the moral and doctrinal corruption that has set in among the hierarchy of the Church. The cure for our ills will involve the fundamental cure of all human sin — namely, humble repentance for deviating from God's holy will expressed in His commandments and a zealous effort to do His will, no matter what sufferings it may cost us. For this, in the end, is how we show our love: "If ye love me, keep my commandments" (John 14:15). The Lord will never turn a deaf ear to anyone who sincerely asks for the grace to keep His law. So important is this prayer that the ancient Roman Rite places it on the lips of the priest right before he receives the Lord in Holy Communion:

> O Lord Jesus Christ, Son of the living God, who according to the will of the Father, through the cooperation of the Holy Ghost, hast by Thy death given life to the world: deliver me by this, Thy most sacred Body and Blood, from all my transgressions and from all evils; make me always adhere to Thy commandments and never suffer me to be separated from Thee, who with the same God the Father and the Holy Ghost livest and reignest God, for ever and ever. Amen.

The paradigmatic change: our conversion

John Henry Newman famously stated: "In a higher world it is otherwise, but here below to live is to change, and to be perfect is to have changed often."[123] This statement is often taken out of context by liberals and progressives who quote it to serve their agenda of continual upheaval in the Church. A glance at the context shows what Newman is really saying: while the essence of the Christian faith never changes, its outward appearances, the amplitude and complexion of its expression, do change — and not in any which way, but in the direction of a fuller, more complete expression. Newman could never legitimately be pressed into support for any "new paradigms" in Christianity. In fact, he left the Anglican church because he came to believe that it had departed from the one and only original Paradigm, which remained alive in the Catholic Church.

Like every Father and Doctor of the Church, Newman believed that mankind had been given, once for all, *the* Paradigm, in the life, death, and Resurrection of Jesus Christ, in His divine teaching and in the divine liturgy, and that it was not up to us to modify it or customize it or update it but rather to accept it in humble faith, internalize it in prayer, and live it in charity, all by the power of God's grace.

Sometimes the customs of fallen human beings, such as chattel slavery, though widespread and taken for granted, stand in contradiction to the Paradigm; therefore, they must give way to its irresistible force. The Paradigm itself stands firm, an immovable rock.

According to Scripture and Tradition, the Christian is one who holds to immovable principles — namely, the divinely revealed truths about God, man, the world, our condition, and our salvation. These principles will *never, ever* change, no matter how much culture, civilization, society, laws, customs, or attitudes may change.[124] The pages of Church history are filled with countless examples of saints who stubbornly adhered to God's Law and who were willing to die rather than act against it or permit anyone else to act against it. This intransigent attitude is displayed notably in all of the premodern popes, who saw the secular world rushing headlong to its destruction — a pessimism amply confirmed by subsequent events down to our time — and who opposed to that world the

[123] *An Essay on the Development of Christian Doctrine* (London: Longmans, Green, 1909), pt. I, chap. 1, sec. 1, no. 7, retrieved at the *National Institute for Newman Studies*, www.newmanreader.org/works/development/chapter1.html.

[124] See "The Cult of Change and Christian Changelessness," in Kwasniewski, *Ministers of Christ*, 235–46.

unchanging Gospel of Christ, with its lofty moral demands and even loftier promise of spiritual help for those who call upon Him and eternal happiness for those who love Him. The Collect of the Fifth Sunday after Pentecost gives consummate expression to the Church's hope:

> O God, Who hast prepared for those who love Thee such good things as eye hath not seen; pour into our hearts such affection of love for Thee, that loving Thee in all things and above all things, we may obtain Thy promises, which exceed all that we can desire.

One of the most popular "memes" in today's preaching in churches is: "God loves you just the way you are." I'm terribly sorry to have to say it, but this is false, and perniciously so. As Anthony Esolen pithily said: "I'm a sinner. I don't want the Church to show me how I can be comfortable with my sins. I want the damned things out."[125] If God loves us just the way we are, religion is over. There is no point to conversion, repentance, or sacrifice. It is precisely because we are *not* fine the way we are that God became man and died on the Cross and gave us the means to join Him in His death and risen life. Yes, Christ died for us while we were still sinners (Rom. 5:6–8) — but in order to make us His friends, that is, with His grace and our sincere effort, *not* sinners (see John 5:14; 8:11). If we are "good to go" as sinners, Christ died in vain, and our faith is in vain.

Nothing unclean may enter heaven (Rev. 21:27). Therefore, we must be cleansed of *all* of our sins, the lingering effects and merest suggestions of sin, if we are to enter heaven. And sorry to break it, folks, but purgatory is not the place where mortal sins are forgiven. That has to happen in *this* life — or it will never happen. If I may paraphrase Newman: "In a higher world it is otherwise, but here below to be saved is to repent, and to be perfect is to have repented often." We repent of our infidelity to the Paradigm, God's Law, the Gospel of Christ, the all-holy God. The Paradigm is the rock, and we bash our sins against it. A "new paradigm," a "paradigm shift" — these are fictions from the devil.

[125] Anthony Esolen, "No Way Out," *The Catholic Thing*, March 22, 2018, www.thecatholicthing.org/2018/03/22/no-way-out.

16

The Kingship of Christ and the Anti-Kingdom of Modernity

Right after the announcement of the Supreme Court's *Obergefell v. Hodges* decision, which required states to license (and thereby recognize) "same-sex marriage," the media quickly reported on the "conciliatory" and "moderate" language of Cardinal Wuerl:

> "The law of the land is the law of the land," says Archbishop of Washington Cardinal Donald Wuerl. "We certainly follow what the law says. That doesn't mean we change the word of God. That doesn't mean we change the scriptures, or the church's millennia-long tradition of what marriage is."[126]

In one sense, this is hardly surprising; we saw the same cardinal take a soft line toward pro-abortion politicians who abuse the Most Blessed Sacrament by receiving It despite their notorious public dissent from immutable teaching on faith and morals. At the same time, however, it should shock us profoundly, as one more instance of a shepherd abandoning the crystal-clear teaching of the Church. The greatest witness to this teaching is, of course, the Angelic Doctor, who writes:

> Human law is law inasmuch as it is in conformity with right reason and thus derives from the eternal law. But when a law is contrary to reason, it is called an unjust law; in this case it ceases to be a law and becomes instead an act of violence.[127]

[126] See Jamie Forzato, "Cardinal Wuerl: Same-Sex Marriage Ruling Is 'Law of the Land,' " *WTOP News*, July 5, 2015, wtop.com/dc/2015/07/cardinal-wuerl-sex-marriage-ruling-law-land.

[127] *ST* I-II, Q. 93, art. 3, ad 2.

> Every law made by man can be called a law insofar as it derives from the natural law. But if it is somehow opposed to the natural law, then it is not really a law but rather a corruption of the law.[128]

Both of these passages are quoted verbatim by John Paul II in *Evangelium Vitae* 72. The same doctrine is found equally clearly in St. Augustine and other Fathers and Doctors of the Church. Indeed, Martin Luther King Jr., in his justly famous "Letter from a Birmingham Jail," cites both Augustine and Aquinas on precisely this point. How shameful it is when the shepherds of the Catholic Church cannot compete with the theological acumen of a Baptist pastor!

The doctrine that an unjust law (or judicial determination or executive action, for that matter) is no law at all but, rather, a corruption of law, an act of violence, an insult to God, and a crime against all citizens is taught most clearly by Pope Leo XIII, the greatest exponent of Catholic social teaching:

> If the laws of the State are manifestly at variance with the divine law, containing enactments hurtful to the Church, or conveying injunctions adverse to the duties imposed by religion, or if they violate in the person of the supreme Pontiff the authority of Jesus Christ, then, truly, to resist becomes a positive duty, to obey, a crime; a crime, moreover, combined with misdemeanor against the State itself, inasmuch as every offense leveled against religion is also a sin against the State. Here anew it becomes evident how unjust is the reproach of sedition; for the obedience due to rulers and legislators is not refused, but there is a deviation from their will in those precepts only which they have no power to enjoin. Commands that are issued adversely to the honor due to God, and hence are beyond the scope of justice, must be looked upon as anything rather than laws.[129]

> The one only reason which men have for not obeying is when anything is demanded of them which is openly repugnant to the natural or the divine law, for it is equally unlawful to command to do anything in which the law of nature or the will of God is violated. If, therefore, it should happen to anyone to be compelled to prefer one or the other, viz., to disregard either the commands of God or those of rulers, he must obey Jesus Christ, who commands us to "give to Caesar the things that are

[128] *ST* I-II, Q. 95, art. 2; see Kwasniewski, *True Obedience*, 12–19.

[129] Leo XIII, Encyclical Letter *Sapientiae Christianae* (January 10, 1890), no. 10.

> Caesar's, and to God the things that are God's," and must reply courageously after the example of the Apostles: "We ought to obey God rather than men." And yet there is no reason why those who so behave themselves should be accused of refusing obedience; for, if the will of rulers is opposed to the will and the laws of God, they themselves exceed the bounds of their own power and pervert justice; nor can their authority then be valid, which, when there is no justice, is null.[130]

Fortunately, the sound reasoning and the Spirit of Truth that led St. Augustine, St. Thomas, and Pope Leo XIII is by no means absent from the Church today. In a homily preached around the same time as Cardinal Wuerl's "conciliatory" language, Raymond Leo Cardinal Burke spoke these uncompromising words:

> Yet almost two hundred years later [after the Declaration of Independence], in 1973, the highest tribunal of the nation took away the right to life from the innocent and defenseless unborn, and on this past June 26th, in defiance of "the Laws of Nature and of Nature's God," the same Supreme Court redefined the nature of marriage and its fruit, the family, the first cell of the life of society. The deadly confusion and error which such decisions represent for the United States of America, and similar confusion and error in other nations, demand from the Church a clear, courageous and tireless witness to the word of Christ, to the truth written upon every human heart, the truth upon which the happiness of the individual and the common good absolutely depend. The Church cannot stand by silent or idle, while a people is destroying itself by lawlessness, even if the lawlessness be clothed in the garment of the highest judicial authority.[131]

The contrast between Cardinal Wuerl and Cardinal Burke speaks for itself. Thanks be to God that the highest tribunal of the land, in *Dobbs v. Jackson Women's Health Organization*, overturned *Roe v. Wade* and cleared the way for the abolition of abortion, state by state. *Obergefell*, however, remains in force, although Clarence Thomas had the courage to say that it, too, and several other dubious decisions, should be reevaluated.[132]

[130] Leo XIII, Encyclical Letter *Diuturnum Illud* (June 29, 1881), no. 15.

[131] See "Cardinal Burke's Sermon at the Fota Conference," *New Liturgical Movement*, July 11, 2015, https://www.newliturgicalmovement.org/2015/07/cardinal-burkes-sermon-at-fota.html.

[132] Matt Lamb, "Justice Thomas says SCOTUS Should Revisit Rulings on Same-Sex 'Marriage,' Sodomy, Contraception," *LifeSiteNews*, June 24, 2022, https://

In the wake of such firestorms — to which the Post-Synodal Apostolic Exhortation *Amoris Laetitia* successfully added more fuel — we can see an ever-increasing challenge for Catholics: How do we live with, how do we respond to, the consequences of a divided hierarchy, a diluted witness, a squandered opportunity, and a mounting persecution? The enemy of human nature will only laugh at compromises as he energetically pursues the corruption of the shepherds, the confusion of the flock, and the damnation of sinners.

In *Libertas Praestantissimum*, Leo XIII explains that it is not man's place to dictate to God what man owes Him, but rather, man must humbly and obediently receive from God the law that must be followed to please Him and attain the happiness for which He created us:

> If the human mind be so presumptuous as to define the nature and extent of God's rights and its own duties, reverence for the divine law will be apparent rather than real, and arbitrary judgment will prevail over the authority and providence of God. Man must, therefore, take his standard of a loyal and religious life from the eternal law; and from all and every one of those laws which God, in His infinite wisdom and power, has been pleased to enact and to make known to us by such clear and unmistakable signs as to leave no room for doubt. And the more so because laws of this kind have the same origin, the same author, as the eternal law, are absolutely in accordance with right reason, and perfect the natural law. These laws it is that embody the government of God, who graciously guides and directs the intellect and the will of man lest these fall into error.[133]

We see in these luminous words the confidence of a pope and of a Church convinced of the reality and primacy of God, the existence of absolute truth, the ability of reason and faith to know that truth, and the ability of even fallen men to live according to that truth with the help of God's grace. We find the same confidence and the same conclusions in John Paul II's masterful encyclical *Veritatis Splendor*.

Early in the twentieth century, Msgr. Robert Hugh Benson proclaimed with inimitable eloquence that one of the greatest exercises of mercy of which the Church is capable is the condemnation of heresy alongside the reconciliation of the repentant heretic:

---

www.lifesitenews.com/news/justice-thomas-revisit-scotus-rulings-on-sodomy-contraception-and-same-sex-marriage/.

133 Leo XIII, Encyclical Letter *Libertas Praestantissimum* (June 20, 1888), no. 17.

> The Catholic Church then is, and always will be, violent and intransigent when the rights of God are in question. She will be absolutely ruthless, for example, towards heresy, for heresy affects not personal matters on which Charity may yield, but a Divine right on which there must be no yielding. Yet, simultaneously, she will be infinitely kind towards the heretic, since a thousand human motives and circumstances may come in and modify his responsibility. At a word of repentance she will readmit his person into her treasury of souls, but not his heresy into her treasury of wisdom; she will strike his name eagerly and freely from her black list of the rebellious, but not his book from the pages of her Index. She exhibits meekness towards him and violence towards his error; since he is human, but her Truth is Divine.[134]

How far we have lost this conception of the Church's primary obligation to God, His truth, and His holiness, and how far we have settled for a worldly compromise with sin and error, can be seen if we consider an astonishing passage from St. John Henry Newman, which, were it written today, would be considered offensive, outrageous, imbalanced, and possibly a form of hate speech:

> The Church aims, not at making a show, but at doing a work. She regards this world, and all that is in it, as a mere shadow, as dust and ashes, compared with the value of one single soul. She holds that, unless she can, in her own way, do good to souls, it is no use her doing anything; she holds that it were better for sun and moon to drop from heaven, for the earth to fail, and for all the many millions who are upon it to die of starvation in extremest agony, so far as temporal affliction goes, than that one soul, I will not say, should be lost, but should commit one single venial sin, should tell one wilful untruth, though it harmed no one, or steal one poor farthing without excuse. She considers the action of this world and the action of the soul simply incommensurate, viewed in their respective spheres; she would rather save the soul of one single wild bandit of Calabria, or whining beggar of Palermo, than draw a hundred lines of railroad through the length and breadth of Italy, or carry out a sanitary reform, in its fullest details, in every city of Sicily, except so far as these great national works tended to some spiritual good beyond them.

[134] Robert Hugh Benson, *Paradoxes of Catholicism* (London: Longmans, Green, 1913; repr. Miami: HardPress Publishing, n.d.), 126.

> Such is the Church, O ye men of the world, and now you know her. Such she is, such she will be; and, though she aims at your good, it is in her own way,—and if you oppose her, she defies you. She has her mission, and do it she will, whether she be in rags, or in fine linen; whether with awkward or with refined carriage; whether by means of uncultivated intellects, or with the grace of accomplishments. Not that, in fact, she is not the source of numberless temporal and moral blessings to you also; the history of ages testifies it; but she makes no promises; she is sent to seek the lost; that is her first object, and she will fulfil it, whatever comes of it.[135]

Note that for Newman, the seeking of the lost means nothing other than *the mission to save sinners from sinning*—to induce them, however she can, by God's grace, to follow His law, and thus to cease from lying, stealing, or any other action that can harm the soul, including the slightest venial sins. What, then, would Newman have said about the legalization of divorce, serial polygamy and polyandry (i.e., "remarriage"), pornography, contraception, sterilization, abortion, sodomy? We are looking at the progressive dehumanization of man, the escalating asphyxiation of society, and the accelerating decomposition of the Church, with the concomitant loss of countless souls to eternal damnation—and yet, there are *still* bishops who do not dare to speak up in defense of God's truth and His immutable rights, or who absurdly claim that "the law of the land is the law of the land," or who are just hoping that if they sit quietly and do nothing, no one will raise a hand against them! One cannot help thinking of the apostasy of the Church in England under Henry VIII. We will have our heroic St. John Fishers and our St. Thomas Mores, along with a greater number of cowards, opportunists, apostates, and traitors.

Pope Leo XIII, Cardinal Newman, and Msgr. Benson, like so many of their age, knew that the Catholic Church was locked in mortal combat with the irreligious and libertine spirit of modernity. They did not parley with it; they did not create committees for joint endeavors; they did not stand on their heads and squint with one eye until they could see something vaguely positive in it. They condemned it as poison, warned against it ceaselessly, and fought its dreadful effects with all their powers. They lost the fight, but only because their cause was betrayed by their own clerical brethren in the twentieth century. The crisis

135 John Henry Newman, *Certain Difficulties Felt by Anglicans in Catholic Teaching Considered*, vol. 1 (London: Longmans, Green, 1901), lecture 8, no. 4.

in the Church is a crisis of bishops; whenever the Church is in turmoil, this will always be at the source of it. St. Gregory Nazianzen bears witness to this sobering fact when he writes:

> The light and eye of the Church is the Bishop. It is necessary then that as the body is rightly directed as long as the eye keeps itself pure, but goes wrong when it becomes corrupt, so also with respect to the Prelate: according to what his state may be, must the Church in like manner suffer shipwreck, or be saved.[136]

Nevertheless, it was Cardinal Newman who, in his *Arians of the Fourth Century*, offered a well-documented and timely reminder that it was primarily the laity, under the guidance of a few stalwart bishops, who kept the true Faith in the horrible time of the Arian crisis. Today it is and will be no different.[137] Let us glory in our baptismal privilege of having and keeping the one true Faith, in union with Christ crucified and risen; let us glory in our Confirmation, which enlisted us in the army of our bloodstained victorious King, to bear Him witness and to fight His battles on earth. "Thus saith the LORD to you: Fear ye not, and be not dismayed at this multitude: for the battle is not yours, but God's" (2 Chron. 20:15).

The superb "Lake Garda Statement on the Ecclesial and Civilizational Crisis"[138] started me thinking about the broad lines of the story in which we find ourselves, characters in a divine drama of light and darkness.

Even if they may have seen it coming, many Catholics were in a state of dismay after *Obergefell.* How did this happen so quickly? How did we end up with a top-down legitimation of sins that cry out to heaven for vengeance, perversions that make a mockery of nature, disorders that unravel the fabric of human society? The world is clearly a mess — hardly Christian even in those

[136] Cited by St. Thomas Aquinas in *Catena Aurea: Commentary on the Four Gospels, Collected out of the Works of the Fathers*, vol. III, *St. Luke*, ed. John Henry Newman (Southampton, UK: Saint Austin Press, 1997), Luke 11:33–36, 415.

[137] See Peter Kwasniewski, *The Road from Hyperpapalism to Catholicism: Rethinking the Papacy in a Time of Ecclesial Disintegration*, vol. 1, *Theological Reflections on the Rock of the Church* (Waterloo, ON: Arouca Press, 2022), 14, 54–55, 77, 96–97, 125, 153, 159–60, 166–67.

[138] Published at *Rorate Caeli* on July 11, 2015, www.rorate-caeli.blogspot.com/2015/07/the-lake-garda-statement.html.

lands once favored by widespread allegiance to the Faith. It is no fairy tale: once upon a time, the Western world was permeated with Christianity; Catholicism had thoroughly shaped governments, laws, economies, the arts and sciences. What happened?

The story of modernity is inherently bound up with the politics and economics of rebellion, revolution, the false messianism of secularization and secularism.[139] "The kings of the earth stood up, and the princes met together, against the Lord and against his Christ. Let us break their bonds asunder: and let us cast away their yoke from us" (Ps. 2:2–3). Thanks to the naïve "opening to the world" of the Second Vatican Council — a move that eviscerated the Church's otherworldly interior — a vast number of Catholics today view history, culture, politics, and economics as *foreign to*, or *outside of*, theology and faith, as if the Church had nothing to say about human nature and life in this world.

Such a narrow mentality, an obvious exhibition of the vices of individualism and spiritualism, is explicitly rejected by a long line of modern popes who saw clearly into our age. Just as no man is an island, Catholicism is not an atomistic thing but a social reality; it has always had and, where truly believed, will always have ramifications in the social order, the life and culture, the laws and structures, of peoples.[140] Due to the fall of Adam, those very structures can become what Pope John Paul II called "structures of sin," *preventing* people from hearing the Gospel or at least making it more difficult for them to live according to it.

One cannot understand the human world around us without grasping how its characteristic ways of thinking and acting have come about and have frequently hardened into structures of sin that hinder the penetration of the Gospel and even the perception of the natural law. The clash between Christian and anti-Christian worldviews needs to be engaged *by theologians*. It is not possible to understand modernity or the Catholic response to it without grappling with the theological-political question — the question of whether the state itself, as a creation of God redeemed by Christ, is bound by an inescapable obligation to seek out the one

[139] See Thomas Storck, *From Christendom to Americanism and Beyond: The Long, Jagged Trail to a Postmodern Void* (Kettering, OH: Angelico Press, 2015), especially "Liberalism's Three Assaults," 22–33; Christopher A. Ferrara, *Liberty, the God That Failed: Policing the Sacred and Constructing the Myths of the Secular State, from Locke to Obama* (Tacoma, WA: Angelico Press, 2012).

[140] See my article "May His Kingdom Come: Catholic Social Teaching, Part VI — Conversion of Culture," *Catholic Family News*, September 25, 2020, https://catholicfamilynews.com/blog/2020/09/25/may-his-kingdom-come-catholic-social-teaching-part-vi-conversion-of-culture.

true religion, adhere to it, and subordinate itself to it.[141] Decisively rejecting this model of harmony between nature and grace, modernity is inherently an anti-Catholic set of choices, ideologies built from those choices, and structures emerging from those ideologies.[142] Both the analytical critique and any realistic solution must be *theological*, not merely humanistic or philosophical.[143]

Social, cultural, political, economic realities are messy and complicated, yes. But they do admit of principled analysis — and one that is properly Catholic and theological. Are we content to stay in the darkness, or do we wish to come into the light of true principles that can illuminate our thinking and acting? We have to descend from the lofty heights of unchanging mysteries such as the Blessed Trinity and the Incarnation of the Word into the concrete situation in which we actually live out our lives as political animals. According to the Church, there is supposed to be a real *interpenetration* between those radiant mysteries and this messy but redeemable social life we lead.

Do Catholics *understand* how we got into a situation in which millions of unborn children are murdered in the womb each year, and people think that men can marry men, or women women? This did not happen overnight, the result of a sudden avalanche of money and political pressure. It is the culmination of a long historical campaign, the accelerating application of a process of rebellion against first principles of nature and grace, beginning with the Protestant Revolt against ecclesiastical authority and Sacred Tradition, achieving its paradigm in the French Revolution's rejection of temporal authority and human tradition, and sliding downhill to the sexual revolution's rejection of social co-responsibility and self-restraint. There is nothing really left except mutilation, madness, and suicide.

[141] That the state is thus bound has been argued persuasively by an increasing number of Catholic thinkers. See Thomas Crean and Alan Fimister, *Integralism: A Manual of Political Philosophy* (Neunkirchen-Seelscheid, Germany: editiones scholasticae, 2020); Thomas Storck, *Foundations of a Catholic Political Order*, second ed. (Waterloo, ON: Arouca Press, 2022); Thaddeus Kozinski, *The Political Problem of Religious Pluralism — And Why Philosophers Can't Solve It* (Lanham, MD: Lexington Books, 2010); Edmund Waldstein, ed., *Integralism and the Common Good: Selected Essays from* The Josias, vol. 2, *The Two Powers* (Brooklyn: Angelico Press, 2022).

[142] As demonstrated by, inter alia, Michael Allen Gillespie, *The Theological Origins of Modernity* (Chicago: University of Chicago Press, 2009).

[143] See, among other papal documents that make just this point, Leo XIII's Encyclical Letter *Tametsi Futura* (November 1, 1900), on Jesus Christ, our Redeemer.

Responding effectively to this multilayered rebellion demands a certain knowledge of the causes of the disease, lest we continue, in open or subtle ways, to buy into the very errors that are causing the evils we decry. The sad truth is that the Catholic Church, as an institution, has, with an ever-lessening resistance, bought into the errors of the secularized and liberal West far more than it has successfully resisted them in the name of natural and revealed truths — the very truths that were preached from our pulpits only a few generations ago, attracting converts weary of modernity, disillusioned with its pomps and empty promises.

One could put the question this way: How did we get from Diocletian to Biden? Not by a direct line, but by a meandering path with heights and valleys that can be evoked by the mention of just a few names or phrases: Diocletian, Constantine, the Arian emperors, Theodosius, Charlemagne, St. Louis IX, Henry VIII, Cromwell, the American and French Revolutions, the modern imperial-nationalistic ideologies, Catholic resistance (García Moreno, Salazar, Dollfuss, Emperor Karl), the dictatorship of relativism. Throughout this bewildering variety of regimes, with every new political-theological solution or dissolution, the Church, faithful Bride of the Lord and servant of His sovereign truth, always held out one and only one ideal: the integral social reign of Christ the King. Something less than this may be tolerated for a time, as one might tolerate a prison, but nothing less can ever be embraced and held up for acceptance without risking the guilt of treason to the King of kings and Lord of lords.

Most Catholic schools today ignore or distort Catholic social teaching, thus producing either useful idiots who keep sawing off the branch they are sitting on or ivory-tower chroniclers who cannot see how to respond to the cultural crisis and do not seem particularly keen to labor for the integral social reign of Christ the King.

If the kingship of Christ is not understood to have profound, immediate, and uncompromisable political and economic ramifications for all mankind, *including Americans* (no "Enlightenment exceptionalism" allowed!), then it is not understood *at all*. Or rather, it has been domesticated, defanged, and declawed by the self-worshiping modern state — a Catholicism rendered harmless as a vague spirituality to which none can object as long as it has no worldly consequences. This purely subjective feel-good "religion" is *not* the incarnational confession of the Son of God by the Church of God, stretching from the first Adam to the last man before the trumpet sounds, and we would do well to spew it forth as the poison it is, knowing there can be no harmony between Christ and Belial (see 2 Cor. 6:14–17). The only antidote is the traditional, authentic, full-bodied, sacramental, incarnational social doctrine of the Church, given its fullest and most classic expression in the magisterium of Leo XIII.

"Here is a call for the endurance of the saints, those who keep the commandments of God and the faith of Jesus" (Rev. 14:12).

17

The Face of True Mercy

Mercy is the heart and soul of Christianity. Out of His unfathomable mercy, Our Lord came down to save us from sin, death, and hell. Notably, St. Thomas Aquinas holds that mercy is the greatest of the divine attributes.[144] The traditional Latin Mass gives consummate expression to this consoling truth:

> O God, who dost manifest Thine almighty power most of all in sparing and showing mercy: multiply Thy mercy upon us, that as we hasten towards Thy promises, Thou mayest make us partakers of heavenly treasures. Through our Lord Jesus Christ, Thy Son, Who liveth and reigneth with Thee in the unity of the Holy Ghost, God world without end. Amen.[145]

The venerable Roman liturgy is saturated with homage to mercy, *misericordia* — far more so than the modern rite that replaced it. Leaving aside the few texts shared in common between the two forms of the rite, here are some of the many invocations of God's greatest attribute that are prayed each time the old Mass is celebrated — and *only* at the old Mass.[146]

> *Indulgéntiam, absolutiónem, et remissiónem peccatórum nostrórum, tríbuat nobis omnípotens et miséricors Dóminus.*
>
> (May the Almighty and merciful God grant us pardon, absolution, and remission of our sins.)

> *Osténde nobis Dómine, misericórdiam tuam.*
>
> (Show us, O Lord, Thy mercy.)

[144] See *ST* I, Q. 21, arts. 3–4; II-II, Q. 30, art. 4.

[145] Collect, Tenth Sunday after Pentecost.

[146] I cite the Roman Canon, too, because, although it is an option in the new Mass, it is rarely used in most communities.

Orámus te, Dómine, per mérita Sanctórum tuórum, quórum relíquiæ hic sunt, et ómnium Sanctórum: ut indulgére dignéris ómnia peccáta mea.

(We beseech Thee, O Lord, by the merits of Thy Saints, whose relics are here, and of all the Saints, that Thou wilt deign to pardon me all my sins.)

Munda cor meum ac lábia mea, omnípotens Deus, qui lábia Isaíæ Prophétæ cálculo mundásti ignito: ita me tua grata miseratióne dignáre mundáre, ut sanctum Evangélium tuum digne váleam nuntiáre.

(Cleanse my heart and my lips, Almighty God, Who didst cleanse the lips of the prophet Isaias with a burning coal: deign so to cleanse me by Thy gracious mercy that I may worthily proclaim Thy holy Gospel.)

Per evangélica dicta deleántur nostra delícta.

(By the words of the Gospel may our sins be blotted out.)

Offérimus tibi, Dómine, cálicem salutáris, tuam deprecántes cleméntiam: ut in conspéctu divínæ maiestátis tuæ, pro nostra et totíus mundi salúte, cum odóre suavitátis ascéndat.

(We offer unto Thee, O Lord, the chalice of salvation, entreating Thy mercy that our offering may ascend with a sweet fragrance in the sight of Thy divine Majesty, for our own salvation, and for that of the whole world.)

Ego autem in innocéntia mea ingréssus sum: rédime me, et miserére mei.

(But as for me, I have walked in my innocence; redeem me, and have mercy on me.)

Te ígitur, clementíssime Pater, per Iesum Christum Fílium tuum, Dóminum nostrum, súpplices rogámus ac pétimus …

(Thee, therefore, most merciful Father, through Jesus Christ Thy Son, Our Lord, we humbly pray and beseech …)

Nobis quóque peccatóribus fámulis tuis, de multitúdine miseratiónum tuárum sperántibus, pártem áliquam et societátem donáre dignéris, cum tuis sanctis Apóstolis et Martýribus … intra quorum nos consórtium, non æstimátor mériti, sed véniæ, quæsumus, largítor admítte.

(To us also, Thy sinful servants, who put our trust in the multitude of Thy mercies, vouchsafe to grant some part and fellowship with Thy holy Apostles and Martyrs … into whose company we beseech Thee admit us, not considering our merits, but freely pardoning our offenses.)

> *Pláceat tibi, sancta Trinitas, obséquium servitútis meæ: et præsta, ut sacrifícium, quod óculis tuæ maiestátis indígnus óbtuli, tibi sit acceptábile, mihíque et ómnibus, pro quibus illud óbtuli, sit, te miseránte, propitiábile.*
>
> (May the tribute of my homage be pleasing to Thee, O holy Trinity, and grant that the Sacrifice which I, unworthy as I am, have offered in the presence of Thy Majesty, may be acceptable to Thee, and, through Thy mercy, bring forgiveness to me and to all for whom I have offered it.)

One could also mention how the penitential litany *Kyrie eleison* is repeated nine times in honor of the Most Holy Trinity and how the *Gloria*, with its beseeching "miserere nobis," is said far more often, usually several times a week. There are many other texts, too, that speak of salvation, remedy, favor, and forgiveness in such a way that the note of mercy is strongly sounded.

Perhaps the reason so few are aware of this magnificent liturgy of mercy is that so few are intimately familiar with the spiritual riches of the traditional Mass — even, one regrets to say, Catholics who may attend it but who take little care to become acquainted with its prayers. It only gets worse when we step outside the traditional enclave. According to certain shapers of Catholic opinion, this outmoded and superseded "Latin Mass" is supposed to be the refuge of intolerant social misfits, judgmental cranks, misogynists, and who knows what other kinds of worn-out relics — a ghetto in which there can be no mercy, because it still clings to absolute dogma, to strict morals against which it is easy to sin, and to a time-honored way of doing things that draws a line in the sand. That the traditional liturgy is, in fact, a veritable school and reservoir of divine mercy, and that those who assist at it frequently discover that it serves as the gravitational center of vibrant communities of friends and families with a heart for outreach, is the very last thought that would occur to them.

Having been reminded of the authentic Gospel by the liturgy that is its flawless mirror, it is difficult not to be reminded, with a sense of betrayal, of members of the Church's hierarchy who today are preaching a false Gospel of pseudo-mercy. Today, the contrast between true mercy and false mercy confronts us everywhere.[147] What the world is really clamoring for is not mercy, however, but indulgence in sin. The sinner wants to be told that he is good, he is fine, he's doing well, he cares about the poor, he tolerates everyone, and therefore

[147] For an extended treatment of this subject, see Christopher J. Malloy, *False Mercy: Recent Heresies Distorting Catholic Truth* (Manchester, NH: Sophia Institute Press, 2021).

it doesn't matter what he believes or how he acts. Moreover, he wants to think that the way to show mercy to others is to tolerate or applaud anything and everything they think and do, because "who am I to judge?" This postmodern feebleness bears no likeness to confessional Christianity:

> "Mercy" is the word of the day that covers a multitude of anti-Catholic thoughts popular within the hierarchy of the present-day Church: it is not merciful to forbid divorced and remarried Catholics from receiving the Eucharist; it is not merciful to forbid Catholic politicians who support abortion from receiving the Eucharist; it is not merciful to leave heterodox theologians outside of visible communion with the Church (even when they do not publicly retract their heresy); it is not merciful to treat homosexual relationships as qualitatively different than heterosexual ones when approaching from a pastoral standpoint, etc....
>
> Mercy, when contrasted with dogma, is set up as an alternate orthodoxy. It is the orthodoxy of the heart, of kindness, of the anti-Pharisaical ethos. But those who would set up this dichotomy never acknowledge that true mercy is always inextricably intertwined with justice, and justice is predicated upon law. These people wish to change dogma to create an inclusive Church. A Church without boundaries, unfocused on rules and sacraments, unwilling to exclude salvation to those who choose not to embrace it, a Church that can lock hands with people of every other faith in a seamless garment of interwoven theology, all respecting each other's "faith walk" progressing on a path to the same "god." And dogma gets in their way, because the real Church looks nothing like that.[148]

We know from Scripture, Tradition, liturgy, and the lives of the saints that God's mercy is quite different. He demands conversion, repentance, abandoning the sin, embarking on the road of virtue, embracing the Cross — and doing this as many times as it takes, stumbling, falling, and yet getting up again, until God is truly the One loved above all things and in all things. His is a mercy that heals by cauterizing the wound, removing debris, resetting broken bones, taking away self-indulgences that are fatal to us: it is, in the famous phrase, a severe mercy.

[148] Steve Skojec, "Modernists Are Tricky. That's Kind of the Point," *Steve Skojec*, July 12, 2014, https://steveskojec.com/2014/07/modernists-are-tricky-thats-kind-of-the-point.

God's mercy is bound up in His penetrating judgment of our souls, which, says Eliot, "questions the distempered part."[149]

St. Augustine never tires of reminding us in his *Confessions* that he himself did not want to be healed, he was running away from God, and yet the divine Lover of souls chased after him and intervened decisively in his life. And he had to change, completely. As he says: "You are ever close upon the heels of those who flee from You, for You are at once God of Vengeance and Fount of Mercy, and You turn us to Yourself by ways most wonderful."[150]

We will never be vessels and ambassadors of mercy to the world unless we act from a right understanding and acceptance of *God's* strong and demanding mercy towards *us*. The traditional liturgy is constantly invoking that awesome mercy, which is our salvation, our consolation, our hope against hope. True mercy heals because it is radiant with the light of truth and so restores us to our Christian dignity.[151] As St. Leo the Great preached: "O Christian, recognize your dignity, and now that you have been made a partaker of the divine nature, do not return to your former base condition by sinning."

Fittingly, the sacred liturgy may be given the final word: "We have received Thy mercy, O God, in the midst of Thy temple; according to Thy Name, O God, so also is Thy praise unto the ends of the earth: Thy right hand is full of justice."[152]

[149] *Four Quartets*, "East Coker," in *Complete Poems and Plays*, 127.

[150] Augustine, *Confessions*, IV.4.7 (Sheed and Foley, 59).

[151] We have a permanent need for *both* God's justice *and* His mercy: "The prospect of justice without compassion sinks the honest soul into the pit of despondency already in this earthly life, and the application of mercy without justice, without bringing forth the fruits of repentance as a new self, renders otiose our God-given freedom and responsibility" (Robert De La Noval, theological introduction to Bulgakov, *Spiritual Diary*, 39–40).

[152] Introit, Eighth Sunday after Pentecost.

18

The Kernel of the Kasperite Heresy

Regarding the debate over marriage and divorce, serial polygamy, and admission to communion, Walter Cardinal Kasper does not dismiss the need for the sacrament of Penance prior to reception of the Eucharist when one is conscious of grave sin. Nevertheless, he does not seem to affirm the necessity of *a firm purpose of amendment* for Penance, since, in the case at hand, such a purpose would demand the renunciation of the use of marriage — the repudiation of adulterous acts. Or, if he does admit the necessity of amendment for serious sins, he must not affirm the objective gravity of divorce itself (a mere fiction of civil law, no more real, in the spiritual order, than a pink elephant) and especially of attempted "re-marriage" or of sexual relations with someone other than one's legitimate spouse. Kasper's error seems to be simultaneously an error about the indissolubility of marriage, the preconditions of absolution, *and* the sanctity of the Holy Eucharist.

There is, moreover, not sufficient clarity in these discussions about the distinction between actual and sanctifying grace. There seems to be in the minds of some a conflation of the fact that "God is working somewhere" with a soul's being in what our catechisms used to call, with supernatural realism, *the state of grace*. After all, God sends actual graces to all human beings, including pagans He is calling to the Christian faith and fallen-away Christians He is summoning to return. Such graces are understood as "pushes" by which God, often gently and sometimes forcibly, moves us to repentance and conversion, to a new understanding of the Faith, to a new practice of the sacraments. Sanctifying grace is a real and abiding quality of the soul, a possession of divine sonship as real as the possession of art, science, prudence, or moral virtues, but deeper and with a far greater capacity for action.

Possibly, too, there is a lack of clarity in these discussions about the qualitative difference between mortal (or grave or serious) sin and venial sin. Has not the Church been practically in a state of denial about mortal sin for fifty years or more? It is rarely mentioned, rarely preached on, forms little or no part in the formation of children and adolescents.[153] No one, it seems, is really such a bad person after all; everyone has their problems, and these problems fully explain our bad behavior. *Voilà,* the guilt evaporates — and not by means of Confession but by means of repression, forgetfulness, denial, or the ruses of pop psychology. This is why, with the exception of conservative and traditional Catholic enclaves, the sacrament of Confession or Penance has vanished as a *regular and defining feature* of Catholic life.

We need, more than ever, a strong affirmation of the reason why those in a state of manifest grave sin cannot receive Communion — namely, the *grave sin* part. Priests are accustomed to meeting with couples in irregular marital situations (or couples planning to enter these situations) and hearing them say something like "Oh, we just can't receive Communion, right?," giving the impression that they don't see that ceremonial detail as connected in any way to the moral quality of their actions.

What a sad world it is when the path of chastity, purity, and self-control is no longer believed to be a viable option for people. Even now, the divorced and "remarried" *are* able to receive Penance and the Eucharist — if they are willing to live in continence, as brother and sister (absent scandal). The real problem is not in Church law or practice or history or theology but in the *will* of those who choose not to live chastely, who will not take up their cross and follow

[153] All the way back in 1946 (!), Pope Pius XII stated in a radio message: "Perhaps the greatest sin in the world today is that men have begun to lose the sense of sin. Smother that, deaden it — it can hardly be wholly cut out from the heart of man — let it not be awakened by any glimpse of the God-man dying on Golgotha's cross to pay the penalty of sin, and what is there to hold back the hordes of God's enemy from over-running the selfishness, the pride, the sensuality and unlawful ambitions of sinful man?" Kathleen N. Hattrup, "Pius XII Was Talking to the United States When He Spoke of the Loss of 'Sense of Sin,'" *Aleteia,* February 16, 2020, https://aleteia.org/2020/02/16/pius-xii-was-talking-to-the-united-states-when-he-spoke-of-the-loss-of-sense-of-sin. Nicola Bux (*No Trifling Matter: Taking the Sacraments Seriously Again* [Brooklyn: Angelico Press, 2018], 117) notes that St. Basil the Great assigned *twenty years of penance* for the sin of abortion: five years of begging people for prayers outside the church; five years of remaining prostrate while the liturgy was taking place; five years of listening to the Mass of Catechumens seated and then departing with them; and finally five years of attending the full Mass, but without receiving Communion. That is how serious the ancients saw the crime of abortion to be. How do *we* see it?

Christ on the narrow and difficult path. The Church should be *supporting* them in knowing, seeking, and living the good of chastity; she should be helping people to experience that living chastely is not impossible — not too much to ask when it is a matter of pleasing God and inheriting eternal life!

Chastity is, at the end of the day, the fundamental issue that none of the progressives want to raise. For them, it is an outmoded category, a relic of an old-fashioned and unhealthy era in which people put restraints on their erotic desires. The unseen premise behind all of the progressivist argumentation is: "People cannot be expected to control their passions, so we must make this or that allowance, exception, relaxation."

In *Veritatis Splendor*, John Paul II gave the lie once and for all to this pernicious error, one of the devil's perennial temptations for shepherds and flocks alike:

> Even in the most difficult situations man must respect the norm of morality so that he can be obedient to God's holy commandment and consistent with his own dignity as a person. Certainly, maintaining a harmony between freedom and truth occasionally demands uncommon sacrifices, and must be won at a high price: it can even involve martyrdom.... But temptations can be overcome, sins can be avoided, because together with the commandments the Lord gives us the possibility of keeping them: "His eyes are on those who fear him, and he knows every deed of man. He has not commanded any one to be ungodly, and he has not given any one permission to sin" (Sir 15:19–20). Keeping God's law in particular situations can be difficult, extremely difficult, but it is never impossible.... It is in the saving Cross of Jesus, in the gift of the Holy Spirit, in the Sacraments which flow forth from the pierced side of the Redeemer (cf. Jn 19:34), that believers find the grace and the strength always to keep God's holy law, even amid the gravest of hardships.
>
> Only in the mystery of Christ's Redemption do we discover the "concrete" possibilities of man. "It would be a very serious error to conclude ... that the Church's teaching is essentially only an 'ideal' which must then be adapted, proportioned, graduated to the so-called concrete possibilities of man, according to a 'balancing of the goods in question.' But what are the 'concrete possibilities of man'? And of which man are we speaking? Of man dominated by lust or of man redeemed by Christ? This is what is at stake: the reality of Christ's redemption.

> Christ has redeemed us! This means that he has given us the possibility of realizing the entire truth of our being; he has set our freedom free from the domination of concupiscence. And if redeemed man still sins, this is not due to an imperfection of Christ's redemptive act, but to man's will not to avail himself of the grace which flows from that act. God's command is of course proportioned to man's capabilities; but to the capabilities of the man to whom the Holy Spirit has been given; of the man who, though he has fallen into sin, can always obtain pardon and enjoy the presence of the Holy Spirit."[154]

The same pope spoke with absolute clarity on the Church's intransigent defense of traditional moral teaching:

> A broken family can, for its part, consolidate a specific form of "anti-civilization," destroying love in its various expressions, with inevitable consequences for the whole of life in society....
>
> This is why the Church never tires of teaching and of bearing witness to this truth [viz., that marriage depends on a sincere gift of self]. While certainly showing maternal understanding for the many complex crisis situations in which families are involved, as well as for the moral frailty of every human being, the Church is convinced that she must remain absolutely faithful to the truth about human love — otherwise, she would betray herself. To move away from this saving truth would be to close "the eyes of our hearts" (cf. Eph 1:18), which instead should always stay open to the light which the Gospel sheds on human affairs (cf. 2 Tim 1:10). An awareness of that sincere gift of self whereby man "finds himself" must be constantly renewed and safeguarded in the face of the serious opposition which the Church meets on the part of those who advocate a false civilization of progress....
>
> No human society can run the risk of permissiveness in fundamental issues regarding the nature of marriage and the family! Such moral permissiveness cannot fail to damage the authentic requirements of peace and communion among people. It is thus quite understandable why the Church vigorously defends the identity of the family and encourages responsible individuals and institutions, especially political leaders and

[154] John Paul II, Encyclical Letter *Veritatis Splendor* (August 6, 1993), nos. 102–3; the interior quotation is from an address to those taking part in a course on "responsible parenthood" (March 1, 1984), no. 4: *Insegnamenti* VII, 1 (1984), 583.

> international organizations, not to yield to the temptation of a superficial and false modernity....
>
> This kind of critical reflection should lead our society, which certainly contains many positive aspects on the material and cultural level, to realize that, from various points of view, it is a society which is sick and is creating profound distortions in man. Why is this happening? The reason is that our society has broken away from the full truth about man, from the truth about what man and woman really are as persons.[155]

The rejection of the possibility of chastity is the reason why *Humanae Vitae* was rejected — at root, there is no other. It is the reason why we have rampant pornography, abortion, homosexual activity, the clergy scandals, and every other sexual aberration. The Church's hierarchy has been complicit every step of the way by refusing to preach chastity "in season and out of season" (2 Tim. 4:2), regardless of the opposition of the world or the incredulity of worldly Catholics. Priests and bishops have (sometimes) condemned the evil *fruits*, but they have refused to name the evil *tree* of unchastity; they would not put the axe to its trunk. And now the tree, having grown unchecked for decades, having been manured and irrigated by its votaries, is an enormous, imposing plant, blocking out the light of the sun and the stars, with abundant dark and sickly-sweet fruits filled with poison. This is the bitter harvest that is ours. We must spit out every last bit of this wretched fruit and begin to hack away energetically at the root with every axe on hand.[156] May God grant us clergy and prelates willing to join with us in the work of clearing and replanting the orchard.

[155] John Paul II, *Gratissimam Sane* 13, 11, 17, 20.

[156] This will include not only the frequent use of the sacraments, of course, but also a more conscientious use of the *sacramentals* Holy Mother Church provides for our many and varied needs. See, for concrete examples, "Living the Virtue of Chastity by the Power of Jesus," in Kwasniewski, *Holy Bread*, 171–78.

19

Rediscovering Modesty from Within

Each year as we enter the warmer months, the problem of modesty in dress arises — ever more acutely, it seems, as Western people lose even the minimal moral bearings and social customs that once guaranteed a modicum of self-respect and consideration for others. We need nothing less than a moral revolution, a rebuilding of our most basic concepts of virtue. This will be difficult, needless to say, and we may not be able to turn the tide of the general culture, more correctly described at this point as an anti-culture. Yet it is by no means impossible to rebuild these concepts within Christian communities, if only there is a courageous willingness to address the issues at stake, with clarity and calmness. I shall attempt an overview.

The notion of "modesty" in dress, speech, or behavior is derived from the notion of *moderation*, of doing something in a fitting, well-considered manner that observes a mean between extremes. Here the extremes are shamelessness (far more common today) and prudery or unhealthy inhibition. Like all moral virtues, the habit of modesty not only gives an aptitude for wanting and choosing what is right in this regard, but it makes us want it and choose it spontaneously; modesty becomes a second nature, an efficacious disposition. Let us not forget, too, that modesty helps us to *appreciate* aptly chosen dress, speech, and behavior, all of which are instruments of virtuous action.

The modest person is one whose actions and appearance consistently reflect self-mastery, good judgment of what is appropriate, a firm command over feelings, a serene ability to express and to *be* oneself without self-advertisement. Hence, true modesty begins in the soul and only later catches the eye's or ear's notice. This inward modesty consists in regulating one's entire life in a manner that is calm, gentle, reverent, and pure. Putting on modest clothing or avoiding immodest dancing is something that "spills over" from that interior condition.[157]

Modern Western societies have discarded the external modesty most required for the basic health of society: dressing and comporting oneself in a manner that will not excite the wrong kind of attention from the opposite sex — an animalistic, possessive, reductive attention. Indeed, as is obvious, the opposite vice is flaunted. Sadly, many sincere Christians who want to lead a chaste life seem to be unaware of the link between purity of heart and modesty in appearance, between commitment to virtue and the way the body is presented to others — an ignorance all the more surprising in that the connection is rather obvious and, in consequence, has been clearly understood in every age other than ours. As Jean Borella remarks: "Clothing falls under the jurisdiction of divine mercy since, by veiling the body, it attenuates the effects of the Fall."[158] There are, for example, young Catholics who try to be pure but who continue to dress as their secular peers do, in provocative or inappropriate styles of clothing. One sees this vividly at World Youth Days, where, in addition to immodesty, there is an astonishing lack of awareness of what is appropriate for the Holy Sacrifice of the Mass and the reception of Holy Communion.

Modern-day people seem to have elevated one criterion above all others: physical comfort. Anything that could cause the remotest discomfort or inconvenience is rejected out of hand. As a result, when dressing in hot weather, Christians all too often fall into the bad habits of their secular peers who think only about what is coolest or easiest, not about what would please God or help oneself and others to remain chaste. As a small part of sound asceticism, Christians ought to reject this sort of pampering of and pandering to the body.

[157] As I will explain, there are different aspects of the virtue of modesty, and it's unfortunate that only the most elementary kind, decency of dress, has tended to receive the name, although one still catches a hint of the older meaning when a man who does not put himself forward is described as "modest." Putting on modest clothing or avoiding immodest dances is not enough; countless men and women have shown a riotous immodesty in private, despite a pristine public demeanor. Research on the prim and proper Victorians has shown that beneath their apparent reserve was a welter of unchastity. Obviously, it is not enough to have the trappings of virtue. One must interiorize virtue; it must become the guiding principle of one's desires and thoughts. Only in this way will the outward dimension correspond to the inward, and vice versa.

[158] Jean Borella, *Love and Truth: The Christian Path of Charity*, trans. G. John Champoux (Brooklyn: Angelico Press, 2020), 237.

St. Paul describes the believer as one who is "always carrying in [his] body the death of Jesus, so that the life of Jesus may also be manifested in our bodies" (2 Cor. 4:10).

Who has not been struck by old black-and-white photographs of pioneer settlers who, in the midst of sweltering summer heat, wore all-covering, full-length outfits? I don't suggest we return to exactly the same wardrobe, but we would do well to heed their witness of propriety and stamina. Obviously, circumstances of hot weather and activities such as long outdoor hikes have to be taken into account, but there are modest and immodest solutions to *any* situation.[159] With our modern materials, dressing modestly need not mean dressing oppressively; for example, dresses of cool, lightweight, opaque material are available that cover the shoulders and come down below the knee or to the ankles.

We cannot pretend that how we treat ourselves bodily, how we eat and dress and look and move, whether we do so with restraint or abandon, with polite regard or thoughtlessness, with responsibility or naïveté, are spiritually irrelevant "fine points." On the contrary, they are essential. They, too, will either manifest the life of Jesus to the world, or promote a contrary spirit. How someone treats, displays, and makes use of the body reveals much about the workings of the soul: who one thinks he (or she) is, what one thinks about oneself and others, what one wants from oneself or others. In more ways than people realize, looks are *not* deceiving: the medium *is* the message. As an observant acquaintance of mine wrote to me:

> We become tacit parties to the sexual revolution when we make use of the extravagant revolutionary dress it introduced as a "uniform." By exposing large tracts of one's skin to the public, I first distance myself from the Christlike ideal of modesty (after all, His disrobing was a *humiliation*), then I divorce myself from cultural continuity with my Christian ancestors, then I forfeit ownership of the particular shapes of my body. This last point is particularly important, because by immodest dress, we force upon others or invite them into a certain intimacy with our bodies they may not want or should not have.

As with every topic of importance, divine revelation is not lacking guidelines. "I desire then ... that women should adorn themselves modestly and sensibly in seemly apparel, not with braided hair or gold or pearls or costly attire but by

[159] The traditional Catholic scouts of Europe set an excellent example in this regard, especially for the young ladies.

good deeds, as befits women who profess religion" (1 Tim. 2:8–10). There is a way of behaving and appearing that is inseparable from the Christian way of life; it is one of the marks of the believer in the world. Modesty, like peacefulness, though primarily a good of the soul, does not stop at the soul but has an effect on all aspects of social life. The modern world needs models of self-control and dignified self-presentation; Christians can and must set the example of seeking the golden mean of virtue. The very absence of excess or of defect is worthy of making its presence known.[160]

The virtue of religion — by which we strive to give back to the infinite God, who has lavished so much upon us, what we, in turn, are able to give by means of internal and external acts of homage — guides the offering up to Him of our persons, our bodies and souls, in faithful love. This is why modesty is both a consequence and a safeguard of religion.

St. Thomas says that holiness denotes two things: *being clean* and *being firm*.[161] "Blessed are the clean of heart, for they shall see God" (Matt. 5:8): blessed are they who firmly preserve their purity of soul and body, for the sake of loving God with their whole being. The sight of God, the great goal and joy of Christian life, is the ultimate reason we must keep our hearts, our words, our movements and appearance pure, undefiled, simple, restrained. When we do, our way of life is conformed to that of Our Lord Jesus Christ and makes present in a fallen, soiled world something of the bright innocence, the serene peace, the incorruptible freshness of the Holy Spirit.

The virtue of modesty, then, is essential, not optional, in the Christian life. It is far from being the most important virtue, yet its presence limits a host of evils, and its absence invites a world of sin. Modesty is a deep human need that is rejected only at great expense to integrity and legitimate self-love. How many women are there whose dignity is wounded and whose memory is loaded with one incident after another of men *using* them for their bodies? They have suffered much on account of poor upbringing, poor education, poor advice. They needed modesty, which is so closely bound up with the fact and the *feeling* of

[160] On the "mean of virtue," see note 112. The view that Christians today should fit in with their surrounding society and, in the case of clothing, wear more or less the same thing as everyone else is acutely critiqued by Anna Kalinowska in "The Art of Dress — Problems with Normalcy," *OnePeterFive*, July 12, 2022, https://onepeterfive.com/art-dress-problems-normalcy. By attending to the need for intentional (and, at the moment, countercultural) beauty, Kalinowska provides a crucial missing piece in discussions on modesty.

[161] *ST* II-II, Q. 81, art. 8.

human dignity. Now that they have suffered from its absence, they need it even more in order to recover their dignity, their sense of worth, their awareness of being a person who deserves to be loved for her own sake. Everyone wants to be loved as a person, not a thing — a who, not a what.

The philosopher Peter Wust speaks of the proper attitude a person should take to his or her own existence:

> Piety towards oneself surrounds the self like a delicate membrane, which must be kept safe from harm if we want to protect our souls from being laid open to great dangers. [This piety is concerned with] values which are, as it were, a heavenly trust within us which we are bound to defend whenever a hostile power threatens to profane them.... Our soul in its ultimate depths is a secret, and this is the inner chamber of the soul which we are, up to a certain point, obliged to preserve religiously. Reverence for ourselves forbids us to unveil the sanctuary of our souls with a rash and impious hand, and to do so would be a real profanation and show an unforgivable lack of modesty.[162]

Many in the Western world, it seems, ignore the need for, or attack the idea of, such an inner modesty, which is the true cause and ground of outward modesty. "The eye is the lamp of the body. So, if your eye is sound, your whole body will be full of light; but if your eye is not sound, your whole body will be full of darkness" (Matt. 6:22–23). Marcel comments: "Against this modesty [of the spirit], in fact, the most active and most opposite powers of our age have made alliance."[163]

The Christian is called upon to proclaim the primacy of the divine over the human and the human over the animal. We proclaim the natural goodness and participation in holiness of a body that receives life and movement from an immortal soul fashioned after the image of God. "The Lord God formed man of dust from the ground, and breathed into his nostrils the breath of life; and man became a living being" (Gen. 2:7). "Thou didst knit me together in my mother's womb.... My frame was not hidden from thee, when I was being made in secret, intricately wrought in the depths of the earth" (Ps. 138:13, 15).

The body is a creation of God, a temple of His Spirit, washed and anointed in Baptism, promised a share of bliss in the final resurrection. Our appearance

[162] Quoted in Gabriel Marcel, *Being and Having*, trans. Katharine Farrer (Westminster: Dacre Press, 1949), 227–28.

[163] Marcel, *Being and Having*, 228.

and way of behaving should bear witness to the uniquely Catholic truth — already unmistakably present in the New Testament — that both marriage and celibacy prize the human body as a worthy offering of love, a channel of grace, a sacred sign, when consecrated by the sacraments of Jesus Christ. "The body is not meant for immorality, but for the Lord, and the Lord for the body" (1 Cor. 6:13). "I beseech you therefore, brethren, by the mercy of God, that you present your bodies a living sacrifice, holy, pleasing unto God, your reasonable service" (Rom. 12:1).

Whether we speak of an organic body, a political body, or the Mystical Body, each in its own way is a unity composed of many distinct parts in hierarchical order and relationship. The human person is, in a sense, a hierarchy of elements of personhood: there are many layers or levels to me, and not all of them should stand in the forefront. A radical anthropological egalitarianism that gives equal weight to body and soul, or to the various faculties of the soul — placing, for instance, imagination or will at the same level as intellect — is no less erroneous than political or ecclesiological egalitarianism.

The bodily dimension of a person carries with it sacramental significance, above all the naked body. The naked body is the most expressive gift spouses can give to each other. In giving *it*, they give *themselves*, since the body is not something I "possess" as if it were my property, but a true part of *who I am*. The human person is not "in" a body but is *bodily*: we are incarnate beings. Here is what St. Thomas Aquinas has to say about that:

> To one asking why there are so many members in a natural body — hands, feet, mouth, and the like — it could be replied that they are to serve the soul's variety of activities. The soul itself is the cause and principle of these members, and what they are, the soul is virtually. For the body is made for the soul, and not the other way around. From this perspective, the natural body is a certain fullness of the soul; unless the members exist with an integral body, the soul cannot exercise fully its activities.[164]

Hence, the body, far more than any other gift that can be given, ought to be unwrapped and taken possession of only by him or her to whom it has been solemnly vowed, even as the Most Holy Eucharist, which is the true Body of our Lord, is to be received only by the baptized who are wedded to Christ in

[164] St. Thomas Aquinas, *Commentary on Ephesians* [1:23], chap. 1, lect. 8, no. 71.

charity. A man's body, teaches St. Paul, no longer belongs to him, but to his wife, and her body to him (1 Cor. 7:4).[165]

It is worth dwelling on the special sacramental bond uniting husband and wife and the all-encompassing modesty, the sensitivity of soul, it demands. Modesty is an essential virtue not because the body or the passions are shameful in themselves but because their very goodness and their potential as ministers of grace impose a duty to protect them from abuse, manipulation, and disorder. Think of the beautiful words of St. Paul, so exalted, so full of God's love for all that He has made and redeemed: "Do you not know that your body is a temple of the Holy Spirit within you, which you have from God? You are not your own; you were bought with a price. So glorify God in your body" (1 Cor. 6:19–20).[166]

Human beings are called upon to guard the secret of their personhood, a precious gift from God, a mystery not for indiscriminate public consumption. To the courting, the betrothed, the newlywed, the lifelong pair, a heavenly trust is given, and they are bound to defend it against hostile powers that threaten to profane it. At their core, man and woman are secrets to be shared in love.[167] Plotinus writes beautifully about what perfect communication would be like:

[165] See chapter 2.

[166] On the rich moral-sacramental-ecclesial teaching of 1 Corinthians, see "St. Paul Tells Us How to Fix Our Liturgical Problems," in Kwasniewski, *Holy Bread,* 35–42.

[167] As Luke Bell writes: "The body communicates in a special way when it is naked. There is a sense in which nudity is sacred.... Nudity is the expression of a privileged intimacy: we reserve it for those from whom we do not wish to hide anything and refuse it to those from whom we wish to remain hidden" (*Mystery of Identity,* 149). Fr. Justine John Dyikuk, a lecturer of mass communication at the University of Jos in Nigeria, writes: "Today, fashion and dressing are purposely made to appeal to the passions.... Shelina Zahra Janmohammed, a writer and commentator on British Islam, makes an important contribution on the challenge of modesty in a western secularist society. She says: 'When I go out on the street there is a demand that my body is public. People want to see my face and my hair, and actually they would probably prefer it if I wore a shorter skirt — to stereotype. And the fact that I won't share my body with people in that way is problematic [for them].' Inquiringly and rhetorically, Janmohammed asked: 'Why should I have to show you my body in order for you to accept me? Why is it insulting to you that I should cover up?' Against the western secularist culture that one's body is public, the Traditional African Society, Islamic, and Christian faiths hold that the body is private and sacred." "Towards a Theology of the Body," *La Croix International,* July 13, 2022, https://international.la-croix.com/news/religion/towards-a-theology-of-the-body/16387.

"Here below we can know many things by the look in people's eyes when they are silent; but There [in the reality of the divine] all their body is clear and pure and each is like an eye, and nothing is hidden or feigned, but before one speaks to another that other has seen and understood."[168] The inner chamber cannot be left open as a public playground. It should be treated with a reverence like that with which we approach the sanctuary and tabernacle of a church.

[168] *Ennead* IV.3 [27].18, 19–24.

20

Vigilance in the Christian Use of Media

All of us could use more silence in our lives. God has so much to tell us, such profound and lofty mysteries, so overflowing with indescribable joy, that He does not engage in chitchat or texting, but speaks "heart to heart": in prayer, in Scripture, in the liturgy. That means if we want to hear Him, we need to open up a space of silence every day — this is why all the spiritual masters say we should commit some sacrosanct portion of the day to quiet prayer — and we should find ways to reduce the constant noise that surrounds us in the form of music, videos, and social media. Back in 1935, Eliot said that moderns are "distracted from distraction by distraction";[169] what would he say *today*, with Facebook, Twitter, Instagram, TikTok, and Lord only knows what else?

Silence is uncomfortable. We flee from it because, sooner or later, it will make us think about ourselves, about God, life, the universe, our happiness or lack thereof, and these are uncomfortable objects of meditation if we are not yet who and what we ought to be. Conversely, for someone who is really striving to be a "just man" like St. Joseph, silence is no longer an uncomfortable no-man's-land but a welcome opportunity to be alone with God, yet never lonely. When we are in the car or taking public transportation, we should not automatically turn on the radio or stick in the earbuds. We can learn to be quiet, to say some prayers or psalms instead. We need plenty of "down time" from social media. It is very hard to pull away from the torrent of news and chats and music tracks — I know it from experience — but the benefits are immense, and even secular people are writing book after book about why we have to do it for the health of our psyche. It's the new form of asceticism: we need to fast from too much media consumption. Some recommend the Sunday shutdown — that is, leaving all devices turned off on Sundays. Go to a park and take a walk in nature, listening

[169] *Four Quartets*, "Burnt Norton," in *Complete Poems and Plays*, 120.

to the natural sounds the world makes. If one doesn't take steps to put up appropriate walls, various kinds of noise will invade one's life and colonize one's mind, turning it into a messy room cluttered with whatever *other* people want to put there, and not much room will be left for oneself or for God.

We must be intelligent and countercultural when it comes to *what* we watch and listen to. Our habits of movies and music need to be in harmony with our Christian faith. This is something St. Paul was already telling the Philippians way back in the early Church, when there were similar problems, such as pagan festivals full of lewdness and the violent games where spectators watched condemned criminals fight each other to the death. St. Paul said:

> Whatever is true, whatever is honorable, whatever is just, whatever is pure, whatever is lovely, whatever is gracious, if there is any excellence, if there is anything worthy of praise, *think about these things.* (Phil. 4:8)

In other words, fill the mind with good things. Just as we all know that eating healthy foods is good for the body, so we should take in only what is healthy for the soul. Implied is a warning: do *not* think about, let alone linger over and absorb like a sponge, the contrary — what is false, dishonorable, unjust, impure, excessive, ugly, slovenly, disgraceful, mediocre, diminishing of human dignity — for that will make our souls less Christian and less fully human. As William Daniel explains:

> The human is made into the likeness, according to Gregory [of Nyssa], of the image — the beauty on which her gaze is cast. This works positively and negatively. To gaze upon evil forms an image of the beholder as depraved and capable only of sinful actions. Casting one's gaze upon God, however, makes manifest the human's true nature — the divine image, a participant in divine goodness.[170]

We don't see in the Church Fathers the false belief that the way to become a "fuller" person is to be "exposed" to a lot of evil, if only vicariously, so that one can better understand it and combat it — the weak argument to which proponents of modern media so often have recourse. This argument, admittedly, has a certain validity in connection with *literary* portrayals of evil, *if* they are tastefully done, because the potency of the content is filtered through the intellect of the reader, who must first understand the words and concepts before he can, to some extent, re-create the scene in his imagination. The medium allows

[170] Daniel, *Christ the Liturgy*, 61.

for the visceral impact of evil to be mediated by a spiritual process. With film or video, however, the image is taken straight in through the eyes, even as the dialogue and soundtrack are taken in by the ears; there is an immediacy that does not filter or interpret the content in the act of reception.

Pope John Paul II asked: "What truth can there be in films, shows, and radio and television programs dominated by pornography and violence? Do these really serve the *truth about man*?"[171] This is a key question. Should not our recreational activities *restore* us, our leisure pursuits lead us more deeply into the truth of things? It would be an evil if the media to which we gave our attention were, in obvious or subtle ways, to take us away from moral and intellectual virtue, the love of beauty, and the ultimate truth for which we are made.

Fr. Dominic Legge explains: "When we watch acts of lust or cruelty, we tend to become more lustful and cruel. What you look on with your eyes, you invite into your soul. How much of the so-called 'entertainment' fare of our age falls into this category?" Appropriately for a member of the Order of Preachers, Fr. Legge here follows the Angelic Doctor, who writes in the *Summa*: "The seeing of sights becomes sinful when it renders a man prone to the vices of lust and cruelty on account of things he sees represented. Hence Chrysostom says that such sights make men adulterers and shameless."[172]

There is, however, an alternative result of watching graphic portrayals of lust or cruelty: one can become indifferent to the matter and even callous about it, numbed to the objective moral evil being portrayed and sluggish in reacting with appropriate disgust and repentance. If I watch movie stars fornicating, I will have one of three responses: I will be moved in sympathy with what they are doing, which is sinful for me, or I will be indifferent to it, which is also sinful, or I will feel disgust. Feeling disgust for evil is right, but we are not supposed to go out of our way voluntarily to seek disgusting things. In the movies, dozens, hundreds, thousands of people get shot up on the screens in front of us: life is cheap, and violence is good entertainment. Should we be surprised when moderns are prepared casually and callously to throw away the lives of unborn

[171] John Paul II, *Gratissimam Sane* 20. This pope was far from being the first pope to address the problem of morals in movies. Two forgotten but still relevant papal documents should be consulted: the Encyclical Letter *Vigilanti Cura* of Pius XI (June 29, 1936) and the Encyclical Letter *Miranda Prorsus* of Pius XII (September 8, 1957).

[172] *ST* II-II, Q. 167, art. 2, ad 2. I copied Fr. Legge's comments from the Internet, from which they have subsequently gone missing.

children or the elderly? Sexual content is treated as a nonnegotiable titillation, and, in general, evil is treated as a spice in the recipe. Should we be surprised at the promiscuity, cheapness, and weirdness of modern sexual behavior, when images of the same are regularly impressed on the imaginations of millions of people? Movies make unreality seem like reality — with the gradual effect, perhaps, of making reality seem like unreality. Movies and life blend together into a flickering phantasmagoria with no moral or eternal consequences.

We should prize and protect our interior purity and quietude.[173] It is difficult for fallen creatures like ourselves to follow St. Paul's injunction to the Colossians: "Set your mind on things above, not on the things of the earth" (Col. 3:2), so that we may remain unstained in the midst of a corrupt generation. It is already difficult enough for us distractible, anxiety-ridden rational animals to achieve inner silence and recollection for prayer. One wonders, then, what the great mystics would say about movies and sitcoms and streaming shows. Think of St. Teresa of Jesus, St. John of the Cross, St. Thérèse of the Child Jesus, St. Elizabeth of the Trinity: would they not consider most of what people watch today to be, at best, a colossal waste of time; at worst, a pollution of the soul? We should adopt for *all* media St. Basil the Great's wise attitude toward pagan writings. He says, with something like Homer's *Iliad* or *Odyssey* in mind:

> When they recount the words and deeds of good men, you should both love and imitate them, earnestly emulating such conduct. But when they portray base conduct, you must flee from them and stop up your ears, as Odysseus is said to have fled past the song of the sirens, for familiarity with evil writings paves the way for evil deeds. Therefore the soul must be guarded with great care, lest through our love for letters [he means pagan literature] it receive some contamination unawares, as men drink in poison with honey.[174]

If that is true of *literature*, is it not a thousand times truer of movies and television and many other forms of today's popular entertainment? Movies

[173] See A. G. Sertillanges, *The Intellectual Life: Its Spirit, Conditions, Methods*, trans. Mary Ryan (Washington, DC: Catholic University of America Press, 1992).

[174] St. Basil of Caesarea, "Address to Young Men on the Right Use of Greek Literature," no. 4, in Frederick Morgan Padelford, *Essays on the Study and Use of Poetry by Plutarch and Basil the Great* (New York: Henry Holt, 1902), 104; text reproduced at *The Tertullian Project*, www.tertullian.org/fathers/basil_litterature01.htm.

exercise a kind of "strong magic" because they fill the soul with hyperdefined imagery, overly potent images. The soul cannot resist the influx of phantasms and is molded accordingly. The medium tends toward a stimulation excessive for the faculties of a rational animal: too much for the animal, too little for the rational. It appeals primarily to the senses of the flesh and thereby induces a pragmatic primacy of matter over mind. Our memories and dreams become saturated with what we watch and listen to.

For St. Paul, the matter is clear. He says to the Ephesians: "Fornication and all impurity or covetousness must not even be *mentioned* among you, as is fitting among saints. Let there be no filthiness, nor silly talk, nor levity, which are not fitting; but instead let there be thanksgiving" (Eph. 5:3–4).[175] He writes to the Corinthians: "Do I make my plans like a worldly man, ready to say Yes and No at once? As surely as God is faithful, our word to you has not been Yes and No" (2 Cor. 1:17–18). If we need sophisticated and elliptical arguments to justify something we are listening to or watching (or, for that matter, reading), we are probably guilty of trying to say yes and no to Christ. How a Christian lives his life, what he spends his time on, where he puts his mind and heart should be utterly consistent with the Faith he professes. The Word of God exhorts us to vigilance, careful discrimination, and a holy ruthlessness with our tendency to cut corners, make excuses, and relax standards.

Nor are the consequences limited to the moral sphere; they extend to the intellectual as well. One watches a movie "effortlessly" — and that is exactly what is wrong with it. How many people today know how to entertain themselves by the use of their *own* intellects and imaginations? Why are we so passive, dependent on a giant money-making industry that homogenizes culture, instead of locally producing beautiful things ourselves, or at least actively assimilating a work of art? Thomas Merton expressed anxiety about what a television culture could do to souls:

> There is a sufficiently general agreement, among men whose judgment I respect, that commercial television is degraded, meretricious and absurd. Certainly it would seem that TV could become a kind of unnatural surrogate for contemplation: a completely inert subjection to vulgar images, a descent to a sub-natural passivity rather than an ascent

[175] Christians are morally required *not* to watch TV shows or movies that display sexually immoral acts: if such things shouldn't even be *mentioned* among those who are called to be saints, what would St. Paul say about *watching* them and taking them into our imaginations and memories?

> to a supremely active passivity in understanding and love. It would seem that television should be used with extreme care and discrimination by anyone who might hope to take interior life seriously. Keep your eyes clean and your ears quiet and your mind serene. Breathe God's air. Work, if you can, under His sky.[176]

So, am I saying we should *never* watch movies or shows? No. Fortunately there are movies that do not indulge in gratuitous evil: a whole library of classic films, more recent ones tastefully done, documentaries, docudramas, stage plays turned into movies, nature films, animated films, and so forth. If one were using media moderately, one would never run out of good films to watch.

As Christians, we need to be engaged in the effort of drawing our dispersed energies and faculties together in a focus on the Holy Trinity dwelling in our soul and outwardly displayed in the beauty of God's creation. Modernity in general, and popular entertainment in particular, wage war on the created order and on our interiority, our "interior castle." The constant buzz and fuzz of worldly images and noise distract us from the pursuit of the *unum necessarium*, the "one thing needful."

[176] Thomas Merton, *New Seeds of Contemplation* (New York: New Directions, 1972), 86. This book was published in 1962 but based on a first edition from 1949.

21

Teaching Children about Sexuality and Its Distortions

"The birds and the bees" conversation that parents need to have with their children, in different ways at different times of maturation, will always be something of a challenge. But Christian parents have several things going for them: first, the graces of the state of matrimony, which support them in all that they must do; second, the simple fact that the truth of the matter, as it comes from God's hand, is already good, fitting, and beautiful, even if it is also marked by the effects of the Fall. When the time is right, smaller children can be told something like this:

> There's a special kind of hug only for husbands and wives — people God has joined in marriage. They become very close to each other, to show how much they love one another and to tell God that they are open to receiving the gift of a baby from Him, because He wants to give them the amazing gift of another person to love. So sometimes God will put a baby into mommy's womb as a gift from this special hug. That's how you came to be here, and your brothers and sisters too.

Beyond this germinal understanding, it can be helpful for parents to think about and discuss sexuality in terms of three major themes: (1) Adam and Eve, (2) Christ and the Church, (3) the evangelical counsels. I'm certainly not suggesting that *all* of the following can be presented at once, but *over* time, these different aspects can be brought out, one by one, as occasion permits.

1. When the first man was created, he was in a state of original solitude — not isolation, since he was with God, but still without a partner "fit for him," of his own nature, with whom he could share a human life. Man's natural "home" is being together with another who completes him as well as other persons who proceed from that union. Home, in fact, is defined by this bond between the first man and the first woman. Fruitfulness is a fundamental natural good that allows the human race to exist; it is also, consequently, a supernatural good,

because it allows Christians to build up the Church by adding members to Christ.[177] This fertility of human nature is an expression of a generous and outward-oriented inner life, by which we can take part in the activity of creating that is proper to God.[178]

2. The ultimate reason the two sexes were created, and the hidden truth that all human couples represent, is the perfect and everlasting union of Christ and the Church (see Ephesians 5). In order for God to express His perfect love for mankind, He had to ensure first that there would be a relationship that is comprehensive, self-giving, fruitful, and stable. Once this was in place, He could point to it and say: "That is how my love is — only better." Unfortunately, this created foreshadowing of the Incarnation was seriously damaged by sin and continues to be so damaged; yet not so much that the comparison is meaningless to us; otherwise, Our Lord, St. Paul, and St. John would not have been able to use it at all.[179]

3. These two points lead, finally, to a third. It is not difficult to see how the truth that Christ is the perfect husband and the Church — in her heavenly glory, and wherever on earth that glory is reflected in the life of grace — is His perfect Bride leads directly to the Catholic teaching on celibate priesthood and religious life. The man who wishes to follow Christ the High Priest should be like Him in not being married to a particular earthly spouse, since he is allowed to share in Christ's unique marriage with His Bride.[180] The priest is *alter Christus*: the image of Christ the Bridegroom. Similarly, the woman who wishes to belong entirely to this heavenly Spouse must be *His* bride and no one else's: that is why the state of consecrated virginity is so noble and privileged in the Church. It isn't merely a spiritual desire to belong to Christ, which everyone should have; it is a gift of oneself in its entirety, body and soul, to Him alone, to the fullest degree possible in this life.

It is clear that Christ sacrificed many goods of human life ("the Son of Man has nowhere to lay His head" [Matt. 8:20]) in order to show us the urgency and absoluteness of salvation. A consecrated, celibate, or perpetually continent life bears consistent and convincing witness to the "one thing needful" chosen by

[177] See chapter 29.

[178] See chapter 27.

[179] To read more about all these themes, see the chapter "This, Too, Reveals God: The Body and Sexuality in Catholic Theology," in Kwasniewski, *Ministers of Christ*, 3–12.

[180] See chapter 25.

Mary of Bethany (Luke 10:42). Although many things matter relatively speaking, only one thing matters absolutely, and that is whether, after we die, our soul will go to heaven (immediately or after purgation) or to hell. There are no other destinies than these two, and a human life is successful when it achieves eternal life, a failure when it loses happiness forever.[181]

By teaching young children, from early on, the beauty of marriage and family as well as the beauty of the calling to religious life or priesthood, there develops a *context* for teaching on more specific aspects of sexuality and the body, which are then able to be seen in their full meaning and appropriateness. This way, one avoids the extremes of excessive anatomical-biological detail on the one hand, and a puritanical spirit of shameful silence or denigration on the other. The Catholic vision of creation, redemption, and sanctification offers us a golden mean.

It should be obvious that children must be shielded from premature exposure to evils, or even to good things, that they are not yet mentally and psychologically ready to process. This is the reason why Christian parents are, or will soon be, morally obliged to homeschool their children: state educational systems are increasingly committed to a militant sexualization based on hedonism, relativism, and nihilism, which is destructive of the innocence and purity of children.

Having discussed some ways in which we can talk to children about the goodness and role of human sexuality in the divine plan, now we must turn to the difficult question of sexual evils, which are, alas, so numerous and prominent in our times that they cannot be entirely avoided.

Our Lord Jesus Christ says: "God alone is good" (Mark 10:18). Every creature can fail, and this includes every human being and every member of the Church, from the least to the greatest. God can transform us by His grace, but He does not force us to be good, much less to be perfect. We have to be willing to work with His grace. St. Dionysius says: "Good happens in one way, evil in all manner of ways."[182] It's hard to get things right but easy to get them wrong. So

[181] See my articles "God Made Us for Heaven," *OnePeterFive*, August 10, 2022, https://onepeterfive.com/god-made-us-for-heaven-2/; "On Hell: Clarity Is Mercy in an Age of 'Dare We Hope,'" *OnePeterFive*, August 7, 2019, https://onepeterfive.com/hell-clarity-mercy/. Purgatory is not a destination but a waystation, a stage of preparation and purification. Those who are in purgatory are already saved; they know they are assured of the Beatific Vision, and this is their surpassing joy in the midst of their sufferings.

[182] As St. Thomas cites him in *ST* I-II, Q. 70, art. 4, ad 2, referring to *On the Divine Names*, chap. 4.

we should somehow convey to children and young adults, when talking about evils, that in this vale of tears we will always be running up against greater or lesser evils but that we can still *know* the good, *love* it, and work toward it — and help others toward it as well.

Talking about good things, even when they are delicate, is relatively easy. The worst job a parent has, in my opinion, is talking about evil — especially the sexual disorders and deviations that constantly show up in the news.

> *Sometimes a man and a woman get together — but they're not married; they're not husband and wife. But they act like they're married, and God gives them a baby, even though they weren't supposed to be acting like that at that time. God is asking them to take responsibility for the baby and to make big sacrifices for him or her.*

Sigh. Complicated and not even coherent. Sin is a mess and makes a mess. Or how about:

> *There are people who are so confused and hurt that they don't actually want to be mommies and daddies, so they do things to prevent God from giving them a baby. It's like keeping the windows shut or the doors locked so a needy person can't get in. This makes them lonely and miserable, and it's very wrong of them to do it.*

It deteriorates from here.

> *Some people, sadly, are not able to have children in the natural way God intended, but instead of accepting this cross or adopting children who need a home, they forcibly make a child inside a glass test tube using material taken from the mother and father.*

I remember dreading the first time the subject of abortion would come up with a child who was unaware of it. It's just so unspeakably evil. What do you say?

> *There are mommies who want their babies to be killed, or who are pressured into it by bullies. They get someone to go into their womb and chop up the baby and suck it out with a kind of vacuum cleaner. Or they take a pill that poisons the baby. And there are so-called doctors who kill thousands of babies as their regular day job. One of them died and they found more than two thousand dead babies collected in his backyard.*

No! One cannot say such a thing. Somehow, one has to find a way to explain it, since it will unavoidably come up. Or how about homosexuality?

> *There are some men who are so confused that they like other men, and there are women who like other women — I mean, not just as friends, but in the way mommies and daddies like each other.*

It only gets more bizarre with transvestites, "sex change" operations, homosexuals' "renting" eggs, sperm, and someone's womb in order to "have" "their own" child, and so on. Such things are repugnant even to think about, let alone verbalize. Truly, in this realm of sexuality, the catastrophe of the Fall shows itself most outrageously, with as many heads as the Hydra.

People often say: "Truth is stranger than fiction." We might also say: "Perversion is stranger than truth." Children will have an instinctive revulsion at perversions; it is only adults who are jaded enough to be unmoved. As a result, your kids are likely to be very judgmental about these evils — and that is a *good thing*. God demands of us judgment between good and evil, and we must be very clear that good is good, and evil is evil; woe to those who call good evil, and evil good, says the prophet Isaiah (5:20). But we can also teach compassion for the sinner by saying:

> *People who do these things are terribly confused, usually very wounded people, with no guidance and bad examples, and are causing themselves and others a lot of suffering. What they are doing is evil, but they are still God's creatures, and they can turn away from their sins to God again.*

As I wrote in a different context:

> We should always encourage praying for the conversion of any sinner we are talking about, or praying for the end of a certain evil — even pausing the conversation at that very moment to pray an Our Father or a Hail Mary or some other prayer. This makes it clear that, just as we learned what was right and wrong from God (either by natural law or divine law), so we are entrusting the evil to God and not acting on the basis of our own rightness or righteousness, or as if we could fix it ourselves.[183]

As a general rule — if we are talking about homeschooled children — it is when the children themselves bring up a topic that they are ready to talk about

[183] "How to Talk to Children about Liturgical Evils," *OnePeterFive*, October 23, 2019, https://onepeterfive.com/talk-children-liturgical-evils/; I have changed a word.

it; if they do not bring it up, it's okay to let sleeping dogs lie, up to a point. There is no need to wake children up prematurely to the fact that the world is not only shattered by the Fall but is in an aggressive growth phase of diabolical wickedness and certifiable madness.

On the other hand, children who are enrolled in schools, whether public *or* private, secular *or* religious — and it is becoming increasingly difficult to justify the morality of keeping them in *any* kind of school, given what is happening among peer groups with unlimited access to social media and, often enough, within the curricula they are made to study — will encounter these evils earlier, and usually long before it would be optimal for them to have to know about them. Parents in that case will need to be much more vigilant and be prepared to discuss any sort of topic at any time. I know of a family that followed the excellent practice of gathering their children every night around the living room to discuss what came up that day in school, especially things that bothered the kids or sounded "off" to them. Since the kids had been well catechized by their parents and the household followed a "low-tech" approach, the kids were happy to sit down and talk about their day, not distracted by their phones, and had a pretty good sense of when they were being fed nonsense in the classroom. As a result, the parents were able to identify and refute errors before those errors had a chance to seduce the mind.

Occasionally one hears about parents whose strategy is (or was) to avoid all discussion of sexuality, sexual morals, and immoral behavior. Perhaps they thought this was the more modest approach. I can assure you that this approach is not modest, but devastating and destructive. Children will learn about such things *either* from their parents, who are equipped by Almighty God with the graces to lead them aright, *or* from the surrounding culture — which generally means, from those who have a vested interest in creating new slaves to vice. Perhaps in a saner age, it would be different, but today's parents cannot avoid taking a strong role in home education.[184]

[184] See Trent Horn and Leila Miller, *Made This Way: How to Prepare Kids to Face Today's Tough Moral Issues* (El Cajon, CA: Catholic Answers, 2018).

III

Virginity and Celibacy

Jesus said to them: Amen, I say to you, there is no man that hath left house, or parents, or brethren, or wife, or children, for the kingdom of God's sake, who shall not receive much more in this present time, and in the world to come life everlasting.

— Luke 18:29–30

I would that all men were even as myself: but every one hath his proper gift from God; one after this manner, and another after that.... The unmarried woman and the virgin thinketh on the things of the Lord, that she may be holy both in body and in spirit. But she that is married thinketh on the things of the world, how she may please her husband. And this I speak for your profit: not to cast a snare upon you; but for that which is decent, and which may give you power to attend upon the Lord, without impediment.

— 1 Corinthians 7:7, 34–35

22

Faith in God and Marriage Follow the Same Logic

Matrimony, as a covenant or a sacrament, has the character of indissolubility, exclusivity, self-renunciation: "What God hath joined together, let no man put asunder" (Matt. 19:6). Of the trust, confidence, and loyalty demanded of spouses toward each other, no more need be said than the heart of any faithful spouse will supply. Marriage, the earthly union of lover and beloved, presupposes and demands the constant exercise of faith. Love can never thrive without a surrender of self in a spirit of trust.

Faith in God follows a similar logic. That is why the Old Testament calls Israel the bride and God the bridegroom, while the New Testament calls the Church the Bride and Christ the Bridegroom. In religious faith, the will holds the intellect captive — "I *believe* in one God, the Father Almighty" — even as the promise "I do" holds the self captive to one's spouse, regardless of difficulty or struggle. "For better or for worse, for richer or for poorer": these words are noble and profound. On their wedding day, the future husband and wife ought to say them with fear and trembling, as they amount to a creed and a baptism immersing the soul in waters deeper and greater than itself.

Many Christian writers have called religion a marriage with God. We make manifest in our words and deeds that we desire to love Him. He courts us with His grace, proposes to be united to our souls, and invites us to the wedding feast. In the end, we must decide to love Him "for better or for worse ..." in this vale of tears, till death brings us face-to-face with the Bridegroom whose love and Real Presence we believed in throughout our lives, though we saw Him not.

As Fr. Thomas Dubay writes:

> It is obvious that our will has a great deal to do with our attainment of religious certitude. This does not mean that our convictions lack objective intellectual bases but that the nature of the evidence allows for a

> free, unforced response. In a similar manner our interpersonal responses on a human level are free and unforced. I can have completely adequate evidence that someone loves me, and yet I remain free to reject the love or to refuse to admit that it exists. We do not reach certitude by a mere choice or an arbitrary decision.... Religious commitment, therefore, is not a blind jump. Nor does the will operate in the dark. The intellectual evidence is there, but frightfully limited and prone to compromise as we are, we need actively willed commitment to truth, if we are to maintain intellectual integrity. Assent to evidence is a duty, and we need our will to assure that we shall act reasonably.[185]

The dogmas of the Catholic religion may seem absurd to carnal reason; mysteries always escape our finite minds, and we do not know how to approach the infinite God, "who dwells in unapproachable light" (1 Tim. 6:16). But mystery is not absurdity, and what is beyond reason is not unreasonable. Love, like religion, is a mystery — indeed love is *the* mystery of life — but love is not absurd. It is greater than we are; it encompasses us and transforms us. If man were the measure of all things, love would be absurd, because true love cannot be measured by man. But who that has tasted real and abiding love can think that *man* is the ultimate measure of all things? Love itself governs the life of the lover.

The husband trusts his wife, and she, for her part, trusts her husband. They believe in each other's words of love. There is no question of a "science" of love. There is a religion of love, a prayer of love, a sacrifice of love, "a peace that surpasseth all understanding" (Phil. 4:7), but there cannot be intellectual comprehension. Love surpasses, one might even say overleaps, comprehension.

One may raise the following objection. In human love, we see and hear the other person, but the situation is entirely different when it comes to religious faith, where we do not see, or in any way come into contact with, the object of our belief in its proper appearance.

In reply, we may ask: What is it a man truly sees in his beloved? Does he see her *belovedness*? Does he even see the *person*? When contemplating a friend or a spouse or a child, we *see* a familiar animal shaped like a human being; we hear it using a conventional language in an attempt to express its hidden thoughts. *That* is what we encounter. The beloved, the love, the *meaning* of words and gestures reside far beneath the surface of the shapes, colors, sounds, and so

[185] Thomas Dubay, *Faith and Certitude: Can We Be Sure of the Things That Matter Most to Us?* (San Francisco: Ignatius Press, 1985), 194–95.

forth. We perceive only *signs* of realities (or, in Scholastic terminology, accidents of substances); the realities themselves are forever beyond touch, sight, smell, taste, and hearing, accessible only to the spiritual part of man, his immortal soul, his divinely crafted mind.

Human love is beyond the realm of a simple problem that the intellect could set itself to "solve" like an equation in physics. Nothing but faith, loyalty, purity, and devotion can get at the heart of reality, the heart of love, the meaning of love, the boundaries of the person created unto God's image and likeness. He knows little of love who thinks it to be nothing other than its signs and tokens.

Not until we reflect on the nature of friendship do we realize how crucial blind loyalty is in the formation and preservation of friendships. I do not mean "blind" in the sense of *refusing* to see — such blindness is never a good thing — but blind as being *unable* to see. It is the difference between being afraid to look at the screen during a horror film and being blind from birth. As intellectual creatures, we stare reality in the face; but the greater part of reality, in fact the best and greatest of it, will always escape our mortal gaze, however acute and probing. Spirit, soul, and God, other persons and their thoughts, not to mention first principles of knowledge and the certitude of our senses, can *never* be directly sensed or experienced as particulars at all. The most important things are the least visible and tangible.

Faith is knowledge *in promise*, "the substance of things hoped for, the evidence of things that appear not" (Heb. 11:1), just as the faith plighted by a bride and bridegroom is *in promise of* a lifetime of knowledge. When Adam knew Eve in a communion of flesh (Gen. 4:1), he physically knew a part of her, the body, but symbolically he knew the whole of her, her future life and her inner destiny. Marriage is the promise to share one's entire life and destiny with another, to make one life and destiny out of two.

Faith in God follows a similar pattern. The believer plights his faith in God, promising firm fidelity to commands that he is nonetheless free to break, just as the husband or wife may violate the nuptial bed by committing adultery. The believer makes the life of Christ his own, as the wife makes the husband's life her own; Christ lays down His life to save those who believe in Him, as the husband sacrifices his life for his wife (see Eph. 5:21–32).

"We walk by faith, and not by sight" (2 Cor. 5:7).

23

Marriage and Consecrated Virginity

As celibacy and virginity come increasingly under fire not only in the secular world but even within the Church and amid her hierarchy, we must renew our understanding of immutable Catholic doctrine and our commitment to "contend earnestly for the faith once delivered to the saints" (Jude 1:3).

In the ancient Church, Jovinian was a heretic who taught equality between sacramental marriage and celibacy for the kingdom of God. His views were roundly refuted by St. Jerome and St. Augustine, and the Church in her Magisterium has consistently taught as they do: one who marries in Christ and brings children into the world does well, but one who altogether relinquishes marriage and family for the sake of following Christ more closely does even better.

Nevertheless, Jovinianism has reared its ugly head throughout Christian history. The Protestant Reformers challenged the traditional doctrine, in spite of its foundation in the words of Christ and of St. Paul. In more recent times, we see among Catholics a pragmatic sort of Jovinianism, which I have discovered in nearly all the students I have ever taught. Perhaps because they have met in their lives so few authentic religious brothers and sisters, they tend to think it wrong to elevate the religious *state* above the married *state* as a means for attaining perfection in charity and contemplation. They are surprised to learn that they are in conflict with the unanimous teaching of the Church Fathers, Doctors, popes, and councils.

One student put the case this way on a final exam: "If I am a married person and I do everything, including change diapers and go to work and embrace my wife and build up a house and garden, all for the love of God, how am I *not* making of myself and my life a 'holocaust,' a total offering, that is just as pleasing as the offering of a religious who gives up family, property, self-determination? As a matter of fact, the religious still has clothes, a bed, a house to live in, probably a lot of books, financial worries in his community, practicalities to take care of, his brethren as a family, and for the most part he does what he wants from day to day, even if the bigger decisions belong (in part) to a superior. So is his life really all that different from mine?"

Sounds plausible, doesn't it? With a vague appeal to the "universal call to holiness" and the "primacy of charity," one can quickly deduce that all Christian states in life are equal. Interestingly, St. Thomas Aquinas also teaches that holiness is for everyone and that charity holds pride of place in becoming holy, but he does not, all the same, reach that egalitarian conclusion.

The student claimed that "marriage, too, is a total holocaust." I ask: In what sense? Is the married man or woman *actually* giving up spouse, children, house, fields, his or her own will? In a way, yes — but in a decisive way, no. When Jesus told His disciples that they who left *everything* to follow Him would receive a hundredfold, He was not speaking metaphorically, but quite literally. Nor was he saying that those who renounced these things up front were permitted to reintroduce them later, through the back door. The hundredfold blessing rests only on the ones who *remain* poor, chaste, and obedient, and to the extent that they are *truly* such.

In order to understand Our Lord's teaching better, let us consider how the evangelical counsels of poverty, chastity (in the sense of perpetual continence), and obedience are *means* for accomplishing the goal of perfection in charity — that is, holiness.

The counsels take away those material and temporal goods that tend to distract or weaken our focus on God or that allow us to rely on them rather than on Him. Unlike the commandments, the counsels do not separate us from *bad* things that are incompatible with love of God. Rather, they separate us from things that are in themselves *good*, even very good, but not the *greatest* good, and thus can hinder a direct focus on the greatest goods and on the Giver of all good things. The reason why separating ourselves from things that are good is helpful for focusing on the highest good and source of all goods, on God Himself, is that we are finite beings with finite capacities for attention and love. Therefore, by removing our attention and love from worldly and temporal goods, the counsels help us to fix them more fully on spiritual and eternal goods, on the divine. St. Thomas beautifully makes this point:

> It is manifest that the human heart is borne more intensely toward one thing, to the extent that it is drawn back from many things. Thus the more a man is freed from the affection for temporal things, the more perfectly his mind will be borne to loving God.... Therefore all the

> [evangelical] counsels, by which we are invited to perfection, have as their aim that man's mind be turned away from affection for temporal objects, so that his mind may tend more freely to God, by contemplating Him, loving Him, and fulfilling His will.[186]

In the present climate, it is important to emphasize that the counsels are not proposed as good because the things we give up by following the counsels are bad but because there is a better way to grow in love than the use of these things. Giving up marriage enables one to grow more in the love of God and neighbor solely because the direct dedication of our heart and mind to God is a better means for growing in love than marriage is, whether considered in itself or as a sacrament.[187] Pope John Paul II taught this quite clearly:

> The reference to the nuptial union of Christ and the Church gives marriage itself its highest dignity: in particular, the sacrament of matrimony introduces the spouses into the mystery of Christ's union with the Church. However, the profession of virginity or celibacy enables consecrated persons to share more directly in the mystery of *this* marriage. While conjugal love goes to Christ the Bridegroom through a human union, virginal love goes directly to the person of Christ through an immediate union with him, without intermediaries: a truly complete and decisive spiritual espousal. Thus in the person of those who profess and live consecrated chastity, the Church expresses her union as Bride with Christ the Bridegroom to the greatest extent.[188]

Implied in these words is, however, a salutary warning. One who has given up marriage — a monk or nun, a priest, a bishop — will not be any better off

[186] St. Thomas Aquinas, *On the Perfection of the Spiritual Life,* chap. 6; translation mine. The original: "Manifestum namque est quod humanum cor tanto intensius in aliquid unum fertur, quanto magis a multis revocatur. Sic igitur tanto perfectius animus hominis ad Deum diligendum fertur, quanto magis ab affectu temporalium removetur. Unde Augustinus dicit in libro LXXXIII quaestionum quod venenum caritatis est cupiditas temporalium rerum, augmentum vero eius est cupiditatis diminutio; perfectio vero nulla cupiditas. Omnia igitur consilia, quibus ad perfectionem invitamur, ad hoc pertinent ut animus hominis ab affectu temporalium avertatur, ut sic liberius mens tendat in Deum, contemplando, amando, et eius voluntatem implendo."

[187] See Pope Pius XII, Encyclical Letter *Sacra Virginitas* (March 25, 1954), nos. 37–39.

[188] John Paul II, *Catechesis on Consecrated Life,* November 23, 1994.

for having done so if he does not use the freedom of his heart to devote himself more fully to God and to the service of the Church. In fact, he will be *worse* off, since he will lack the great good of marriage *as well as* the greater good of virginity or celibacy "for the kingdom," which is the orientation that alone makes it so great a good.

Moreover, assuming good intentions to begin with, the intensity and steadfastness of the resolve to pursue the goal of holiness using whichever means one chooses is of greater importance than the means as such. To be more concrete: it will go better for the one who seeks holiness wholeheartedly in marriage than it will for the one who seeks holiness halfheartedly in religious life.

Our Lord has provided us with two ways, noble and nobler, good and better, of entering into the mystery of His indissoluble nuptial union with the Church: through a sacramental image of it in marriage and through a mystical participation in the very union itself in consecrated life.

It is quite common nowadays for people to speak of "the vocation of marriage" and "the vocation of religious life" as if they were equivalent, as if we are using the term "vocation" univocally (with the same meaning). This is simply not true, and it runs directly against Catholic teaching.

A vocation, just looking to the etymology of the word in the verb *vocare* (to call, to summon), refers to a call from God addressed to an individual. God is calling that person out from a *natural way of life* to a *supernatural state or condition.*

Thus, we rightly speak of a "baptismal vocation" because Baptism establishes a person in the Christian state, a supernatural condition that is a pure gratuitous gift from God and not something imminent to our nature or merited by our humanity. Again, we speak of a "vocation to the religious life" — that is, the life constituted by the evangelical counsels of poverty for the kingdom of God, chastity in the sense of perfect continence, and obedience as a sacrifice of self-determination in the world — because this state goes beyond what is natural to men and women as social animals living in this world: it is a gratuitous gift from God, summoning to a divine way of life, in imitation of the God-Man, Jesus Christ, who lived His life on earth entirely and exclusively for the glory of the Father and for the salvation of mankind.

In contrast, marriage — understood in its essence as the lifelong bond between a man and a woman for the procreation and education of children and for the mutual help and comfort of the spouses — is a *natural* condition for human beings. We were made for it, and it well suits the conditions of our mortal existence. Marriage, for that reason, is not a vocation in the strict sense, a gratuitous gift that elevates one beyond what is native to our social and earthly life.

It is true, of course, that Our Lord elevated the natural state of marriage to the dignity of a sacrament. But the Church traditionally understands the sacrament as rendering the conjugal union of a baptized couple a grace-bearing and grace-bestowing reality for them; in other words, a way to sanctify temporally what remains, in itself, a state tied to this world and this passing order, which the laity are deputed to "conquer" for the kingdom of God.[189] Marriage thus points to the union of Christ and the Church, but it does not *realize* this union in the personal and eschatological way that the religious life does. Put differently, the religious is already beginning to live, on earth, the life of the world to come, where no one "marries or is given in marriage" (Matt. 22:30).[190]

This is why we can say that religious life is the fullest and most perfect living out of the baptismal vocation possible, for Baptism consecrates a man or woman to God, and the religious life completes this by consecrating the totality of his or her life to God, with no "thought," as it were, for the temporal order that passes by. He or she no longer lives as befits life in the present age, by acquiring and possessing private property, bringing children into the world by marital union, and retaining freedom of personal disposition (where I will live, what my job will be, etc.).

As the *Catechism of the Catholic Church* states: "The precepts [the Ten Commandments] are intended to remove whatever is incompatible with charity. The aim of the counsels is to remove whatever might hinder the development of charity, even if it is not contrary to it."[191] Or, in the words of John Paul II: "In the economy of the Redemption, the evangelical counsels of chastity, poverty, and obedience constitute the most radical means for transforming in the human heart this relationship with 'the world.'"[192]

The doctrine of the universal vocation of all the faithful to holiness of life, regardless of their position or social situation, has been advanced very much

[189] See "Lay Ministries Obscure Both the Laity's Calling and the Clergy's," in Kwasniewski, *Ministers of Christ*, 83–102, and "May His Kingdom Come: Catholic Social Teaching, Part VI — Conversion of Culture." See also chapter 7.

[190] For a complete account, see Kwasniewski, "St. Thomas on the Grandeur and Limitations of Marriage."

[191] *CCC* 1973, referring to St. Thomas, *ST* II-II, Q. 184, art. 3.

[192] John Paul II, Post-Synodal Apostolic Exhortation *Redemptionis Donum* (March 25, 1984), no. 9; cf. St. Thomas, *ST* II-II, Q. 186, art. 7.

in modern times, and this is as it should be. Nevertheless, Paul VI sounded a note of caution and offered an important clarification:

> We must be on guard lest, for this very reason, the true notion of religious life as it has traditionally flourished in the Church should become obscured. We must beware lest our youth, becoming confused while thinking about their choice of a state in life, should be thereby hindered in some way from having a clear and distinct vision of the special function and immutable importance of the religious state within the Church.... This stable way of life, which receives its proper character from profession of the evangelical vows, is a perfect way of living according to the example and teaching of Jesus Christ. It is a state of life which keeps in view the constant growth of charity leading to its final perfection. In other ways of life, though legitimate in themselves, the specific ends, advantages, and functions are of a temporal character.[193]

The foregoing helps us to see the precise mistake made by those who speak of marriage and religious life as if they are simply diverse vocations: "Marriage is better for some people, and religious life for others, so as long as you do what you are 'called' to do. The two ways are equally good ways of growing in virtue and in love for God." Such a view marks a recrudescence of the Jovinianism against which St. Jerome battled in his day.

The "calling" to marriage is inscribed in human nature, and that is why it is altogether good. It is our *nature*, fashioned by God the Creator, that impels us to start a family, and it is by God's universal Providence that we meet a spouse, get married, and have a family with His blessing. The desire to do all this is rooted in our need for completion and in our power of fruitfulness, as we see them presented in the creation accounts in Genesis. In a sense, to speak of a "vocation" to marriage from God would be much like speaking of a "vocation" to eat and drink, or to work and rest, or to think and love. This need and this power are meant to teach us, under the guidance of divine faith, about a need that is more definitive and all-encompassing: the hunger for God, the thirst for union with Him, the yearning to see Him face-to-face in heaven.

We know that all are called to the *end of holiness* by their Baptism and that, for some individuals, marriage will help them to achieve holiness better than religious life. Even so, religious life still offers a better *means* for attaining the end

[193] Paul VI, Address to General Chapters of Religious Orders and Congregations (May 23, 1964).

of holiness. In itself, the state of Christian virginity or celibacy is preferable to that of marriage, since this state "frees the heart of man in a unique fashion (cf. 1 Cor. 7:32–35) so that it may be more inflamed with love for God and for all men."[194] In order to accomplish this function and to serve this end, it must be embraced with the proper motivation — namely "for the sake of the kingdom of heaven" (Matt. 19:12) and as a way of giving oneself entirely to God. The total gift of self in the religious life depends on *love* — the basis on which every one of us will be judged and rewarded by the Lord.

To devote oneself wholeheartedly to a life of virginity or celibacy requires a special charism, a grace of enlightenment and movement of the heart, which is not given to all — a special "mode" of divine love that disposes one to devote oneself exclusively to Christ and His Church and enables one to make a firm choice of this way of life. This charism is not to be understood as a higher degree of love, as though all who embrace the virginal or celibate state love God more than those who do not. Nor is this charism to be understood by way of subtraction, as if those called to belong wholly to Christ were either incapable of making a gift of themselves to another human being in marriage or were not inclined to do so. A lack of the natural inclination toward marriage would *impede* the virginal or celibate self-giving to Christ and His Church. This charism is rather to be understood by way of an *addition* to the love, an *excess*, which is capable of specifying the love, giving it a more completely spousal mode.[195]

In our age, when the word "marriage" and the reality it signifies have been perverted in countless ways, a man's or woman's intention to marry a member of the opposite sex, in the Church, for the sake of having children and bringing them up in the fear and love of God, will be looked upon as abnormal by unbelievers and perhaps as heroic by the timid. Think of how much stranger, even *offensive*, it will seem to many when someone announces the intention to give his or her entire life to Jesus Christ alone! This was already a stumbling block in the ancient world, and so it has become again in the post-Christian West. John Paul II recognized this when he said:

> Jesus calls attention to the gift of divine light needed to "understand" the way of voluntary celibacy. Not everyone can understand it, in the sense

[194] Vatican II, Decree on the Adaptation and Renewal of Religious Life *Perfectae Caritatis* (October 28, 1965), no. 12.

[195] The preceding paragraph and a half were adapted, word for word, from Fr. Joseph Bolin's *Paths of Love: The Discernment of Vocation according to the Teaching of Aquinas, Ignatius, and Pope John Paul II* (N.p.: CreateSpace, 2008).

> that not everyone is "able" to grasp its meaning, to accept it, to practice it. This gift of light and decision is only granted to some. It is a privilege granted them for the sake of a greater love. We should not be surprised then if many, who do not understand the value of consecrated celibacy, are not attracted to it, and often are not even able to appreciate it.[196]

We believe in the glorious example of Christ and of His immutably true promises, which are stronger than culture, stronger than fashion, stronger than false philosophy. His voice continues to call unbelievers to conversion and Baptism, believers to fuller commitment, and individual Christians to the most radical gift of self, in imitation of Him.[197]

[196] John Paul II, *Catechesis on the Consecrated Life*, November 16, 1994.

[197] For further elucidations, see my article "On Discerning Vocations: How to Think about 'States of Life,'" *OnePeterFive*, January 23, 2019, https://onepeterfive.com/vocations-better, and my book *Ministers of Christ*.

24

Poverty, Chastity, and Obedience in Marriage

In the Middle Ages, every member of Christendom lived under a common law: the law of the Gospel as taught by the Church. There were not two worlds, two standards, the sacred and the profane; there was but one world, woven of various secular and ecclesiastical strands on the loom of the Cross. Hence, this society was hierarchical but not clericalist. Clericalism is the sclerosis of hierarchy. It occurs when hierarchy ceases to be a vital, internal principle of cohesion, recognized as the mouthpiece for a commonly held Christianity, and becomes instead an externalized imposition.[198]

If we follow St. Thomas Aquinas's theology of marriage, which was fairly representative of the age in which he lived, we can say that married life was *not* seen as worldly to the exclusion of the demands of the sacred, nor was clerical and religious life seen as sacred to the exclusion of this world's needs. Rather, *both* were perceived as sacred realities belonging to the Church as expressions of Catholic life, and *both* were meant to bear fruit for the kingdom of heaven: marriage by helping spouses to beget and educate citizens of this kingdom, the clergy and religious by seeking first the kingdom of God in their liturgical prayer and then teaching and feeding the faithful with spiritual goods (and often enough, material goods). Marriage itself will no longer exist in the heavenly kingdom, but, with the exception of Adam and Eve, who were fashioned directly by God, all who are in the kingdom are the welcome *fruits* of marriage, and this is precisely its great dignity: to be the unsurpassably vivid symbol and humble handmaid of ultimate heavenly joy, an indispensable midwife to the glorious City of God.

Hence, marriage in the period of Christendom was understood within the logic of the Gospel. It was not viewed as a worldly affair of self-determination

[198] On true and false meanings of clericalism, see Kwasniewski, *Holy Bread*, especially 203–13.

and pleasure at one's will; it involved penance and self-control, even as clerical and religious life did. During the Middle Ages, Catholic spouses were routinely expected to abstain from marital relations many times during the year, including the whole of the Lenten season. Abstinence from the "use of marriage" appears to have been expected, if not obligatory, for a total of several months each year. Sexual self-restraint was an ascetical routine of periodic continence that we have not seen the likes of for hundreds of years, and a good case can be made that this loss has been detrimental to the spiritual lives of the married (cf. 1 Cor. 7:5; 7:35).

The main point is that marriage was then recognized to be a true *via crucis*, a way to carry one's daily cross in the footsteps of Christ. For all their differences, the married state and the religious and clerical states enjoyed a profound unity — the unity of the Christian virtues, with charity as their queen mother. The love of man and woman, and their love for their children, had to be a love of *charity*, not a mere earthly affection. All the demands of supernatural charity, beginning with the very demand that it have primacy over all aspects of human life, were in force in the domestic church.

However much the beautiful face of Christendom has been disfigured by wars, plagues, and revolutions over the last five hundred years, this primacy of charity remains true today, since the intrinsic nature of sacramental Marriage has not changed, nor have its lofty aims and requirements.

An important consequence was seen clearly by St. Thomas in his treatise *On the Perfection of the Spiritual Life* — namely, that even if only a few Christians embrace the evangelical counsels of poverty, chastity, and obedience to their full extent in imitation of the Redeemer's way of life on earth, *all* Christians are called to live out their essential meaning. No less than those "dead to the world," Christians living *in* the world must also be poor in spirit, pure in heart, and obedient to God's Word and the word of the Church. More specifically, they must strive to be frugal in bodily goods, ready for bodily continence, and obedient in the family structure. In other words, poverty, chastity, and obedience are to be lived, both in spirit and in flesh, by *all* Christians according to their states in life and the needs and demands of different stages in their lives.[199]

Married couples know this from experience: such circumstances as illnesses, injuries, pregnancies, travel or work demands, and the simple fact of aging make abstinence unavoidable. Moral virtue is required if the spouses are to accept

[199] See chapter 11.

these periods with a generous spirit of charity and self-denial and turn them into meritorious temporary continence for the kingdom. The same is true with the use of wealth and the relinquishment of independent activities outside the home that no longer suit the common good of the family.

It is a tragedy that much of the teaching of Sacred Scripture on the family, as well as much of the wisdom of the patristic and medieval tradition, has been discarded due to plain embarrassment or, worse, a modernistic view that the moral dictates of Scripture are culturally determined and thus replaceable by the more "enlightened" code of behavior that men and women of the modern West deem themselves to possess. Even the *Catechism of the Catholic Church* succumbs at times to this temptation to follow the zeitgeist instead of the Holy Ghost.[200] Fortunately we are possessed of a rich and consistent heritage that guides the faithful aright, even when churchmen at a particular moment in history are culpably confused.

What would the reaction of Catholics be if they were told that the *Roman Catechism* produced after the Council of Trent, in addition to a substantial fast from food, calls for a fast from "the use of marriage" (i.e., sexual intercourse) for *a few days* prior to reception of the Most Holy Eucharist?

> Our preparation should not, however, be confined to the soul; it should also extend to the body. We are to approach the Holy Table fasting, having neither eaten nor drunk anything at least from the preceding midnight until the moment of Communion. The dignity of so great a Sacrament also demands that married persons abstain from the marriage debt for some days previous to Communion. This observance is recommended by the example of David, who, when about to receive the showbread from the hands of the priest, declared that he and his servants had been clean from women for three days. The above are the principal things to be done by the faithful preparatory to receiving the sacred mysteries with profit; and to these heads may be reduced whatever other things may seem desirable by way of preparation.[201]

200 See "What Good Is a Changing Catechism? Revisiting the Purpose and Limits of a Book," in Kwasniewski, *Road from Hyperpapalism*, vol. 2, chap. 40.

201 *The Catechism of the Council of Trent*, trans. John A. McHugh and Charles J. Callan (Rockford, IL: TAN Books, 1982), 248.

Such a practice — commended by all the Scholastic theologians, enforced and widely followed in the Middle Ages — is continued to this day, in varying degrees, by the married clergy of the Eastern Orthodox and Eastern Catholic Churches, who are required to abstain from the use of marriage prior to serving the Divine Liturgy.

Apparently, it is not uncommon nowadays to hear some Byzantine clergy say that this form of asceticism is out of date and need not be practiced. But is it not strange that in the West, the question does not even *occur* to us? And that if it were suggested, we would dismiss it as nonsense unworthy of our consideration? The more sophisticated might consider it a remnant of Manichaean or Jansenist contempt for the flesh and a sign of insufficient "maturity."

But is that really true? The reason behind the old discipline was quite down-to-earth. Original Sin inflicts several wounds on human nature. One of these is called "disordered concupiscence." We are inclined too much toward sensible goods; we tend to get bogged down in the desire or the enjoyment of them, to the detriment of our spiritual life and at the expense of self-control. In short, since all material things are good and reflect God in some way, we are sorely tempted to make an idol of them, forgetting the one true God, who made our hearts and alone satisfies our thirst for happiness.

The Church, our Mother, like any good mother, is realistic about the needs of her children. Over the ages, she established limits, demanded sacrifices to tame and discipline disordered concupiscence. Fasting and abstinence throughout Lent, on Ember and Rogation Days, and on vigils before great feasts established the distinctively Catholic pattern of fasting and feasting, of withdrawing for spiritual purification and then enjoying (one hopes moderately!) the good things that the Lord abundantly provides. The Church asked that even good things be given up for the sake of those that are better — in the case of the Most Holy Eucharist, which is God Himself, *infinitely* better.[202]

To so great an extent has our awe before the Blessed Sacrament evaporated and our assumption about the naturalness of "free" sexuality ballooned that we can no longer enter into a Christian mindset of at least a thousand years' duration! A sign of how far we have drifted: in Catholic circles, a husband and wife seeking to develop their interior lives to the fullest could almost never mention the idea of abstaining for a time from sexual intimacy so as to dedicate themselves more intensely to prayer (cf. 1 Cor. 7:5) without fear of being

[202] On fasting and other forms of preparation for Eucharistic Communion, see Kwasniewski, *Holy Bread,* 71–88, 159–70.

laughed or scolded out of the room. If, moreover, a couple believed that God was calling them to a Josephite marriage — something that the Catholic Church has honored in dozens of married saints, beginning, of course, with Our Lady and St. Joseph — how much worse would be the total incomprehension they would receive![203]

Truly, our age has not simply ceased to practice sexual asceticism; it has ruled it out as unhealthy, misguided, and, frankly, impossible. The whiff of Freud is unmistakable. It has not helped that popularizers of the "theology of the body" have, at times, come near to making an idol out of sex, rather than portraying it as a created good that, like all created goods, has a definite and limited place in human life and must be subordinated to certain other goods, especially the demands of the spiritual life. To adapt a familiar saying, sex makes a good servant but a terrible master.

I do not know what to propose as a solution today, since many of our pastors who should be preaching self-control and sacrifice seem to be paralyzed by uncertainty about the value of asceticism, how to preach it, and how to practice it, or even worse, are bent on satisfying their own disordered concupiscence or winking at those who do. Universally, we seem to be suffering amnesia when it comes to the timeless wisdom of Holy Mother Church.

Until Catholic tradition is more broadly restored (which I firmly believe will happen someday), I think the best we can do is to follow this wisdom of periodic continence in food, drink, and the use of marriage according to what we believe the Lord is calling us to do for love of Him, always with the consent of one's superior or spouse and ideally in consultation with a reliable spiritual director.

To avoid any misunderstanding, it should be stated clearly that there is no requirement from natural law, divine law, or current ecclesiastical law to forgo the marital act in the day or days leading up to the reception of Holy Communion, nor is it ever sinful for spouses to make legitimate use of the God-given right they have over one another's bodies. This is particularly true at a time when daily Communion among disciples of Christ is more common than it has been for over a millennium.[204]

Rather, we are speaking here about an ancient discipline of restricting the use of a good thing that belongs to this world and the domain of the flesh, in order

[203] See chapter 26.

[204] See my article "Tensions in the Catholic Tradition on Frequent Communion," *New Liturgical Movement*, September 5, 2022, https://www.newliturgicalmovement.org/2022/09/tensions-in-catholic-tradition-on.html.

to intensify our spiritual preparation for an immense spiritual good, our longing for it and savoring of it. One could put it this way: if we never do anything to emphasize to ourselves the magnitude of what we are doing when we receive Our Lord, and we never take pains to subordinate the lesser to the greater, we could run the risk of trivializing the sacrament and not actually making it the "font and apex" of our entire Christian life.

The point is not to take on extreme penances but to recognize that we will glorify God and benefit our souls by forcing ourselves to lean less on the corruptible flesh and more on the immortal spirit.[205] This is not an unhealthy dualism but a level-headed Christian sense of priorities in life — what might be called a "preferential option for heaven." In the words of St. Paul: "Mind the things that are above, not the things that are upon the earth. For you are dead; and your life is hid with Christ in God" (Col. 3:2–3).

[205] See Peter Kwasniewski, "Should We 'Despise Earthly Goods and Love Heavenly Ones'? A Liturgical Lesson for Lent," *OnePeterFive*, March 2, 2022, https://onepeterfive.com/despise-earthly-goods/.

25

The Treasure of Priestly Celibacy in the Western Church

In the past, Western Catholics have at times tried to force their own discipline on Eastern Catholics; the name of Bishop John Ireland still haunts the conversation. We now recognize that this was a mistake — and one that is not likely to be repeated, given the correct insistence that Catholicism thrives within a diversity of rites and disciplines.

At the same time, it should come as no surprise that Latin-rite Catholics have developed, over the course of many centuries, a *positive* understanding, and with it a substantive defense, of the practice of clerical celibacy. For us, it is not just "a discipline"; it has profound theological and spiritual foundations that are recognized and advanced in formal magisterial documents. To contradict the Western tradition on this matter would be tantamount to calling into question Catholicism as a whole. The Eastern Orthodox are only too glad to do so; they already dispute papal primacy, the Filioque, Purgatory, Original Sin, the Immaculate Conception, and a host of other "errors," as they see it. But it is disedifying, to say the least, when Eastern Catholics jump on their bandwagon.

I encountered this personally in the years when I taught theology in central Europe to mixed classrooms of Latin-rite and Byzantine-rite students. The Byzantine students almost always came in with views identical to those of the Eastern Orthodox — the only difference being that they prayed for the pope in the Divine Liturgy — and only after much patient conversation could they be brought around to recognizing the truth contained in (even if not exhausted by) the Western positions and the cogency of Western responses to Orthodox apologetics. For example, one could assume, at the start of a course in Trinitarian theology, that many Greek Catholics would have a knee-jerk reaction against the Filioque; by the end of the course, nearly all of them would agree that the Filioque is implicit or explicit in the Greek tradition itself.

Obviously, there is much to be said on the topic of celibacy, and many books have been written, presenting both accurate and inaccurate material. One especially helpful book is Fr. Gary Selin's *Priestly Celibacy: Theological Foundations*,[206] which deserves to be better known. The subtitle is a bit misleading in that Fr. Selin does not limit himself to pure theology but looks at the history of the question, starting from the Old Testament, proceeding through the Greek and Latin Church Fathers and councils, and prudently assessing later developments.

Starting from the celibacy of Jesus Christ, the celibacy of the Apostles John and Paul, and the common belief that the married Apostles, on meeting the Lord, gave up their conjugal lives and practiced perpetual continence thereafter (it was none other than St. Peter, known to be married, who said: "Lo, we have left all things and followed you," a statement to which Our Lord replied: "Amen, I say to you, there is no man that hath left house, or parents, or brethren, *or wife, or children*, for the kingdom of God's sake, who shall not receive much more in this present time, and in the world to come life everlasting" [Luke 18:28–30]), Fr. Selin presents evidence that deserves to be taken with utmost seriousness, not only by Latin Catholics, but also by their Greek brethren:

> In the fourth century the first conciliar legislation concerning a consistent practice of clerical continence and celibacy appears in the Latin Church. With the lessening and eventual cessation of the persecution of the Church, provisional councils and synods were convened and record keeping was facilitated. The regional Council of Elvira (305), although convened during continuing persecution, produced the first written law in the East or in the West concerning clerical continence. In canon 33 the council required perfect continence for all married clerics under pain of deposition: "It has seemed good absolutely to forbid the bishops, presbyters, and deacons, i.e., all clerics who have a position in the ministry, to have [sexual] relations with their wives and beget children. Whoever in fact does this is to be removed from the honor of the clerical state."
>
> This disciplinary canon dealt with an infraction of an apparently existing ecclesial law. Neither it nor any other canon gave an explanation or justification for the law; it simply demanded obedience. It is unlikely that it was an innovation that would have deprived married clerics of a long-established right. Further, it is a characteristic of law that the origin

[206] Washington, DC: Catholic University of America Press, 2016.

> of a legal system consists in oral traditions and in the transmission of norms that only slowly receive a fixed, written form.
>
> The Second Council of Carthage was convened amidst the crisis of the decline of the Church in North Africa. On June 16, 390, the bishops of northern Africa gathered under the presidency of Genethlius. Bishop Genethlius said: "As was previously said, it is fitting that the holy bishops and priests of God as well as the Levites, i.e., those who are in the service of the divine sacraments, be continent in all things, so that they may obtain in all simplicity what they are asking from God; what the apostles taught and what antiquity itself observed, let us also endeavor to keep." The bishops declared unanimously: "It pleases us all that bishop, priest, and deacon, guardians of purity, abstain from [conjugal intercourse] with their wives, so that those who serve at the altar may keep perfect chastity." . . .
>
> The teaching of Saint Epiphanius of Salamis (c. 310–403) is significant insofar as he, an Eastern Father, gave testimony to the unity of the Western and Eastern Churches on the matter of clerical continence, rooting it in divine Revelation: "[The Church] does not accept as deacon, priest, bishop, and subdeacon, be he the husband of a single wife, the man who continues to live with his wife and to beget children; the Church accepts him who, as monogamist, observes continence or widowhood; this is observed above all wherever the canons of the Church are kept faithfully."[207]

Then Fr. Selin touches on a sore subject in East-West dialogue:

> The earliest legislation that permitted *periodic* continence for married clerics appeared at a regional council of the Eastern Churches, namely the Second Council of Trullo (691–692). This council upheld the traditional discipline that required bishops to be unmarried, or if married, to live apart from their wives, and continued the ban on remarriage for all major clerics whose wives had died after their ordination. However, the bishops also introduced a law that was unprecedented in previous

[207] These four paragraphs were supplied to me by Fr. Selin as a summary of some of the major historical points he covers at greater length in the book. The quotation from Epiphanius's *Panarion* is from Roman Cholij, *Clerical Celibacy in East and West* (Leominster: Gracewing, 1989), 20. For additional Eastern testimonies, see John Chrysostom, *Homiliae in I Tim.* Prol., *PG* 62:503ff.; *Hom. 2, in Tit.* I, *PG* 62:671; Eusebius of Caesarea, *Demonstratio Evangelica* I, 9, *GCS* 23:43.

> local or ecumenical councils. Canon 13 mandated that married priests, deacons, and subdeacons were not permitted to separate from their wives and were to observe periodic rather than perpetual continence. The reigning pope, Saint Sergius I, a Syrian by birth, did not accept the Trullan canons on clerical marriage, nor did his successor, John VII (c. 650–707), who returned the Acts of the Trullan Council unsigned. However, Adrian I (c. 700–795), while rejecting the canons on clerical marriage, did accept with qualification other Trullan Acts that were free of anti-Roman canons.

The Western requirement of perfect and perpetual continence was clear from early on, and it was maintained ever more strongly, in spite of abundant evidence of noncompliance and the constant need for reform movements. The East, in contrast, opened a way of *periodic* continence that does not obviously harmonize with the teaching of the New Testament, the witness of the Fathers, or previous regional legislation. This real or perceived disharmony was sufficient reason for *three popes* to refuse their recognition of the policy. Even those who entertain skeptical views about papal primacy as it developed later on cannot deny that the pope's endorsement of conciliar decrees in the first millennium was taken with utmost seriousness. It was seen as *very important*, to say the least, that the pope of Rome should "sign off on" whatever declarations, anathemas, and canons were accepted by the bishops in council.

The history of the Latin Church reveals not only a consistent exaltation and requirement of perfect and perpetual continence for the clerical state but *always* a theological and spiritual interpretation of it. Clergy are to be celibate *not* for practical pastoral convenience (although much can be said from that point of view), but as a manner of living out the *imitatio Christi* expected of the *alter Christus*. Like fasting before Communion, celibacy is a bodily-spiritual expression of the necessary striving for the ritual purity demanded by that divine worship in which a man dares to enter the presence of the Living God on behalf of the people and to offer up a pleasing sacrifice to the Lord. Indeed, it comes to be seen as a sacramental conformity to the High Priest and Victim, the one Bridegroom of the Church, whose nuptials are celebrated on the Cross, as St. John the Evangelist reveals to us in the parallelism of Cana and Calvary. The Western theology of *clerical* celibacy, therefore, also reflects the unanimous Eastern-Western theology of *episcopal* celibacy: it is in the West that the identity of the presbyter as the one who assists the bishop and, later on, represents the absent bishop is most perfectly preserved.

I emphasize these points because, whatever may have still been within the realm of possibility in the year 250 or 500, it is certainly no longer possible today, after the lived experience and theological development that have passed behind us, to regard the Latin position on celibacy as solely disciplinary. A striking sign of this truth is the formulation of the 1917 *Code of Canon Law*: "Clerics constituted in major orders are prohibited from marriage and are bound by the obligation of observing chastity, so that those sinning against this are guilty of sacrilege." This is not the language of a mere convention, a dictate of legal positivism.

Thus, I was pleased to see the following remarks by Mark Brumley:

> Personally, I am happy to have the tiny number of ex-Anglican married priests we have in the Latin Rite, by way of exception to the norm of priestly celibacy. Apparently, certain folks find that paradoxical. Balthasar explained it decades ago when he spoken of them as exceptions, even while he defended the norm of mandatory priestly celibacy in the Latin Rite. He did not envision [that] men in the Latin Rite who have always lived as laymen would be ordained even by exception.
>
> And of course Eastern Catholicism sees things differently regarding married priests. The Catholic Church, despite being overwhelmingly Latin Rite, and despite a theological valuing of priestly celibacy and not simply working from a practical administrative appreciation, hasn't regarded the Eastern Catholic view as "communion-dividing." That does not, however, mean Latin Rite Catholicism and the various Eastern Rites see celibacy and priesthood in the same way. They differ.
>
> It should surprise no one, then, that the theologians and leaders of the Latin Rite will, as John Paul II did, see priestly celibacy in the Latin Rite the way the Latin Rite's understanding of it has theologically developed. That's part of why it's the Latin Rite. Its theological tradition and understanding of priesthood doesn't get gainsaid just because Eastern Catholicism has a different view or because a tiny number of Protestant ministers/priests are ordained as an exception. Of course, exception in one circumstance doesn't automatically justify an exception in another circumstance. Though some will insist illogically it does.[208]

Brumley is correct. One can find Eastern Catholics claiming that Cardinal Sarah's arguments on behalf of celibacy are "intemperate," "erroneous,"

[208] Comments posted on Mr. Brumley's Facebook page.

"insensitive," "offensive," and so on.[209] Is this not a sign, richly ironic, that the East has internalized the inversion of Latinization and now refuses to be content until the West is Easternized — or at least until the West confesses that its own practice lacks a theological and spiritual foundation of its own, one that is thoroughly traditional? Yet it is a basic sign of maturity in East-West dialogue when each side *respects* the other side's *theological* interpretation of its practice (if such an interpretation exists). If the East has a truly theological argument for its married clergy, let it bring it forth, and let the West respect it and allow it to stand *for the East* (since we will never agree with it for ourselves); if the West, for its part, has a truly theological argument for clerical celibacy, let it be put forward without apologies and without embarrassment, and let the East respect it as a valid, if not exclusively valid, perspective.

Is this a form of doctrinal relativism? I do not think it has to be seen that way. The great Mystery of Faith uniting all orthodox Christians is lived out variously in diverse traditions, all of which remain in sacramental and ecclesial continuity with Christ and the Apostles. We see such diversity in many examples: the use of leavened bread or unleavened bread, the giving of Communion under both kinds or under one kind. These traditions are defensible from different angles; they are worthy of preservation within their own context, where the meaning is (generally) understood and (hopefully) preserved from misinterpretation. This is why I have always advocated "letting Latins be Latins, and Greeks Greeks."[210]

It is also possible that multiple traditions can be legitimate, while nevertheless one tradition is superior, on the whole, to another — put differently, that one way is better than another because it rests on a deeper foundation or coheres better with other aspects of the Faith. This is what Western Catholics believe to be true about the Latin rule of clerical celibacy. To say it is better does not mean that the Eastern rule is wrong and must be overturned, but only that it is less good — even as asserting the superiority of the life of evangelical poverty, chastity, and obedience over the state of marriage does not entail that marriage be something evil. Marriage is still a divinely blessed sacrament, and married

[209] Referring to the work jointly authored with Benedict XVI: *From the Depths of Our Hearts: Priesthood, Celibacy, and the Crisis of the Catholic Church*, trans. Michael J. Miller (San Francisco: Ignatius Press, 2020).

[210] For a fuller explanation, see Peter Kwasniewski, *The Once and Future Roman Rite: Returning to the Traditional Latin Liturgy after Seventy Years of Exile* (Gastonia, NC: TAN Books, 2022), 179–88, 304–9.

clergy are still clergy in the full sense of the word, empowered to do all that the clergy are divinely appointed to do.

Ultimately we have to recognize that it's not really the Eastern tradition that inspires those Western Catholics today who seek to abolish or optionalize clerical celibacy, just as neither was it the East that inspired Paul VI's liturgical reform, which was, in its most salient features, profoundly anti-Byzantine.[211] The roots of the Bergoglian synodal Church are to be found not in Eastern Orthodoxy but in Modernism, itself deriving from liberal Protestantism.[212] St. Pius X already gave his judgment: "There are some who, echoing the teaching of their Protestant masters, would like the suppression of ecclesiastical celibacy."[213] If we want to understand the push for married clergy, the *Novus Ordo Missae,* and many other aspects of the Vatican II era, we will find more illumination in dusting off the works of Martin Luther than in perusing the catalog of St. Vladimir's Seminary Press.[214]

On July 18, 2019, Fr. Anthony Ruff published at the blog *Pray Tell* a translation of the "16 theses" advanced by historian Hubert Wolf, a passionate critic of mandatory clerical celibacy, in his book *Zölibat: 16 Thesen.* Currently the book is available in German and Italian, but having already attained the status of a number-one best seller, it will no doubt soon appear in English to cause further confusion, factionalism, and dissent among the faithful.

Wolf's theses are full of misconceptions, factual errors, leaps of logic, and ideological baggage. Due to the apparent popularity of his book and the explosive nature of the topic, it is important not to let his theses pass unchallenged. I find it disappointing but not surprising that Fr. Ruff deleted the two comments I left at *Pray Tell,* in which I briefly and nonpolemically responded to Wolf's theses, thus demonstrating once again that there is no intolerance like that of today's proponents of "dialogue" and "mercy."

211 See Kwasniewski, *Once and Future Roman Rite,* 279–304.

212 See Kwasniewski, *Road from Hyperpapalism,* vol. 2, chap. 62.

213 Pius X, Encyclical Letter *Pascendi Dominici Gregis* (September 8, 1907), no. 38.

214 Joseph Cardinal Ratzinger recognized this widespread Catholic "revitalization" of Luther in his masterful paper "The Theology of the Liturgy," given at the Journées liturgiques de Fontgombault, July 22–24, 2001, and republished in *Collected Works,* vol. 11, 541–57. Since that time, we have seen Pope Francis expressly honor the memory and teaching of Luther. See Kwasniewski, *Once and Future Roman Rite,* 45–46, 196–215.

Below, I will quote each thesis in Fr. Ruff's translation, then add to it a short refutation, in some cases recommending further reading.

Thesis 1. *Taboos have fallen. The priest shortage and accusations of abuse force the Vatican to address celibacy.*
There has *always* been a priest shortage, above all in missionary areas. Nevertheless, it did not occur to our predecessors in the Faith, including the most dedicated missionaries, to abolish the discipline of celibacy or to relax any other standards.[215] I will address the bugaboo of abuse below, but suffice it to say that neither the Vatican nor episcopal conferences have had the honesty or the courage to address the most statistically relevant factor in abuse — namely, homosexuality.

Thesis 2. *The mother-in-law of Peter. Celibacy cannot be justified biblically, since there are of course married bishops, priests, and deacons in the New Testament.*
The roots of celibacy are certainly to be found in the New Testament, even if the theological foundations and implications have taken time to develop in full, as has been true for many aspects of Catholicism. To sideline the Gospel and epistle passages that commend celibacy chosen for the kingdom of heaven and to downplay or ignore the evidence for apostolic continence and the testimony of the early Church — especially the voluminous Patristic witness[216] — is nothing other than shoddy advocacy scholarship.

Thesis 3. *Celibacy is not the same as celibacy* [i.e., the term is equivocal depending on context]. *Not only were there entirely different understandings of it in various eras; the regulations had to be repeatedly renewed, modified, and implemented against great resistance.*
One would have thought that a self-professed modern like Wolf would appreciate development in understanding over time, with a gradual deepening of appreciation for Church discipline. Nor should it surprise us that a discipline marked by self-restraining chastity has encountered resistance in every age. Has Wolf perchance heard of "disordered concupiscence," one of the concomitants of Original Sin? It's a phenomenon that shows up now and again.

[215] See Phillip Campbell, "There's Always a Priest Shortage in Missionary Areas," *Unam Sanctam Catholicam*, June 20, 2019, http://unamsanctamcatholicam.blogspot.com/2019/06/theres-always-priest-shortage-in.html.

[216] See Phillip Campbell, "The Truth about Priestly Celibacy in the Early Church," *Unam Sanctam Catholicam*, July 5, 2014, http://unamsanctamcatholicam.com/the-truth-about-priestly-celibacy-in-the-early-church.

Thesis 4. *Pre-Christian origins. The notion of cultic purity of the priest derives from Jewish and pagan antiquity and no longer fits our era.*
So, according to Wolf, we don't learn from and have some continuity with pagan sages and Jewish forebears? A hint of revived Marcionism and anthropological parochialism there, no doubt! This thesis is nothing more than propping up the corpse of the old liberal Protestant claim that Christianity abolishes cult, sacrifice, and priesthood.

Thesis 5. *Jesus was no Stoic. The ideal of the ascetic priest goes back to notions of the philosophical life in antiquity and does not correspond to the model of Jesus.*
The morality preached by Christ was the most demanding the world has ever seen — and it would be insanity to ask people to embrace it, if He had not promised divine gifts (grace, the Holy Spirit) for living it out and conferred upon His ministers the power of remitting sins. Here, once again, we see in Wolf the liberal Protestant idea of Jesus as a nice moral teacher who hands out prizes all around and makes no demands that require self-denial.

Thesis 6. *Economic roots. Abstention from marriage in the Middle Ages and early modernity ensured that clergy would not bequest church resources at their disposal to their children.*
Economic questions cannot be so easily dismissed. How many dioceses are ready to financially support a cleric with his wife and large family (since we should presume they would joyfully follow the teaching of *Humanae Vitae*)? Or are we assuming that married clergy should conform to the current U.S. average of 1.89 children?

Thesis 7. *Flying the flag in doctrinal battles. In the Reformation and Counter-Reformation era, celibacy served as a mark of distinction from Protestants.*
While this is largely true, it is also irrelevant. First, Catholics will always hold that Protestants are mistaken in many of their views, which is hardly surprising for sects based on the fissiparous principle of *sola Scriptura*. Second, John Henry Newman and certain other Protestant pastors have historically chosen celibacy, recognizing its biblical foundation and spiritual value.

Thesis 8. *Priests too have human rights. Since the Enlightenment, the critique of celibacy as violation against nature has radicalized advocates of celibacy.*
The Enlightenment's conception of "nature" is exceedingly narrow, prescinding from the dual perspective of creation and redemption. God created man to find himself by giving himself away in love. This takes place in any Christian life worthily lived, but most obviously in the state of Holy Matrimony and in

the state of consecrated virginity (of which clerical celibacy is the echo). The only "radicalization" found here is the radicalism of love itself, which wishes to give all to the beloved.

Thesis 9. *The leap into other realms. Since other justifications no longer held, Paul VI exalted celibacy spiritually.*
Celibacy has been exalted by many great spiritual authors, not just Church authorities. Paul VI would have considered himself last and least within a millennium-striding tradition. One need only study, for example, the writings on priestly spirituality from the great French School of the Grand Siècle.

Thesis 10. *It works without celibacy too. In the Eastern Catholic churches there are married Catholic priests as a matter of course.*
The Eastern Churches place more ecclesiological emphasis on the bishop, who must always be celibate. Ironically (since the East is always boasting of its antiquity), the Western practice harks back to the earliest way of looking at priests — namely, as "substitutes" for the bishop in places where he could not be present for liturgy. The Roman Catholic priest bears more clearly the image of the bishop, who, representing Christ par excellence, is wed to the Church alone.

Thesis 11. *Ever more exceptions. Protestant and Anglican pastors who convert to Catholicism receive priestly ordination with a papal dispensation.*
Married convert clergy themselves often defend the practice of celibacy on both practical and speculative grounds. I recommend, as an example, Ray Ryland's "The Gift: A Married Priest Looks at Celibacy."[217]

Thesis 12. *Developments in sexuality. Since the Second Vatican Council, marriage is seen as an image of the covenant between Christ and his church and cannot be the reason to prohibit priestly service.*
St. Thomas Aquinas, among other great theologians of the tradition, already presented the loftiest theology possible of Matrimony as a sacramental representation of the union of Christ and the Church.[218] It is absurd to say marriage has not been appreciated until Vatican II. One would expect an author who takes "Vatican II" as his badge to embrace the "ressourcement" or return to the best sources of Christian theology, rather than proclaiming deracination from the past.

[217] *Crisis Magazine,* October 1, 2006, www.crisismagazine.com/2006/the-gift-a-married-priest-looks-at-celibacy.

[218] See my article "St. Thomas on the Grandeur and Limitations of Marriage."

Thesis 13. *Not a dogma. Catholic church teaching allows for the abolition of celibacy at any time.*
The Catholic Faith is made up of many things that are not "dogmas" in the strict sense, the removal or optionalizing of which would nevertheless cause great harm to the fabric of the religion. Canonist Ed Peters well expounds why we should not trivialize Church discipline.[219] This is all the more true the longer it has endured.

Thesis 14. *Dangerous promises. Obligatory abstention from marriage is a risk factor with respect to sexual abuse by priests.*
We have now seen report after report about sexual abuse in Protestant communities, among the Eastern Orthodox, Mormons, Jews, Muslims, atheists, and Boy Scouts. The presence or absence of marriage does not seem to make an appreciable difference in the overall statistics, but the presence or absence of homosexuality certainly does — which is why the abuse crisis will be surmounted only when the lavender mafia is finally overthrown. Avoiding abuse is not about being married but about being chaste in any and all states of life.

Thesis 15. *Weighing goods. Faced with a choice between ameliorating the priest shortage or retaining celibacy, the Church must decide in the interest of the Eucharist (which is necessary for salvation) over celibacy (which is not).*
See number 1 above. No reputable theologian has taught that the Eucharist is necessary for salvation with a necessity of means — that is, such that one could not be saved without it. While the Eucharist is the end and perfection of all the sacraments, the only sacrament strictly necessary for salvation is Baptism — and for this reason, it can be administered by anyone.

Thesis 16. *The old system has come to an end. The abolition of celibacy as an instrument of retaining power must be part of a foundational reform of the hierarchical clerical system.*
Indulging in Marxist-flavored canards about clericalism betrays a mentality of postmodernism, which distrusts authority and discipline in principle. For those with such a perspective, ontological distinctions in ministries and states of life are seen as inherently contrary to human dignity in a democratic age. There is no way, however, of preventing such a mentality from invading and undermining

[219] Ed Peters, "Sure, Celibacy Is 'Disciplinary,' but Then, So Is . . . ," *In the Light of the Law*, April 10, 2014, https://canonlawblog.wordpress.com/2014/04/10/sure-celibacy-is-disciplinary-but-then-so-is/. .

all distinctions, exactly as we have seen take place in debates over homosexuality and transgenderism. Christianity is inseparable from a robust acceptance of natural and supernatural differentiation and hierarchy.

In short, *Zölibat: 16 Thesen* is the work of a Wolf in scholar's clothing. In spite of its crippling weaknesses, however, Fr. Ruff regards Wolf's work in a kindly light: "This [book] seems intended as a somewhat provocative or even polemical statement of the author's strong opposition to mandatory celibacy. In the context of the [at that time] upcoming Amazon synod, ongoing scandals, and Pope Francis's efforts to renew and reform the church, the book is timely."[220] Be that as it may, more timely still would have been a book that clarifies and defends the truth. Fortunately, such resources already exist, as the bibliography at the end of the present book indicates.

[220] Fr. Anthony Ruff, "16 Theses on Celibacy," *PrayTell*, July 18, 2019, www.praytellblog.com/index.php/2019/07/18/16-theses-on-celibacy/.

26

The True Marriage of the Virgin Mary and St. Joseph

In the traditional Roman liturgical calendar, October 11 is the feast of the Divine Maternity of Our Lady — a "modern" feast instituted by Pope Pius XI in 1931 to commemorate the fifteen hundredth anniversary of the Council of Ephesus (431), at which the Blessed Virgin Mary was declared to be *Theotokos*, the God-bearer, *Deipara* or *Dei genetrix*. Unlike Pius XI's *other* new feast, that of the Kingship of Christ, this one did not survive the sharp scissors of the liturgical reform. That this Marian feast was chosen by Pope John XXIII expressly to invoke Our Lady's intercession for the Second Vatican Council at its opening on Thursday, October 11, 1962, makes its abolition and the subsequent placement of *his* feast on the same date ironic in the extreme.[221]

Whatever we may think of that, the feast of our Lady's Motherhood reminds us of a truth of outstanding importance in this time of confusion about marriage and family: our Lady was *not*, as some ignorant preachers are fond of saying, an "unwed mother." When expecting the Child Jesus, she was betrothed to St. Joseph, which, in the Jewish context, gave her the legal right to be regarded and treated as his spouse. Her wifehood, in other words, was as real as the foster fatherhood of Joseph or the adoptive relationship of so many saints of the Old Covenant; she could not, with any justice, be referred to as a mere fiancée.[222]

This truth nevertheless prompts a question: How can we say that Mary and Joseph were *ever* married at *any* point in their lives? Is not the consummation of a marriage part of its definition? In fact, a couple of college students in a class

[221] See "Feast of the Divine Maternity — or of Papa Roncalli?," *Road from Hyperpapalism*, vol. 2, chap. 45.

[222] For a refutation of the erroneous view that Mary "had a baby out of wedlock," see "A Sermon by Cardinal Burke: On the Marriage of the Virgin Mary with St. Joseph," *New Liturgical Movement*, January 23, 2015; https://www.newliturgicalmovement.org/2015/01/a-sermon-by-cardinal-burke-on-marriage.html.

discussion once suggested that maybe Mary and Joseph were "just friends" all their lives, engaged but never married—yet letting people *think* they were. I said: "No, that's not right; the tradition of the Church (as we can see in the liturgy) always refers to Joseph as 'the husband of Mary' and to the three as 'the Holy Family' and always holds up Mary and Joseph as exemplars for *spouses*."

But the argument from authority, although sufficient, can be unsatisfying, so here is a proper explanation. According to St. Thomas, Mary and Joseph "consented to the conjugal uniting, but not expressly to the fleshly uniting save on condition that it should please God"; hence their marriage really came into existence. Thomas clinches his argument with a quotation from Augustine:

> All the goods of marriage are fulfilled in these parents of Christ: offspring, fidelity, and sacrament. The offspring we know to have been the Lord Jesus himself; fidelity, because there was no adultery; sacrament, because there was no divorce. Only marital intercourse was not present there.[223]

A modern reader is tempted to say: "*Only?* If this is lacking, how can the rest of it be a true marriage?" Indeed, Aquinas himself raises the same objection in this context: "Where the final consummation is lacking, there is no true completion."[224]

St. Thomas can argue the way he does because, in his view, the consent to marriage is not a consent to carnal intercourse, but a consent to the marital *consortium* or *societas* that implies such intercourse, or put differently, a consent to the mutual power of the spouses over each other's bodies that is explicitated in the *commixtio carnalis*:

> As fleshly uniting stands related to marriage, so likewise the consent that causes marriage stands related to consent to fleshly uniting. Now marriage, as was said above, is not essentially the fleshly conjoining itself, but a certain association of a man and a woman with a view to fleshly uniting

223 *ST* III, Q. 29, art. 2, citing *On Marriage and Concupiscence* I; see *In IV Sent.*, Dist. 30, Q. 2, art. 2; *Super Matt.* 1, lec. 4, no. 92. At *In IV Sent.*, Dist. 31, Q. 1, art. 3 we read: "From the very fact that through the conjugal pact the spouses hand over to each other, in perpetuity, power over one another, it follows that they may not be separated, and so it is that marriage is never found without inseparability; whereas it is found without fidelity and offspring, because the being of a thing does not depend upon its use."

224 *In IV Sent.*, Dist. 30, Q. 2, art. 2, arg. 3.

> and the other things that pertain, as a consequence, to the husband and wife, according as power is mutually given to them with respect to the fleshly uniting; and *this* association is called the conjugal union. Hence it is clear that those men spoke well who said that to consent to marriage is to consent *implicitly* to fleshly uniting, not explicitly. For the latter ought not to be understood [as given] except in the way that an effect is implicitly contained in its cause: for the power of fleshly uniting, to which one consents, is the cause of the fleshly uniting, as the power of using one's own possession is the cause of its use.[225]

And: "Although the act of fleshly uniting is not of the essence of marriage, still the *power* for this is of its essence; for through marriage power over the other's body is given to both of the spouses with a view to fleshly uniting."[226]

These things premised, Aquinas maintains it was not inconsistent for Mary and Joseph to *know* that God wanted them to remain virgins, and yet for them to keep their hearts so open to the divine will that they did not *insist* on maintaining this virginity "at all costs."

> She [Mary] planned on virginity, unless the Lord should arrange otherwise; hence she entrusted herself to the divine arrangement. To the idea that she consented to fleshly intercourse, one should say that she did not; she consented to marriage directly, but to fleshly intercourse implicitly, so to speak, if God should will it.[227]

Again:

> While virginity is best in and of itself, nevertheless at that time [before Christ's birth] marriage was preferred to it because of the expectation of a blessed offspring to come by way of generation; and thus the Blessed Virgin vowed virginity as the thing most excellent and most acceptable

[225] *In IV Sent.*, Dist. 28, Q. 1, art. 4.

[226] *In IV Sent.*, Dist. 34, Q. 1, art. 2, ad 1. A simple example will show that we intuitively recognize the rightness of Thomas's reasoning. If two people had just exchanged wedding vows but were then suddenly parted by the arrival of enemy troops in their town and were carried far away from each other, we would still say they are married; we would call them husband and wife and lament their separation. If they were virtuous people, each would consider him- or herself bound in fidelity to the other and destined for the procreative union proper to the married. They could not be called unmarried.

[227] *Super Matt.* 1, lec. 4, no. 93.

to herself, yet not simply speaking, but under a most noble condition — namely this: unless God should ordain otherwise.[228]

Hence Mary and Joseph, fully consenting to be each other's spouses, thereby *became* spouses, but because it was the Lord's will that they not unite sexually, they remained "in suspension" as regards the bodily exchange that normally follows upon this consent.[229] In fact, if Mary had not, in wedding Joseph, willed to remain open to the procreation of children by him if God wanted this, then their marriage would have been invalidated through her rejection of one of the essential goods of marriage, the good of offspring (*bonum prolis*).[230] It may be noted that this curious state of being "in suspension" with regard to legitimate earthly goods typifies the entire eschatological orientation of the Christian condition. For this reason, the marriage of Mary and Joseph is, paradoxically, an exemplar of religious life no less than it is of married life.

In at least one place Aquinas presents the objection that Joseph and Mary's marriage was imperfect because it lacked children that were an effect *of that* marriage.[231] His response is that this good was partially present there due to the education of offspring that took place, and that (to paraphrase) we ought to expect things to be unique in the family of the Son of God. This response helps us to remember that the classic catechisms and codes of canon law always said that the primary purpose of marriage is the "procreation *and education* of children."[232] Bringing children into the world is only the first step; the more important step, completive of the first, is rearing them and educating them in the Catholic Faith, moral virtues, and how to live in one's society (as well as other subjects of instruction or apprenticeship, depending on circumstances). It is because we implicitly recognize this hierarchy of obligations that we regard adoptive parents as truly parents.

In the mind of believers reflecting on the Holy Family, an obvious question ought to arise: Are we supposed to learn from the celibate marriage of Mary

[228] *In IV Sent.*, Dist. 30, Q. 2, art. 1, qa. 1.

[229] See *In IV Sent.*, Dist. 30, Q. 2, art. 1, qa. 1, ad 1–3.

[230] See *In IV Sent.*, Dist. 30, Q. 2, art. 1, qa. 2, ad 2.

[231] *In IV Sent.*, Dist. 30, Q. 2, art. 2, arg. 4.

[232] For a tightly argued defense of this traditional teaching, see Jennaya Arias, "On the Primary Purpose of Marriage," *Catholic Culture*, https://www.catholicculture.org/culture/library/view.cfm?recnum=5822.

and Joseph a lesson that is actually *applicable* to married laypeople? Put differently, could their "Josephite marriage" have anything to say to us here and now?

St. Thomas answers in the affirmative: "By this example [of Mary and Joseph] the faithful are taught that if after marriage they remain continent by mutual consent, their union is still marriage and is rightly called such, even without intercourse of the sexes."[233] Peter Lombard goes further: "Without carnal commingling, marriage is holier, as is said in the text [of the *Sentences*]."[234] In two places, Aquinas even formulates the view in his own words, albeit buried in objections as premises to which he does not take exception: "It is even better for spouses to restrain themselves than to make use of marriage"; again, "those marriages are more perfect that are accompanied by a vow of continence (*pari voto continentium*)."[235] It is hard to know the extent to which Aquinas personally endorses this opinion, but there are reasons to think he could not have rejected it altogether.

This being so, we are left with matter for reflection. If, as occurred fairly often in former centuries, a Catholic couple today felt drawn by the Lord to a deeper life of prayer and contemplative intimacy with Him and were convinced that He had given them the desire and strength to remain perpetually continent, would we, as a friend or spiritual director, counsel them in favor of this choice or against it? Would we view it as a case of confused vocational identity, of mistaking for superior virtue what is in reality a retreat from the demands placed on Christians living in the world? A too-quick answer about "medieval Manichaeism" or "contempt of God's good creation" or "staying in line with one's state in life" might well bring to light a superficial spirituality that does not respect the divine initiative and the Spirit's free giving of gifts, not to mention a failure to comprehend a rare but defensible application of ascetical-mystical doctrine.

The saints are given to the faithful as luminous exemplars of Christian life, practitioners of heroic virtue worthy of our prudent imitation. Now, it is well known that many saints in all periods of history have lived perpetual continence either for the whole or for a notable part of their married lives.[236] We are

233 *ST* III, Q. 29, art. 2, sed contra, quoting Augustine with approval.

234 *In IV Sent.*, Dist. 26, q. 2, art. 4, sed contra 2.

235 *In IV Sent.*, Dist. 32, art. 2, arg. 2; *In IV Sent.*, Dist. 34, art. 2, arg. 1.

236 See, for abundant examples, Ferdinand Holböck, *Married Saints and Blesseds through the Centuries*, trans. Michael J. Miller (San Francisco: Ignatius Press, 2002).

bound, therefore, by our very trust in the Church's recognition of sanctity, to see in this (admittedly atypical) path a genuine "vocation within a vocation," a different mode of nuptial love to which the Lord has called and will continue to call some Christians.

We could understand a Josephite relationship in this way: as Christian marriage, with its divinely graced bodily-spiritual intimacy, is the privileged earthly sign of that heavenly reality of which religious life is the superior anticipation and realization, so a Josephite marriage is the mutual and voluntary surrender or sacrifice of spousal rights in order that the spouses — precisely as representing the perpetual gift of self, total yet nonsexual, that subsists between the Bridegroom Christ and His bridal Church — may become *for each other* more transparent signs of the ineffable intimacy awaiting them in their final beatific destiny, an intimacy with God and with each other in Him that is more lofty and profound than any earthly communion they might enjoy. It would be, then, the renunciation and offering up of a way of life that is rooted in the sanctified and sanctifying but necessarily transitory and imperfect communion of man and wife, in order to achieve *another* kind of communion of brother and sister in the Spirit; and this for no other reason than that both may strive more wholeheartedly to attain, in their common life, an ever-fuller participation in the divine holiness and beatitude that knows neither beginning nor end.[237]

Such was indubitably the calling of Joseph and Mary and of certain saints who followed in their footsteps. We could not dare, for fear of sinning against Love, to state categorically that such a vocation is no longer possible or no longer given. The parents of St. Thérèse, Louis and Zélie Martin, are sometimes ridiculed for the vow of continence they made at the start of their marriage. But their very openness to renunciation, together with an ongoing discernment, was a crucial part of their sanctity, and when they came to see that it was God's will for them to have children, they embraced *that* vocation without demur, giving to the Church the gift of five daughters who entered religious life — one of whom became the greatest saint of modern times.

In the midst of synodal confusion and chaos, this topic is more pertinent than ever, due to the flawed reasoning of certain leaders in the Church who seem to take for granted that chastity and continence either outside of marriage or even within it are simply impossible, off the table.[238] If we adopt a broader perspective,

[237] For the metaphysical and theological principles underlying this claim, see chapter 11.

[238] See chapters 14 and 18.

we can see that history furnishes us with more than a few examples of the reality of such "platonic" unions, which can be models for couples in situations of remarriage who wish to be fully reconciled with God and the Church and thus be able to enter into communion with Our Lord in the Most Holy Eucharist.

27

The Devil's War against Celibacy, Marriage, and the Eucharist

Many readers will have seen this quotation from a letter written by Sr. Lucia, the Fatima visionary: "The final battle between the Lord and the reign of Satan will be about marriage and the family. Don't be afraid, because anyone who works for the sanctity of marriage and the family will always be contended and opposed in every way. This is the decisive issue." Few, however, will be familiar with Pope Siricius (334–399), who described his opponent Jovinian as a tool of "the ancient enemy, the adversary of chastity, the teacher of luxury," because he had attacked the celibacy of the clergy. Is there a connection between Sr. Lucia's insight and the devil's age-old campaign against celibacy and virginity for the kingdom of heaven?

In order to answer this question, we need to look at the devil: who he is and how he operates.

Lucifer hates consecrated virginity and priestly celibacy because this charism and state of life is the one *most intrinsically opposed* to the pride that brought about his fall, his eternal loss of beatitude, his damnation. The devil desired to receive beatitude as a reward for his own natural greatness, not as a pure gift of grace undeserved by any creature. He desired to be the "firstborn son" who received the homage of inferior creation — perhaps even to be a mediator between the human race and its Creator. When God revealed that He Himself would enter into friendship with rational animals, so vastly inferior to the angels, and grant them beatitude; that his own Word would become flesh, passible flesh; that this Word-made-flesh would raise up the human race by suffering and dying for it — Lucifer would not tolerate it. His love of self turned inward. In his pride, he said: *Non serviam:* I will not serve God; I will not serve such a God; I will not serve such a plan. Lucifer rejected the supernatural in favor of the natural.

The man or woman who chooses virginity or celibacy for the kingdom of God is doing the opposite. In a way, he or she is setting aside the natural in favor of the supernatural. The virgin or celibate is relinquishing that which is most natural to the human being — to live in partnership with another of the opposite sex, finding in this community a friendship and fruitfulness intended for man from the beginning, written into his very bodily nature, as we see in the account of Eve's being fashioned from the side of Adam and then brought to him as his wife. Just as nothing is more natural to man than marriage, nothing more supremely testifies to the offering of oneself to God in love than relinquishing it for His sake.[239] The life of the virgin or the celibate is a holocaust in imitation of Jesus Christ, the Lamb of God. As the Word became flesh for our sakes, the consecrated soul makes of his or her own flesh a living word of total consent and surrender to God. The virgin or celibate is the supreme human sign of God's radically self-emptying redemptive love — and the complete antithesis of Lucifer's self-inversion.

But as the saints pray without ceasing and generate prayer in others, so the devil, who is a liar and the father of lies (John 8:44), lies without ceasing, and fathers ever more lies in his victims. He persuades people to think that celibacy or virginity is a denigration of marriage, that those who promote this higher state and calling are casting aspersions on the order of creation, the goodness of nature, the beauty of married love. He presents himself, at times, as a *defender* of these things, but only in a distorted way, as Luther was. The devil wants the exclusive commitment of priests and religious to the Lord and His people to be diluted or abandoned, so that he can amplify and multiply his own infernal rebellion against the clothing of grace in favor of a naked nature he can call his own — and an army of followers he can call his own, who follow him to the emptiness and frustration of eternally denuded nature. Most of all, however, he

[239] We can see a similar paradox operative in the mystery of transubstantiation itself: the natural (namely, the substance of bread and wine) is subordinated to the supernatural (the substance of Christ) without canceling out the goodness of the natural, whose accidents become the privileged means by which the Lord nourishes us with the food of His flesh, the drink of His blood. In fact, speaking poetically, one might say the bread and wine surrender themselves to give way to that which is divine, yet the characteristics of food and drink remain as signs to tell us what God is for us. In His ineffable humility, He chooses to come into our midst under the form of a good to be used and enjoyed by us. The natural elements are spent in their use as means but carry us beyond them to the end for which we were made.

sows the lie that man cannot be fulfilled apart from sex, from sexual experience and expression — that humans are maimed and impoverished if they do not enjoy the fleshly presence of another man or woman.

See how subtle the strategy of Satan is! For the ultimate impoverishment of man is, in reality, *to live without God,* to live without knowledge of or desire for eternal communion with God in heaven. Now, the priesthood and the religious life are both directly ordered to living out and proclaiming the reality and primacy of the kingdom of heaven. It is therefore *crucial* for the well-being of mankind that priests and religious be unambiguous signs of our ultimate destiny — for in heaven, as Our Lord teaches, there is neither marrying nor giving in marriage (Matt. 22:30; Mark 12:25; Luke 20:35). The one all-sufficient marriage in heaven is the perfect union of Christ and His Church.

This marriage of Christ and the Church has two special signs on earth that point to it: the sacrament of Matrimony and the sacrament of the Eucharist. Therefore, the devil attacks both of them. He attacks marriage by undermining the goods of marriage: offspring (through contraception and abortion), fidelity (through fornication and adultery), and sacrament (through divorce and pastoral practices that countenance divorce). He attacks the Holy Eucharist, which is the fleshly presence of the Savior and fully capable of satisfying our hunger for love in this life, by attacking the sacred liturgy, by tempting people to make it into an anthropocentric, horizontal self-celebration through which its very meaning is undermined, even if the sacrament may still have been effected.

Thus, the devil's strategy is multifaceted. He works to undermine the indissoluble covenant of heterosexual marriage, which is the sacramental sign of the indestructible and superabundantly fruitful union of Christ and His Church. The contemporary war against marriage is also, indeed more deeply, a war against the nuptial union of Christ and the Church — a vain but frenzied effort to erase from the minds of men any memory of this glorious union consummated on the Cross. He works to undermine the Most Holy Eucharist, which is the sign and cause of our communion with Christ and our highest participation in His self-oblation on the Cross. He works to undermine the priesthood and religious life, which exemplify and effectively bring about in this world the ordering of all creation, through Christ, to the Father, who is the beginning and end of all things. The common element in all these attacks is the devil's fury that anyone or anything *natural* should ever be subordinated to that which is *supernatural* — that a faithful, radical self-sacrifice should be the path of salvation and blessedness.

By refusing to serve the God of fruitfulness and sacrificial love, Lucifer merited his own everlasting isolation and barrenness, and he ever seeks to draw human souls into his realm of selfishness. In particular, the refusal to subordinate the natural to the supernatural is his defining trait, and it explains why he hates celibacy and virginity more than anything else in the world.

Satan hates marriage for analogous reasons: it, too, is a life of self-sacrifice made possible only by divine blessing, a state ordered to the multiplication of children of God who will have the potential to receive supernatural elevation by grace and to enjoy heavenly glory, of which the devil deprived himself. The power of generation in man — how mysterious it is! To be invited into partnership with the Author of life; to stand, in procreation, at the origin of being *ex nihilo*: this is a power no angelic spirit has. It is a direct participation in God's creative act. Its burgeoning fruit directly opposes the fruitless introversion of the devil. *Ex ore infantium et lactentium perfecisti laudem propter inimicos tuos, ut destruas inimicum et ultorem*: "Out of the mouth of infants and of sucklings thou hast perfected praise, because of thy enemies, that thou mayst destroy the enemy and the avenger" (Ps. 8:3).

As the great Thomist theologian Matthias Scheeben explains, if Adam and Eve had not fallen, their activity of generation would not only have transmitted natural life to their offspring but would also have occasioned the gift of supernatural life: their children would have been conceived and born in a state of grace.[240] This is why the devil so hated Adam and Eve, resplendent in grace as

[240] "He [the Holy Spirit] willed to communicate justice to other men precisely as descendants of Adam.... Therefore He dwelt in Adam as in a person especially endowed by Him with grace, but at the same time associated His spiritualizing, supernatural power of animation and generation with Adam's generative power, so that the effect of the former might be transferred to the product of the latter. He overshadowed Adam's natural fecundity with His own supernatural fecundity, so that the fruit of the former might issue from the originating principle immediately glorified and sanctified.... It was rather in pursuance of a free, gratuitous, mysterious decree that God attached the transmission of grace to the transmission of nature, that He rendered fellowship in grace dependent on mankind's fellowship in nature, and made the propagation of nature, as it were, the vehicle of grace. It was a new grace for Adam that grace was intended not for himself alone, but also for his posterity as such, and consequently that he, who was the principle of nature, was also, to some extent, to be the principle of grace for the whole human race." Matthias Scheeben, *The Mysteries of Christianity*, trans. Cyril Vollert (St. Louis: B. Herder, 1946), 231–32, 235.

they were: he knew that from their loins would spring an entire race of beings destined for immortal glory with the angels. Even though we are now fallen and no longer conceive "sons of God," the privilege of procreation and the freedom to cooperate with Christ in the sanctification of our children remain ours. As Pope Pius XI eloquently testifies in the greatest papal document ever written on marriage and family:

> How great a boon of God this [good of offspring] is, and how great a blessing of matrimony is clear from a consideration of man's dignity and of his sublime end. For man surpasses all other visible creatures by the superiority of his rational nature alone. Besides, God wishes men to be born not only that they should live and fill the earth, but much more that they may be worshippers of God, that they may know Him and love Him and finally enjoy Him for ever in heaven; and this end, since man is raised by God in a marvelous way to the supernatural order, surpasses all that eye hath seen, and ear heard, and all that hath entered into the heart of man. From which it is easily seen how great a gift of divine goodness and how remarkable a fruit of marriage are children born by the omnipotent power of God through the cooperation of those bound in wedlock.
>
> For although Christian spouses even if sanctified themselves cannot transmit sanctification to their progeny, nay, although the very natural process of generating life has become the way of death by which original sin is passed on to posterity, nevertheless, they share to some extent in the blessings of that primeval marriage of Paradise, since it is theirs to offer their offspring to the Church in order that by this most fruitful Mother of the children of God they may be regenerated through the laver of baptism unto supernatural justice and finally be made living members of Christ, partakers of immortal life, and heirs of that eternal glory to which we all aspire from our inmost heart.[241]

Satan does what he can to thwart this plan — and so he will do with each of us, if we let him. The devil opposes natural as well as supernatural generation: he seeks to prevent men and women from using the gift of their sexuality to bring more life into the world; he seeks to prevail upon them to kill the fruit they bear; he seeks to lead them away from the source of immortality in the sacraments of the Church. Hating procreation, he has bent all his efforts toward either

[241] Pius XI, Encyclical Letter *Casti Connubii* (December 31, 1930), no. 12.

preventing it through contraception or destroying its fruits through abortion. Contraception is an abomination of desolation in the midst of the temple, which is the human body sanctified by the Holy Spirit: by means of contraception, the Lord and Giver of Life is cast out as if He were an evil spirit, and in his place is welcomed the spirit of lust and avarice, to make its home in the barren womb, like a church with no tabernacle and no Real Presence.

Contrary to the demonic spirit of selfishness, spouses give up their right of self-determination over their own bodies when they vow their faithful love to each other until death, come what may. When a Christian man and woman marry "in the Lord" — that is, when they embrace their calling to the full, embracing each other and the children God gives them — they do the greatest and noblest thing on earth, from the vantage of the capacities God has planted in human nature itself. The marriage is elevated by Christ, the Bridegroom, into a living sign of His unbreakable union of love with His immaculate Bride, the Church. In this way, Christian spouses show forth to each other and to the world the central mystery of reality: the love that moves the sun and the stars, the love that multiplies itself in the joy of giving, the love that overcomes self-isolation.

Christ, too, is faithful to His Church, come what may, and never gives up on her sinful members until all who are destined for glory have reached the fatherland. In light of God's faithfulness to sinful Israel and Christ's faithfulness to His still-imperfect Church on earth, divorce is an unredeemable fiction, adultery an abomination, and Eucharistic Communion for those who are "remarried" an act of sacrilege by which the Savior is spat upon, scourged, crowned with thorns, and crucified in His Sacrament.

Let us make no mistake about it: Lucifer, with the pseudo-patience of an immortal spirit, has slowly built up an anti-religion, a counterfeit Catholicism, that has for its purpose the eternal damnation of men, just as the Catholic religion has for its purpose their eternal salvation. Divorce, and with it, adultery, is the anti-sacrament of Marriage; contraception, and from it, abortion, is the anti-sacrament of Baptism; the self-indulgence of masturbation and homosexual activity is the anti-sacrament of Confirmation, which produces self-control and fortitude; euthanasia is the anti-sacrament of Extreme Unction. In place of Holy Orders, there is negligent fatherhood and man-hating feminism; in place of Penance, there is the hedonistic satisfaction of every bodily appetite; in place of the Eucharist, there is idolatry of the world, the flesh, and the devil.

It is far from coincidental that the sacred liturgy had to fall into ruins first before the devil could carry out his full-scale attack on virginity and celibacy.

These latter have no meaning, no purpose, apart from the wedding feast of the Lamb, to which the liturgy gives us access. When the liturgy is drained of adoration, beauty, and contemplation, it can no longer awaken, nourish, and direct an all-consuming hunger and thirst for God's kingdom. It will no longer stir up priestly and religious vocations or sustain them to the end. The Mass and the Divine Office had to be brought low before celibacy and virginity could be felled. The "irreversible liturgical reform" had to predate the supposedly irreversible decline in "traditional models of ministry and service."[242]

In reality, the Church's authentic liturgy, in all its depth and splendor, always summons forth abundant vocations to the priesthood and the religious life. This, again, is why the devil hates the *usus antiquior* with such implacable fury. Wherever the traditional liturgy returns, celibacy and virginity blossom anew — as do marriages in which husband and wife sacrificially welcome many children. Satan hates it all and is at work, sleeplessly, to fight against it, using every means at his disposal.

We are now in a better position to see the connection between Sr. Lucia's statement that "the final battle between the Lord and the reign of Satan will be about marriage and the family" and Pope Siricius's castigation of Jovinian for denying the superiority of the celibate or virginal life dedicated to God. False teachings on marriage and the "relaxation" of the required discipline of clerical celibacy are two flanks of a single army laying siege to the City of God on earth. Any word, any action against the sanctity of marriage, the good of the family, or the exalted vocations of clerical and religious life finds its origin in the general of this army, the enemy of mankind. As we endure the worst doctrinal confusion, moral laxity, and liturgical uprootedness the Church has ever suffered, may the Lord, mighty in battle (Ps. 23:8), save His people and bless His inheritance (Ps. 27:9).

If, as argued in chapter 22, faith in God and marriage follow the same "logic," we would expect infidelity to God and sexual promiscuity to do the same — an intuition validated by almost every page of the Old Testament. As the spiritual marriage and the sacramental marriage resemble each other, so, too, do the betrayal of our Maker and the fornication, the adultery, the breaking of vows, that hold His law and His love in contempt.

[242] On these points, see Kwasniewski, *Ministers of Christ*, 219–34.

One of the most astounding passages in the Gospels is where Jesus says to Judas, an intimate companion and His betrayer: "What you are about to do, do it quickly" (John 13:27). It almost sounds as if Jesus were giving Judas a command to betray Him: "Do it quickly." Or as if there were a hint of fear in His voice, anticipating the struggle that would come in the Garden of Gethsemane.

The Lord knows that His hour has come. He is eager to embrace it, to drink the cup of suffering, to accomplish the long-awaited redemption of mankind. He has the eagerness of a bridegroom before the wedding feast, longing for the consummation of His love and the fruitfulness of the union. He sees before him generations of righteous men and women born in His heart, raised from His blood. He sees with full clarity the unspeakable pain of soul and body that He must undergo, and He already tastes it. "Do it quickly": do not delay the supreme sacrifice that unites heaven and earth. "Do it quickly": I am ready to enter my Passion and can brook no delay.

Shortly after this saying of the Lord, St. John adds the haunting words "And it was night" (John 13:30). Night fell on the light of the world. The clouds of malice and scorn surrounded the Sun of Justice and hid Him from view. We are plunged into utter darkness — the darkness of a world from which God has hidden His face, a world consigned to the outer darkness as long as it does not know its Savior and freely bow before its King. "And it was night," not only because of the impending doom of the betrayal, scourging, and Crucifixion, but even more because of the fallen state of mankind, "the people sitting in darkness and in the shadow of death" (Matt. 4:16).

"As soon as Judas took the bread, Satan entered into him. So Jesus told him, 'What you are about to do, do quickly.' " There will *always* be Judases in the midst of the disciples. There will always be those who allow themselves to be conquered by Satan, who allow themselves to be his instruments for betraying Christ and trying to rid the earth of His presence. What happens to Our Lord is not limited to His own time but is archetypal for all time. His Mother is always in our midst; His apostles are always in our midst; and His betrayer is always in our midst — or at least those who act his part.

Today they may be wearing papal white, princely red, or clerical black, but they are no less culpable for that outward symbol of holiness. Quite the contrary: the higher the station, the more sinful the deviation. For us, too, it is night, and the Son of Man is betrayed into the hands of sinners — metaphorically, by false teaching and evil example and, literally, whenever Our Savior in the Holy Eucharist is placed into the hands of unrepentant mortal sinners, to be crucified anew. The words of St. John Vianney on this subject should be enough to prompt a serious examination of conscience and sincere recourse to the sacrament of Penance![243]

The following text from St. Thomas Aquinas is especially suitable in our times:

> The sin of the fornicator receiving Christ's body is likened to Judas kissing Christ [in the Garden], as to the resemblance of the sin, because each outrages Christ with the sign of friendship.... And this resemblance in crime applies no less to other sinners than to fornicators: because by other mortal sins, sinners act against the charity of Christ, of which this sacrament is the sign, and all the more according as their sins are graver. But the sin of fornication to some extent makes one *more* unfit for receiving this sacrament [than other sins], because thereby especially the spirit becomes enslaved by the flesh, which is a hindrance to the fervor of love required for this sacrament.[244]

This observation of Aquinas goes a long way toward explaining why many Catholics today derive no benefit from receiving the Eucharist but, rather, heap up punishment for themselves until they repent. If they are guilty of sins such as sexual self-gratification, premarital sex, contraceptive sex, adultery, or homosexual acts, they cannot have charity in their souls, and in this way, they "outrage Christ with the sign [but not the reality] of friendship." They are imitating Judas by giving the Lord a false kiss.

"And it was night." We are indeed immersed in an ecclesial night that stretches on wearisomely, year after year, decade after decade. We might have forgotten what the day looks like; we might wonder if the dawn will ever come; we could be deceived by the evil one into believing that night has won and the day has been vanquished. That is what the disciples believed in their weakness, when they were scattered and went into hiding. Our Lord let them remain in darkness for a time, to make it absolutely clear that without Him, all *is* night and will remain night. He rose again on the third day to show where the only light of the world will ever come from. "Salvation is found in no one else, for there

243 *Eucharistic Meditations: Extracts from the Writings and Instructions of St. John Vianney*, ed. Abbé H. Convert, trans. Sr. Mary Benvenuta (Wheathampstead, Hertfordshire: Anthony Clarke Books, 1923, repr. 1964), 92–96; quoted in Kwasniewski, *Holy Bread of Eternal Life*, 187–90.

244 *ST* III, Q. 80, art. 5, ad 2.

is no other name under heaven given to mankind by which we must be saved" (Acts 4:12).[245]

Nothing will change this everlasting truth. Even the Judases in our midst will be the means by which Divine Providence brings about, again and again, the triumph of the Cross until the end of time.

[245] See Kwasniewski, *Road from Hyperpapalism*, chaps. 4–8, 16–19, and 21.

IV

Contraception and Abortion

It was not enough for them to err about the knowledge of God, but whereas they lived in a great war of ignorance, they call so many and so great evils peace. For either they sacrifice their own children, or use hidden sacrifices, or keep watches full of madness, so that now they neither keep life, nor marriage undefiled, but one killeth another through envy, or grieveth him by adultery: and all things are mingled together, blood, murder, theft and dissimulation, corruption and unfaithfulness, tumults and perjury, disquieting of the good, forgetfulness of God, defiling of souls, changing of nature, disorder in marriage, and the irregularity of adultery and uncleanness.

—Wisdom 14:22–26

28

The Gift That Completes the Nuptial Mystery

St. Benedict in his *Rule* tells the monk that all the possessions of the monastery are to be treated with the same care that a monk would give to the vessels of the altar. The monk owns nothing — not even his own body or his own will, says the saint.[246]

The human body is a liturgical vessel. It is part of the sacrificial offering we bring to God, not just at Mass but throughout our lives: "I beseech you, therefore, brethren, by the mercy of God, that you present your bodies as a living sacrifice, holy, pleasing unto God, your reasonable service" (Rom. 12:1).

Now, what do we offer to God upon the altar of sacrifice? Moldy bread and sour wine? How could *that* be something suitable for consecration? But the same question should be asked of that which a husband or wife offers to the other. Is it some artificially segregated portion of ourselves, sexual functionality separated from its procreative purpose or from the person as a whole? A hungry selfishness? Will they offer themselves in the totality of their human nature, body and soul, together with the children who may come? "Let the little children come to me, and do not hinder them" (Matt. 19:14) — let them come into being!

As the priests and rulers God has placed in this world, we are to offer the whole of creation. What is worthy of the Divine Liturgy, the cosmic liturgy? The bees, the grain, the grapes, the olives are not selfish; they yield everything they are to man and to God. Consider the lilies of the field. They prodigally offer their scent and shape, giving glory to their Maker and comfort to their beholder. They do not feel the need to hold back or to do this at their pleasure.

Each time a husband and wife embrace each other, it is a reenactment of the sacrament of their marriage, as each Eucharist is a reenactment of the sacrifice of the Cross. What do we offer God and each other in this act? In what condition

[246] See *Rule,* chaps. 31 and 33.

is the matter we offer? "This holy and unspotted host," "an unblemished lamb." If God deserves gold and silver vessels for the Eucharist, and pure wine and bread, then at least we can say that husbands and wives deserve worthy intentions and honest fleshliness without chemicals or barriers.

Should not the giver of the most intimate gift give his or her *best*? What is best in man is not just his flesh or his "heart" but the *whole man*, body and soul, flesh and spirit, mind and will, the power to unite and the power to give life and receive it. We are not dualists: man is not two things but one. If he is to give *himself*, he must give *all* of himself, surrendering *who* and *what* he is to the beloved, that the union may be a complete and perfect union — not a business contract or a prostitution or a recreation, none of which has anything to do with true love of a person for the person's *own sake*, for who he or she is in the fullness of his or her being.

Nature-defying, man-denying, God-hating nihilism is at the root of "recreational sex" as well as "sex ed." People who do not love one another for who and what they are live in a world without realism, love, or hope. They learn the cynical arts of distraction and dissipation to forget the miserable isolation of their condition. If one has nothing worth giving up one's life for, the only thing left is a ceaseless pursuit of pleasures or frenetic business. In this way, one tries to escape the asking and answering of existential questions such as: Who am I? Why am I here? What is the purpose of my life? What does death mean? The reason religion seems to be irrelevant to so many people today is that *religion exists to ask and to answer these questions*. When people no longer ask them, religion has nothing to say to them.

The action of nuptial union carries with it immense meaning and responsibility, which is why it ought to be freely and consciously chosen with the full weight of one's being and with an unspoken but vital awareness of *what it is*. The best of Christian customs and pious traditions surrounding marriage always underlined this truth; Christians today should thoughtfully retain or recover them as they plan and celebrate their weddings and embark on the pilgrimage of married life in Christ.[247] Those who are engaged or betrothed[248]

[247] See, for example, my article "The Return of the 'Care Cloth' at the Traditional Nuptial Mass," *New Liturgical Movement*, September 13, 2021, www.newliturgicalmovement.org/2021/09/the-return-of-care-cloth-at-traditional.html.

[248] On the act and state of betrothal and for references to further reading on the subject, see Sharon Kabel, "Rite of Betrothal," *Latin Mass Wedding*, https://www.latinmasswedding.com/rite-of-betrothal/.

and not yet married do not *really* know what the Lord will ask of them, what the burden of joy and suffering will be, until it has come upon them. But when they receive humbly and trustingly the mysteries handed down from eternity to time, from one age to another, they also receive the grace to be broken and healed, to hold on and let go, to die and rise again. It is a lifelong initiation into the paschal mystery, and its fruit is perfect conformity to the Bridegroom and the Bride, the oneness of eternal life, and a family beyond all earthly families.

The language of the living body

French patrologist Jerome Alexandre observes:

> The flesh, like language, acts as a sign. It signifies a reality that only trust can attain. This is why the substantial difference between soul and flesh is so important: the soul knows that the flesh attached to it is other than itself, that it can neither take full possession of it nor separate itself from it. It must hence resolve to trust it, respect it, and love it.[249]

My flesh is part of who I am — it is not an appendage or a machine or a piece of property, but myself in matter. At the same time, my consciousness of myself is not the same as the flesh; we know there is a distinction between my thoughts and my body. As a result, my flesh, like the language I speak with my lips, is itself a sign of me and of my intentions and my priorities. What I do in the flesh and to it and with it signifies what *I* think and desire. It is not only *not* irrelevant to my personhood; it is the primary language through which my person speaks, even before a particular word is uttered.

Therefore, the flesh is also a reality that must be *respected*. I do not absolutely "own" it, nor can I live without it (at least, in a natural way; how we live after death is mysterious and certainly no longer simply "natural"). I have to acknowledge the reality and goodness of the flesh, "trusting" it as I go through life, trusting that my embodiment is part of my perfection, and that the body's limitations, as regards both pleasure and pain, are also for my benefit, if I have learned to respect and love it for what it is.

We might consider, then, how contraception and abortion contradict Alexandre's insight. What are you saying about your own flesh when you impede what is the most normal and natural functioning of your body — namely, to

[249] Quoted in Antoine Arjakovsky, *What Is Orthodoxy?: A Genealogy of Christian Understanding*, trans. Jerry Ryan and Penelope Cavill (Brooklyn: Angelico Press, 2018), 170–71.

give rise to other human beings and to nurture them into existence, to maturity? What are you saying about your *self* when you treat your flesh, which is part of yourself, as a locus of threat, danger, antagonism, competition? What this says is that a person is profoundly sick, divided from himself or herself, internally at war. Or it might say that the soul would treat the body as an industrialist treats raw materials, stripping them from nature, exploiting them and extracting every last benefit without regard to the health of the "body politic."

Take it one step further. What is the person who thus divides himself from himself (or herself from herself) saying to a partner, a spouse, about the other's flesh? *Your* flesh is also the enemy of my soul, my desire, my self-conception; there is something in you that I do not trust, respect, or love. I will take your appetite, I will take the comfort of your matter, but I will not take you yourself in your wholeness. I will do violence to your materiality, as I do (or am willing to do) violence to mine, so that we can be disembodied and embodied together. Is there not in all this a *hatred* of the flesh mixed in with the love of it?

The language such a couple speaks to each other is a language of desperate half-truths and evasions, politely covered over with conventions, but reducible to self-interest — and as we have seen, not even the interest of one's entire self.[250]

It gets worse with abortion, for here the hatred of one's own flesh is magnified to include the flesh (and soul) of another. To seek to rid oneself of the flesh of a child is to hate the child himself or herself, since the body is the person in his or her material aspect. Thus, the civil war that began in the person in whom disordered desire has created self-hatred extends to encompass the person with whom he or she lies (in both senses of the term) and all the persons implicit in this relationship, which is naturally fruitful and must be violently attacked to preclude or excise the fruit.

If the flesh, then, is a language, what are contracepting and aborting couples saying to themselves? What are they saying to each other? What are they saying to their potential or actual offspring? "I do not trust you. I do not respect you. I do not love you."

Voluntary barrenness

One day, when I was standing on a train platform in New Jersey, waiting to catch a train into New York City, I noticed well-dressed young women waiting at the platform on their way to work, and I thought: How many of these women are

[250] See Edmund Waldstein, "Natures as Words, Contraception as a Lie," in Waldstein and Kwasniewski, *Integralism and the Common Good*, vol. 1, 83–89.

committing themselves to a life of singlehearted devotion to Mammon, the god of the world, without reaping any of the benefits that would arise from a life dedicated to the true God?

They are celibate, after a fashion, but they are not virgins; they make sacrifices day after day but reap no salvation from them and bring no immortal souls into the world. They might have sex, but they have no children; thus, they lose the chief glory and merit of the married woman. Once they have a child, they then frequently hand over the burden of childcare to someone else, losing the greatest opportunity and privilege of all, that of nurturing and educating their own offspring.

So many modern women are a set of absolute contradictions: their lives are consecrated, but to a false god who takes away the blessings of virginal faith; they are lying down with their boyfriends or husbands, but they choose barrenness; when they bear children, they do not nurse and educate them. In a satire upon their own existence, they are unvirginal celibates, unfruitful wives, uncommitted mothers — and all this *by choice.*[251]

In many of his sonnets, Shakespeare urges the recipient to beget children in order to pass on beauty and not waste it on oneself. The sonnets assume that sexual intercourse is naturally and quite happily linked with the conception of children; that marriage, all things being normal, leads to family (to think otherwise just would not have made any sense to a person living in a traditional culture); that a spouse will not only bear but rear children with complete dedication. What would Shakespeare have said to these women on the train platform? "You should get married"? But they *are* married, many of them, yet they have no children. "You should have children"? But some of them have — one or two, and they think this is "more than enough." The whole structure of social relations, the most elementary moral responsibilities, the most basic human realities have disappeared; Shakespeare would have almost no way of entering the minds of these people.

Let me emphasize that I am talking only about what might be called voluntary barrenness, the de facto sterility chosen by those who either do not

[251] I fully acknowledge that there are Catholic women who *do* want to get married and have a family but who cannot find a morally upright decent man to marry; obviously the crisis of Christian manhood means that it is no easy task to find a spouse today. Here I am speaking about modern women unbelievers as well as confused Christian women excessively aligned with feminism, to whom I believe the critique made here does apply.

want children or do not wish to shoulder the burden of commitment. Obviously, those who deeply desire to have children and cannot must bear this cross with the help of God's grace, for their infertility is certainly neither chosen nor blameworthy. Childlessness is in truth the deepest sorrow and burden for those who have a worthy conception of marriage and human life. The perversity of the modern attitude consists in viewing children as a losing proposition, as a throwing away of one's life.

When the prophet Isaiah uses the metaphor of a mother for God's tender love, it relies upon the fact that the bond between mother and child is known and felt to be the strongest, the most sacred, the most intimate of all bonds. It is perhaps the noblest model of love available to us, and thus, God can make use of it and expect to be immediately understood. No mother forgets her child; how, then, could God? When Scripture says, "Can a woman forget her infant, so as not to have pity on the son of her womb? and if she should forget, yet will not I forget thee" (Isa. 49:15), it is arguably making a *reductio ad absurdum* argument: no mother worthy of the name forgets her child, and, since this is true, how much more will God remember us, since He is our Maker and sustains our being? Today, the very basis for making this comparison — the natural and beautiful bond of mother and child — is openly mocked and repudiated. We are, alas, very far away from what was self-evident to the prophet, to whom the yearning of the mother for her child so readily served as a vivid image for the tender mercies of God toward lost and wayward Israel.

Somewhere in the human heart, no matter how calloused and cynical, there is an ember of that yearning, a spark of that love. We need to breathe on those embers and throw tinder on those sparks as much as we can, by witnessing constantly to the great gift of human life, the beauty of motherly and fatherly love, and the hard-won but deeply satisfying joy of living outside of oneself, for the sake of another.

Unashamed communion for life

Adam spoke "up" when he spoke with God and "down" in the naming of the animals, but it was not until the creation of Eve, "bone of my bone and flesh of my flesh" (Gen 2:23), that he had a dialogue with an *equal.*

Adam and Eve had no proper names of their own before they met each other (see Gen. 3:20). The animals were altogether *other*; he was himself; but Eve was, in a way, himself and yet other — formed from him and for him by God, just as the Father and Son, though distinct, are not separated from each other, the One ever proceeding from the Other and turned toward Him, from and for Him. The unity of the Father and Son in the Love of the Holy Spirit is the source of our dialogue, communion, and fruitfulness.

For Adam and Eve, their awakening was an ecstasy, a going out of themselves in love; their state was not the monism of manipulative autonomy but the oneness of unashamed communion (see Gen. 2:21–25). This is the nuptial state to which husbands and wives are striving to return, just as the Church on earth is striving for it with her Bridegroom: "that they may be one, even as we are one" (John 17:22).

Consecrated life is eschatological: it is a sacramental sign and anticipated reality, here and now, of our future condition in heaven. Marriage, too, is eschatological, foreshadowing the ultimate rest of the Beatific Vision and the ultimate perfection of the Church in her embrace of Christ.

Just as the love "until the end" manifested in the Last Supper (cf. John 13:1) presupposed the Cross yet to come, so the fleshly union of husband and wife presupposes sacrifice through children yet to be received — later in time but already present in intention, present in eternity (cf. Eph. 1:4). From this we can see the perversity of the intentionally barren union. He who partakes of the flesh unworthily partakes of his own damnation (cf. 1 Cor. 11:29). The communicant must be willing to bear the Cross of Christ, for that is the meaning of the gift of which he partakes. Spouses, too, must be open to the crown and cross of children, for that is inherent in the gift they give to each other; the child is excluded or thwarted only by doing violence to the gift.

Would we receive Holy Communion as casually as some receive their partner into bed? There are those who do one or the other, or both. But neither of these should be done casually. When we come into contact with God, we are touching fire.[252] When we come into contact with another person, we are touching *God's* property, *God's* image, *God's* sacrament, and in this way, we are handling fire. It is no mere recreation for the sake of pleasure; it is a self-revelation and a self-emptying, the most intimate in its immediacy and the most cosmic in its implications. The Church does not "intrude" into this sphere (as her enemies say). Rather, she shows how this sphere extends to the depths and opens to the heights. Spousal friendship is the only vehicle great enough, stable enough, strong enough, to sustain the full impact of this communion, which is meant to increase the life of God within us.[253]

[252] See "Eating Fire and Spirit," in Kwasniewski, *Holy Bread of Eternal Life*, 5–11.

[253] One recent writer, drawing on Wendell Berry, contrasts what she calls "communitarian sexuality," by which spouses are connected "to one another, to forebearers,

The dwelling together of spouses is a sacramental domain. The Holy Spirit moves over the face of these waters and, according to His inscrutable mercies, takes away their formlessness, the reproach of their emptiness, even as bread and wine in the divine liturgy are transformed by the power of the same Spirit into the Flesh and Blood of Christ. The child is the gift that consecrates and completes the nuptial mystery, making it come alive in the astonishing wonder of new life.

---

to descendants, to the community, to Heaven and earth … the fundamental connection without which nothing holds, and [for which] trust is necessary," with "the cult of liberated sexuality," which, having no moorings in trust and stability, spins out of control and destroys itself, or more precisely, destroys the happiness of persons. See Kelli Buzzard, "Abortion's Bed of Lies," *Crisis Magazine*, May 24, 2022, https://www.crisismagazine.com/2022/abortions-bed-of-lies.

29

The Original Sin of Contraception and Its Remedy

Man was created in a relationship of love with God: this is what we call original justice and original innocence. This relationship was meant to be fruitful spiritually *and* physically: all true love, which is interior, rooted in the heart, bears fruit that magnifies and expresses that love in the world. All love is bound up with conception, the generation of new life of some kind that incarnates the love.

When Adam and Eve cut off their relationship to God, they performed (in a manner of speaking) the first act of contraception by refusing to be fertilized by the love and grace of God. They wanted to be the measure of how much love they would give and receive; they wanted to be "in charge" of the conceiving of their world, all by themselves. It's as though each had begun to think, in the depths of a heart already bent before any hand reached out to take hold of the fruit:

ADAM. God is always seeking to bear more fruit inside our souls; He is engendering His offspring in us. Should we not take control of this situation and decide when *we* want to have *His* children?

EVE. Why should He have this intrusive privilege, which makes us vulnerable to His seed, to His life-giving and commitment-demanding words?

ADAM. Indeed, He has demanded that we not eat of the tree of the knowledge of good and evil, as though we should sacrifice our autonomy and freedom to choose when and what we shall eat and should receive only what *He* wants to give us.

EVE. Let us take charge of our reproductive freedom and receive His seed when it is convenient for us, on our terms.

ADAM. Maybe we will *allow* a few offspring to be born in us, but only if it will not require too much interior sacrifice.

> EVE. In any case, we should start by eating of that forbidden fruit, since when we do, we will know all His secrets of good and evil, and then we can take care of ourselves — can freeze our knowledge and inseminate ourselves whenever we wish.

Perhaps the serpent, too, used this tactic: "If you go ahead and eat that fruit, you will be as *gods*, you will be able to conceive on your own terms." In saying this, he blasphemed the ecstatic generosity of the Most Holy Trinity, of whose eternal and infinite giving and receiving our entire universe is but the shadow and echo. When the couple ate of the fruit, they were suddenly ashamed of their nakedness, that is, the sudden deprivation of their spiritual fertility, the loss of the spiritual children God had given them and was going to give them.

The original sin of spiritual contraception is repeated in modern marriages when spouses want to decide what is sexually right and wrong, instead of obeying the divine law inscribed in their hearts, written into the very structure of their bodies (for the body itself is a revelation of God, a messenger of divine purpose), and stamped upon their souls. Yes, their *souls* — for we see that in all healthy societies throughout history, people love and delight in large families, and children themselves, as they grow up, long for this, and barrenness is felt as a bitter disappointment. Wherever nature has not been perverted by evil custom, propaganda, or public (mis)education, men's and women's souls impel them to the natural good of children and extended families. Folk songs, age-old prayers, poems all bear witness to this fundamental love of and delight in offspring.

As Pius XI taught with outstanding clarity in *Casti Connubii*, man and woman are *not* the ones who decide what wedded love is or how it ought to be used. God is the *sole* author of human nature, of natural marriage, and of marriage's interwoven purposes; no less is He the author of the sacramental dignity of marriage between Christians, in whom the momentous truths inscribed into our bodies and souls are supernaturally elevated and fecundated for eternity.

If each Christian can say, through Baptism, "I bear the marks of the Lord Jesus in my body" (Gal. 6:17), and if a new identity is given to the soul in the sacrament of Marriage — the identity of one spouse in relation to the other — then how reverently ought husband and wife to embrace one another! He who partakes unworthily partakes of his own damnation, not discerning the body of the Lord (cf. 1 Cor. 11:29), for your spouse is a member of His Body (1 Cor. 12:27), and sins against him or her are sins against Christ (cf. Matt. 25:45). In receiving the spouse unworthily, one receives Christ unworthily: whatsoever you do to the least of these, you do *unto me* (Matt. 25:40). One eats and drinks, i.e., uses and enjoys, damnation. *Corruptio optimi pessima:* the corruption of the best is the worst.

The contrary, however, is also true: since, according to St. Thomas, the right use of the nuptial act, like any act of charity, causes an increase of grace in the soul, and since Christ is the author of grace and the goal for which it is given — that is, the purpose of grace is to join us to Him — it therefore follows that by communing worthily with one's spouse, one is spiritually joined to Christ, to whom the beloved belongs as a member of His Body.[254]

Marriage is spiritually fertile and life-giving to the extent that it is consecrated to the one heavenly Spouse of the Church, who endows all things with being, life, and generative power. Thus, parents who conceive a child *not* for love of this Spouse but for some lesser end run the risk of viewing themselves as the cause and the end of generation, and their offspring as *their own product*, to be handled, disposed of, or brought up as they see fit. In imitation of Adam and Eve, they want to be the measure of the good and evil of their own destinies and of the life of their child, whereas "no one is good but God alone" (Luke 18:19). He alone is the measure of good and evil destiny; He alone the giver of life and its goal.

God is the creator, lawgiver, ruler, protector, perfecter, and ultimate end of all that belongs to the unitive and procreative aspects of marriage. Such are the great and beautiful truths by which Christian spouses live in fellowship, seeking, in their own little corner of the universe, the common good of one and all: first in their mutual gift of self, then in the family that arises from it, and outward from there, circle by circle, reflecting the integral, superabundant love of Christ for His Bride, the Church.

Offspring as a common good for the spouses

Several centuries before Christ, Aristotle had observed in his *Nicomachean Ethics*: "Children seem to be a bond of union. Hence sterile couples separate more readily, for children are a common good of both parties; and what is common maintains friendship." In the thirteenth century St. Thomas commented as follows on this passage:

> [Aristotle] indicates a means of making this friendship [of marriage] strong. He remarks that children seem to be a cause of a stable and

[254] For the relevant texts and commentary thereupon, see Kwasniewski, "St. Thomas on the Grandeur and Limitations of Marriage."

> lasting union. Hence, sterile couples who fail to have children are separated more readily. In fact, divorce was granted in former times because of sterility. And the reason for this is that children are a common good of both husband and wife whose union exists for the sake of children. But what is common continues and preserves friendship which also consists in sharing (*communicatio*), as has been pointed out.[255]

A moral philosopher who was well acquainted with both Aristotle and Aquinas, John Paul II, seemed to have just this thought in mind when he wrote in his *Letter to Families*:

> *In the newborn child is realized the common good of the family*. Just as the common good of spouses is fulfilled in conjugal love, ever ready to give and receive new life, so too the common good of the family is fulfilled through that same spousal love, as embodied in the newborn child.[256]

Even the Enlightenment philosopher Baruch Spinoza (1632–1677) — a hard-core modern who asserted that things in nature do not act for an end and that final causes are the products of our fantasy — could not deny in his *Ethics* that marriage is inherently bound up with children. It was as if the facts themselves compelled his assent:

> As concerning marriage, it is certain that this is in harmony with reason, if the desire for physical union be not engendered solely by bodily beauty, but also by the desire to beget children and to train them up wisely; and moreover, if the love of both, to wit, of the man and of the woman, is not caused by bodily beauty only, but also by freedom of soul.[257]

We are thus not completely unprepared for the rather sharp observation of Blaise Pascal (1623–1662) in his *Pensées* that children are so much the good of marriage that married people who avoid them selfishly are worse than child-seeking fornicators:

[255] St. Thomas, *Commentary on the* Nicomachean Ethics, trans. C. I. Litzinger (Chicago: Henry Regnery, 1964), bk. 8, lect. 12, no. 1724.

[256] John Paul II, *Gratissimam Sane* 11.

[257] See Benedict de [=Baruch] Spinoza, *Ethics*, pt. IV, Appendix, no. 20, in *On the Improvement of the Understanding; The Ethics; Correspondence*, trans. R. H. M. Elwes (New York: Dover Publications, 1955), 240.

> It is not the nuptial benediction [of the Church] which takes away the sin from procreation, but the desire to procreate children for God, which is only genuine in marriage.... The daughters of Lot, for example, who only wanted to have children, were purer without marriage than married people with no desire for children.[258]

What is the problem with such a lack of desire? What does it tell us? We could begin with the probing remarks of Gabriel Marcel, who detects the contradiction of contraception:

> The advocates of birth control claim more or less sincerely that it is out of pity for their possible descendants that they refuse to give them the chance of existence; but we cannot help noticing, all the same, that this pity which is bestowed at small cost, not upon living beings but upon an absence of being or nothingness, is found in conjunction with a suspiciously good opportunity for indulging the most cynical egoism, and can scarcely be separated from an impoverished philosophy which measures the value of life by the pleasures and conveniences it provides.[259]

What Marcel is pointing to is the inherent selfishness of wanting to "keep marriage just for the two of us." This is contrary to its very nature as a good thing, since good things are meant to be shared, spread out, multiplied, and perpetuated. If we do not want to multiply the loaves and fishes that God has given us a natural power to multiply, we are starving ourselves and others. If we do not seek a living image of our love, by which it can transcend itself and demand still more love, we are purposefully throwing up a barrier to the maturation of friendship, the increase of virtues, the growth of our humanity. In short, it is self-crippling, self-enclosing, self-imploding. It is all about me, a little about you inasmuch as you serve my perceived needs, and nothing about anyone else. No wonder Aristotle and Aquinas think such a relationship unstable and ready to break apart.

Granted, this description would apply in full only to those who are in the grip of an extreme anti-family mentality, of which, sadly, there seem to be an increasing number in the contemporary Western world. But it is the nadir, the limit case, of a trend of thinking and feeling that fails to see or refuses to see how spousal love is literally "embodied in the newborn child."

[258] Blaise Pascal, *Pensées*, trans. A.J. Krailsheimer (New York: Penguin, 1966), Lafuma fr. 713, p. 250.

[259] Marcel, *Homo Viator*, 90–91.

The wisdom of the Catholic Church is far different from the folly of the world. Her teaching inspires, challenges, and consoles, confirming our God-given intuitions. In a passage quoted earlier, Pope Pius XI voices this wisdom:

> God wishes men to be born not only that they should live and fill the earth, but much more that they may be worshippers of God, that they may know Him and love Him and finally enjoy Him for ever in heaven; and this end, since man is raised by God in a marvelous way to the supernatural order, surpasses all that eye hath seen, and ear heard, and all that hath entered into the heart of man. From which it is easily seen how great a gift of divine goodness and how remarkable a fruit of marriage are children born by the omnipotent power of God through the cooperation of those bound in wedlock.[260]

What a privileged way of sharing the greatest of goods — to baptize sons and daughters, bring them up in the fear and love of the Lord, and set them on their way to eternal life with Him and the whole company of the blessed — and to do so as a couple, as a family!

[260] *Casti Connubii* 12.

30

Why the Church's Peace and Unity Depend on *Humanae Vitae*

How often in conversations have we heard someone say he cannot see any meaningful difference between natural family planning and contraception? It is a problem one encounters even among Catholic traditionalists who maintain that *any* use of NFP is impermissible because it is contrary to the primary end of marriage. I will attempt here to explain the difference as clearly and simply as I know how to do.

The couple using NFP chooses *not* to engage in marital relations at a fertile time; the couple using contraception engages in them but tries to prevent a natural result from happening. In one case, there is a nonaction; in the other, an action. It is a difference as absolute as that between being and nonbeing.

From this ontological difference, there stems a moral difference. The NFP user intends to *avoid* a pregnancy, while the contraceptive user intends to *prevent* a pregnancy. The one, presumably for good reasons, respects a rhythm inherent in nature itself; the other, let us even presume for equally good reasons, uses technology to interfere with the order of nature. NFP is founded on an attitude of humility in the face of the mystery of fertility, whereby human beings cooperate with God in the creation of an immortal being destined for heaven. This is why NFP users are fundamentally pro-life: respecting the order inscribed in their bodies and acknowledging God as the sole Lord of life, they are ready to welcome any children He will send, even at a time when they may have wished to avoid conception.

Contraception, in sharp contrast, is the result of a Baconian-Cartesian "mastery of nature" mentality that puts man in God's place. It makes man the one who determines the meaning, function, and goal of the sexual act: if he wants it to be for him and his partner *only*, excluding the child, he will find a way to carry out his intention. But in so doing, man is no longer pro-life, pro-human, and pro-divine; God Himself, the human nature He created, and the life He fashions in the womb all stand contrary to that contraceptive intention.

Finally, NFP *can* be abused if the mentality behind it happens to be anti-life, but it *need* not be so abused. Contraception, on the other hand, is an abuse in and of itself, since it treats fertility as a problem to be overcome or thwarted. And this is objectively offensive to the Creator of human nature. In short: the use of NFP can be rendered evil by a bad intention, but the use of contraception is evil in and of itself.

In spite of its derivation from the law of human nature and its confirmation in the divine law consistently handed down by the Catholic Church for two thousand years,[261] the message of Pope Paul VI's *Humanae Vitae* has struggled for a hearing from the day it appeared in print to the present. A combination of outright dissent and cowardly inaction has silenced its truth. As Fr. Hardon points out, contraception is "fatal to the Faith" and "fatal to salvation":

> The practice of contraception is a grave sin. Those who indulge in the practice are in danger of losing their immortal souls.... Christianity has always held, holds now, and always will hold, that contraception is a serious offense against God. Unless repented, it is punishable by eternal deprivation of the vision of God, which we call eternal death.[262]

Commenting on this passage, John Galvin writes: "It is intolerable that the Church should stand by passively as the vast majority of its members — amounting to hundreds of millions of souls — conduct lives that must lead to eternal perdition."[263]

[261] Pope Pius XII made this absolutely clear in his Address to Midwives of October 1951: "Our Predecessor, Pius XI, of happy memory, in his Encyclical *Casti Connubii*, of December 31, 1930, once again solemnly proclaimed the fundamental law of the conjugal act and conjugal relations: that every attempt of either husband or wife in the performance of the conjugal act or in the development of its natural consequences which aims at depriving it of its inherent force and hinders the procreation of new life is immoral; and that no 'indication' or need can convert an act which is intrinsically immoral into a moral and lawful one. This precept is in full force today, as it was in the past, and so it will be in the future also, and always, because it is not a simple human whim, but the expression of a natural and divine law."

[262] John Hardon, "Contraception: Fatal to the Faith and to Eternal Life," *Real Presence Association*, www.therealpresence.org/archives/Chastity/Chastity_004.htm.

[263] John Galvin, "*Humanae Vitae*: Heroic, Deficient, or Both?," *Latin Mass Magazine* 11, no. 1 (Winter 2002): 6–24; www.latinmassmagazine.com/pdfs/

Can anyone deny that this, all by itself, demonstrates the massive apostasy of all too many shepherds of the Church since 1968, their refusal to shoulder the responsibility of their office to "preach the truth in season, out of season" (2 Tim. 4:2), their abandonment of the sheep to the savage wolves of modern egoism and hedonism? This situation has always been intolerable, it is still intolerable, and it always will be intolerable. It is the root cause of much of the crisis in marriage and family.

Today we face a worsening situation: in addition to the usual widespread refusal to teach the truth, there is a new siege on *Humanae Vitae* by moral theologians emboldened by the "new paradigm" attributed to *Amoris Laetitia* and other acts of the Bergoglian pontificate, whereby the perennial moral teaching to which *Veritatis Splendor* bears witness is being dismantled, plank by plank.[264]

At one point in *Humanae Vitae*, Paul VI makes the prescient remark: "If men's peace of soul and the unity of the Christian people are to be preserved, then it is of the utmost importance that in moral as well as in dogmatic theology all should obey the magisterium of the Church and should speak as with one voice" (no. 28). John Paul II returns to this point repeatedly:

> In their effort to live their conjugal love correctly, married couples can be seriously impeded by a certain hedonistic mentality widespread today, by the mass media and by ideologies and practices contrary to the Gospel. This can also come about, with truly grave and destructive consequences, when the doctrine taught by the Encyclical [*Humanae Vitae*] is called into question, as has sometimes happened, even on the part of some theologians and pastors of souls. This attitude, in fact, can instill doubt with regard to a teaching which for the Church is certain; in this

Humane-Vitae-TLM-2002-Winter.pdf. The pages referred to include Janet Smith's and Ronald McArthur's responses. I do not necessarily endorse Galvin's critique of the inadequacies of Paul VI (Galvin maintains that this pope's doctrine is not sufficiently traditional and therefore maims the pro-life cause), but I think his case deserves serious attention.

264 See Michael Haynes, "Pontifical Academy for Life Defends New Book Supporting Contraception: 'What Is Dissent Today, Can Change,'" *LifeSiteNews*, July 11, 2022, www.lifesitenews.com/news/pontifical-academy-for-life-defends-new-book-supporting-contraception-what-is-dissent-today-can-change; cf. Diane Montagna, "New Academy for Life Member Uses *Amoris* to Say Some Circumstances 'Require' Contraception," *LifeSiteNews*, January 8, 2018, www.lifesitenews.com/news/new-academy-for-life-member-uses-amoris-to-say-some-circumstances-require-c.

> way it clouds the perception of a truth which cannot be questioned. This is not a sign of "pastoral understanding," but of misunderstanding the true good of persons. Truth cannot be measured by majority opinion.[265]

Again:

> By describing the contraceptive act as intrinsically illicit, Paul VI meant to teach that the moral norm is such that it does not admit exceptions. No person or social circumstances could ever, can now, or will ever, render such an act lawful in itself. The existence of particular norms regarding man's way of acting in the world, which are endowed with a binding force that excludes always and in whatever situation the possibility of exceptions, is a constant teaching of the Tradition and of the Church's Magisterium which cannot be called in question by the Catholic theologian.[266]

If the unanimous, uninterrupted, unequivocal, exceptionless Magisterium of the Church on the intrinsic evil of contraception is not obeyed, *peace of soul cannot be preserved, any more than the unity of the Church*. Those who are leading souls away from this Magisterium, which is founded in the "objective moral order" (*Humanae Vitae* 10) — whoever they may be, whatever uniform they may wear on the outside — are producing the bad fruits of warfare, unrest, confusion, anxiety, that tremendous lack of interior and exterior peace that characterizes all who flee from the divine law or dare to assault it. "By their fruits ye shall know them," said Our Lord (Matt. 7:16).

[265] Discorso di Giovanni Paolo II ai partecipanti al IV Congresso Internazionale per la Famiglia d'Africa e d'Europa, March 14, 1988, www.vatican.va/content/john-paul-ii/it/speeches/1988/march/documents/hf_jp-ii_spe_19880314_famiglia-africa-europa.html. Elsewhere he writes: "The Church's teaching on contraception does not belong to the category of matter open to free discussion among theologians. Teaching the contrary amounts to leading the moral consciences of spouses into error" (Discorso di Giovanni Paolo II ai partecipanti ad un incontro di studio sulla procreazione responsabile, June 5, 1987, www.vatican.va/content/john-paul-ii/it/speeches/1987/june/documents/hf_jp-ii_spe_19870605_procreazione-responsabile.html). These two texts and the one following were translated from the Italian by John F. Kippley.

[266] Discorso di Giovanni Paolo II ai partecipanti al II Congresso Internazionale di Teologia Morale, November 12, 1988, www.vatican.va/content/john-paul-ii/it/speeches/1988/november/documents/hf_jp-ii_spe_19881112_teologia-morale.html.

The Holy Spirit inspires joyful obedience to *each and every* moral truth traditionally taught by the Catholic Church. By following the way of sacrificial love, Christians produce good fruits in abundance for the glory of God. The Holy Spirit also inspires implacable hatred for sin, the devil, and heresy. To these, a Christian's heart can offer no hospitality.

Discussions of natural family planning often rapidly turn into a tug-of-war between strong proponents and strong opponents. On the one side, there are those who defend NFP as morally upright, as a healthy practice from which couples positively *benefit*. On the other side, there are those who think NFP is a subtle form of contraception from which couples *suffer loss*, since they would always do better to "trust in God's Providence alone."

As with the so-called theology of the body, discussed earlier,[267] here, too, I find myself in sympathy with both sides — not because I agree simply with either but because each is raising a relevant point while arguably failing to integrate the truth they see into a larger picture.

Without beating around the bush, let us admit, first of all, that selfishness or false priorities can lead to an abusive reliance on NFP, when it is chosen as a more natural way to avoid children. Godless hippies could do this because it's environmentally sound and healthier for human bodies.

Nevertheless, NFP, even when chosen for selfish reasons, cannot be (or be called) contraceptive in an unqualified sense. In its moral species, contraception is intrinsically or *per se* immoral because it directly and categorically opposes one of the defining goods of marriage. NFP is more ambivalent and ambiguous: by consulting natural rhythms, the couple is not *doing* anything to the natural act to thwart its procreative end. To have intercourse during infertile periods is in no way an act of violence or obstruction against the generative powers of the human person, since these powers themselves, by divine design, are sometimes capable of leading to conception and sometimes not. Neither the act (or rather, non-act) of abstaining during fertile times nor the act of coming together during infertile times violates the procreative *nature* of the sexual act as intended by the Creator, whereas the use of contraception obviously does, as its very name indicates: *contra*-[con]ception. For that reason, contraception, by interfering with a natural process, is inherently *against* nature, whereas NFP is *in accord with* the order of creation, since periods of fertility and infertility are natural rhythms of the woman's body.

[267] See chapter 10.

That being said, "naturalness" is not the only relevant aspect to consider; it establishes the context but does not complete the analysis of the free human act. One must ask the properly *moral* question: Is this (admittedly natural) approach to regulating procreation being used for a *good* reason or for a *bad* reason? When used in circumstances that are not serious in comparison with the primary end of the great vocation of marriage in the Church, namely, the begetting and educating of children, NFP is being abused.

Let me offer some concrete examples. Sometimes a newly married Catholic couple will say they want to "enjoy each other's company" or "get used to being married" before they "shoulder the burden of children." Sometimes spouses want to postpone children so both can pursue graduate degrees simultaneously. Sometimes the virtue of "prudence" is tied to assumptions of an upper-middle-class American lifestyle — e.g., an annual expensive vacation, the ability to pay in full for college tuition, or maintaining the mother's career outside the home.

Such intentions do not seem honorable when weighed against the serious obligations of the state of life into which the spouses have solemnly entered. The doctorate-seeking couple, for instance, might be better off postponing or forgoing marriage if their scholarly work is believed to be of such importance that they feel it could not be interrupted, or, in some cases, canceled out, by a sacrament whose fruitfulness in imitation of the fruitful love of Christ and the Church would become the *primary form of their sanctification*, their *primary calling in life*. It could almost be called a sacrilege to set the chief good of marriage at a level below that of personal ambitions and private goods, however legitimate these may be at the right time and place.

As Donald Asci explains in his unsurpassed treatment, NFP involves a *moral* imperfection, that is, a sin, when there is *an anti-life will* — in other words, if the conception of a child is actually nilled, or willed against.[268] A rough and ready way to see if an anti-life will is present is to formulate this question: Were a couple to conceive a child "by accident" or "unexpectedly" (from their vantage), would they welcome their child with joy as a gift from God? If they can honestly answer *yes*, then even the avoidance of conception via NFP is not the expression of an anti-life will. If they would answer no, or feel uncertain of the answer, we are most likely dealing with a contraceptive intention.

[268] See Donald P. Asci, *The Conjugal Act as a Personal Act: A Study of the Catholic Concept of the Conjugal Act in the Light of Christian Anthropology* (San Francisco: Ignatius Press, 2002).

Yes, these questions have a subjective dimension, and given the nature of things, they *have* to have a subjective dimension to them. God deals with human beings as individuals, as personal subjects. He does not care too much when Rover dies, as long as dogs remain (see 1 Cor. 9:9). But God cares very much when Peter, James, John, Mary, Martha, or Lydia dies. The only ever-valid, universally binding law — the one altogether *objective* law — is the law of charity, which confronts the subjectivity of each person with a question that *only that person* can answer. Unlike modern governments, the Lord does not view people as numbered taxpayers or draftable soldiers. He views each one with a father's love, and He asks of each what each is ready and able to give for the common good of the Church and the world. Assuming that spouses are abiding by the teaching of *Humanae Vitae,* there is one and only one law by which they are judged, and that is the law of charity, which is addressed to the heart of each person. There can be no compromise or evasion when it comes to the demands of this law, which includes the unreserved gift of self in marriage.

Should a couple have as many children as the Lord sends them, without a thought for when they come? Would they be prudent to postpone the next child because the father is unemployed or the mother is physically weak or psychologically overwhelmed at a given juncture in life? Or might they delay the next child by remaining continent instead of using NFP; or take up a longer period of continence in order to devote more time to prayer, study, teaching, hospitality, or some other ministry for which a desire has been planted within them by the Lord?[269] In regard to any particular choice to make or path to follow, there is and can be only one criterion of discernment and judgment: Does this choice or this path — thinking about it, choosing it, living it — have the effect of increasing my charity for God and for my spouse and my family, bringing me closer to them and making me more responsive to their needs and rights? Does it make of me a more prayerful and a more loving person?

This is a question that has to be asked constantly by *all* Christians; it is the ultimate examination of conscience.

[269] Regarding this point, the history of the Church has offered numerous examples of saintly couples who have lived their married life in continency. I know couples for whom such a life has proved immensely fruitful in spiritual goods. Most modern Catholic writers on marriage dismiss this kind of married life as a regrettable holdover from Manichaeism, when, in fact, it is a legitimate way of life *if* the Lord is calling the spouses to it. To assert that married couples *must* continue their procreative uniting is an arbitrary assertion that fails to take into account the mysterious working of the Holy Spirit in the sanctuaries of His temples. See chapter 26.

31

Abortion's War against Reality, Reason, and Rights

"Out of sight, out of mind." This simple saying accounts for much in the battle over the unborn. As long as people can make themselves *not think about* the tiny baby human they do not see, they can pretend he or she doesn't exist — or pretend the child is "something" vague, indefinite, blobbish, not yet human. This explains, to a large extent, the opposition to laws that require an ultrasound image for women considering abortion. The proponents of abortion do not want them to *see*.

In one of his most profound works, *The Mystery of Being*, Gabriel Marcel draws the reader's attention to "the mysterious character that attaches to the presence near one of a sleeping person, especially of a sleeping child." He goes on to say:

> From the point of view of physical activity, or at least in so far as the notion of physical activity is defined in relation to the possible grasping of things, the sleeping child is completely unprotected and appears to be utterly *in our power*; from that point of view, it is permissible for us to do what we like with the child. But from the point of view of mystery, we might say that it is just because this being is completely unprotected, that it is utterly at our mercy, that it is also invulnerable or sacred. And there can be no doubt at all that the strongest and most irrefutable mark of sheer barbarism that we could imagine would consist in the refusal to recognize this mysterious invulnerability.[270]

[270] Gabriel Marcel, *The Mystery of Being*, vol. 1: *Reflection & Mystery*, trans. G. S. Fraser (Chicago: Henry Regnery, 1960), 266. Plato makes a similar point in the *Laws* VI (777d–e), where he has the Stranger remark: "Proper treatment of servants consists in using no violence towards them, and in hurting them even less, if possible, than our own equals. For it is his way of dealing with men whom

David Hume (1711–1776), a skeptical agnostic whose philosophy is opposed in almost every respect to Marcel's, nevertheless makes a similar point in *A Treatise of Human Nature*:

> 'Tis an aggravation of murder, that it was committed upon persons asleep and in perfect security; as historians readily observe of any infant prince, who is captive in the hands of his enemies, that he is more worthy of compassion the less sensible he is of his miserable condition.[271]

This is — or should be — evident to all. Hume's predecessor John Locke (1632–1704), a founding father of modern liberalism who defends an almost absolute right over one's own property and one's own body, nevertheless stresses that parents have no power over the lives of their offspring, for whose well-being they are accountable.[272]

---

it is easy for him to wrong that shows most clearly whether a man is genuine or hypocritical in his reverence for justice and hatred of injustice. He, therefore, that in dealing with slaves proves himself, in his character and action, undefiled by what is unholy or unjust will best be able to sow a crop of goodness — and this we may say, and justly say, of every master, or king, and of everyone who possesses any kind of absolute power over a person weaker than himself." Cited in Stephen R. L. Clark, *Cities and Thrones and Powers: Towards a Plotinian Politics* (Brooklyn: Angelico Press, 2022), 135.

271 David Hume, *A Treatise of Human Nature*, ed. David Fate Norton and Mary J. Norton (Oxford: Oxford University Press, 2000), 239.

272 John Locke, *Second Treatise of Civil Government*, ed. C. B. Macpherson (Indianapolis: Hackett Publishing, 1980). Locke emphasizes that, so far from parents having a power or right of disposal over the lives of their children, they are rather bound to care for them and are accountable for their good: "From him [Adam] the world is peopled with his descendants, who are all born infants, weak and helpless, without knowledge or understanding: but to supply the defects of this imperfect state, till the improvement of growth and age hath removed them, Adam and Eve, and after them all parents were, by the law of nature, under an obligation to preserve, nourish, and educate the children they had begotten; not as their own workmanship, but the workmanship of their own maker, the Almighty, to whom they were to be accountable for them" (sect. 56); "The power, then, that parents have over their children, arises from that duty which is incumbent on them, to take care of their offspring, during the imperfect state of childhood. To inform the mind, and govern the actions of their yet ignorant nonage, till reason shall take its place, and ease them of that trouble, is what the children want, and the parents are bound to" (sect. 58); "The nourishment and education of their children is a charge so incumbent on parents for their

Skepticism and sophistry

Yet the gradual degeneration of thought that has resulted in the almost universal acceptance of abortion, in which a child asleep in the womb is brutally murdered, is at least in part Hume's fault. Hume was the first modern thinker to say that *causality* is a fabrication of the mind, a mere custom of thinking. That is, we can never *know for sure* whether one thing (say, a flame on the stovetop) is responsible for another (heating up the pot of water); it's all a matter of the way we *look at* things. We can't even know if a thing that appears to be the same — a dog or a cat, for instance — *remains* the same as itself over the passage of time; it might be different every day, as when the ancient philosopher Heraclitus said that the sun was new each day, extinguished at night and newly born at dawn.

Whether they realize it or not, many people today have in the matter of abortion adopted Hume's skepticism, although they would reject it in almost every other case of practical life. Just as we know that a man of eighty is essentially the same human being he was when eight years old, in spite of the changes that have taken place over the course of seventy-two years — a fact we acknowledge by calling him by the same name the whole time — so, too, we know that an embryo or fetus *is* an unborn child or baby, which *is* a human being endowed with a face, a heart, hands and feet, already named or ready to be given a name.[273] "Embryo," "unborn child," "adolescent," "youth," and "man" or "woman" are words that refer to different stages of the *same developing reality*; they refer to *one thing*, an enduring individual identity.

In spite of this commonsense view, people talk and act as if a fertilized egg had nothing to do with a child or a human being, although it would be difficult to think of a more obvious fact of nature.[274] I read a newspaper article about a couple who had frozen a fertilized embryo many years ago and decided to thaw it out and "have a second child" rather than "destroy the embryo." In one and the same sentence, we read: the couple decided to "*have* a second *child*" rather than "*destroy* the *embryo*." But if an embryo is not a human being, where would that "second child" have arisen from? Could a couple choose to have a second

---

children's good, that nothing can absolve them from taking care of it" (sect. 67); and so forth.

[273] Philosophically, it does not matter how well developed the child is. See my article "Hominization, or Man at the Moment of Conception," *OnePeterFive*, May 13, 2020, https://onepeterfive.com/hominization-conception.

[274] And thanks to technology, it doesn't even have to be left to the imagination: to see an unborn child through the ultrasonic window on the womb is to *see* him or her as a little child resting peacefully within his or her mother.

child if there was no *child* to be had? There is nothing in the child that was not already present in some way in the embryo.

Not only have modern embryology and genetics done nothing to shake a truth so evident to all; they support it a thousandfold. That is what the eminent geneticist Jérôme Lejeune bore witness to in courts all over the world: modern science shows unequivocally that there is no fundamental biological discontinuity in the entire process from fertilized ovum to born child. If one invents a right to kill the former, one logically must invent a right to kill the latter. There are now university professors who are coldly "rational" enough to draw the conclusion: since we have legalized abortion, we ought to legalize the killing of small children when they are severely disabled or perhaps simply unwanted. If one can kill the latter, there is no end to what life-extinguishing policies governments may approve, as we already see in the spread of euthanasia. Dr. Lejeune saw that you must either defend human life consistently from beginning to end — conception to natural death — on the grounds that innocent human beings have a dignity and rights that no one may violate, *or* you have to maintain that limits on any killing are purely arbitrary and can be changed at will by legislative fiat.[275] In a world that prides itself on the fragile construct of a "social contract" in which we all belong to the state in exchange for protection of our basic rights, this amounts to selling all your goods in order to purchase a field of quicksand and then walking into it.

Language games

Let us go back for a moment to the newspaper article that not so cleverly combined in one sentence the phrases "have a second child" and "destroy the embryo." Imagine a parallel construction. If someone were to say: "I decided to take care of my grandmother, instead of injecting that bag of bones with lethal drugs," we would think that person, just to *have* such a thought, was heartless, insane, or criminal — for it is abundantly clear that the insulting phrase refers to the grandmother, and the intention to inject lethal drugs is murder.

But if a woman should say: "I have decided to have the fetus dismembered by a knife or destroyed by acid, instead of going ahead with my pregnancy and giving birth to a baby boy," the media, the government, and a good portion of society would remain calmly aloof or perhaps even burst into applause. "That's each woman's decision."

[275] For a current example of how legislators try to push the envelope, see Calvin Freiburger, "California Bill That Could Legalize Infanticide Advances Again," *LifeSiteNews*, April 27, 2022, www.lifesitenews.com/news/california-committee-votes-to-advance-bill-that-could-legalize-infanticide.

What strange tricks of thought, what bizarre self-deceptions are practiced in the modern world! As long as language and experience mean *anything*, we *know* what a pregnant woman is: a woman "with child," a woman whose body is now fully geared toward nourishing and protecting that unborn child until the child is viable outside of the womb. Yet language itself has been twisted and distorted past recognition. Pregnancy is now considered a "medical condition" or, according to some radical feminists, a disease or an act of foreign aggression.[276] It is hard to believe that people could be so alienated from nature, so far removed from the simple facts of biology, that they would be able to overlook the obvious structure, the procreational design, of the male and female bodies. The female body is *structured* to conceive and bear children, and any healthy woman would rejoice in this fact, recognizing the indescribable dignity it confers upon her as a "mother of the living."[277]

It is hard to imagine a woman being ignorant about the meaning of pregnancy — namely, that she is now *with child*, as the rich old saying has it. How many births are spoken of every day! How many barren couples long for children to adopt! How many mothers do people know — beginning with their own! Yet a constant stream of propaganda has projected a pitch-black shadow of ignorance into millions of minds. If a woman believes a seemingly reasonable doctor who tells her that abortion is a simple procedure to remove an unwanted blob of tissue in the same way a cosmetic surgeon removes a mole on the skin, who can say how vast a cloud of darkness this poor woman's mind has fallen under? She has been led astray by the individual in whom primitive societies always place their unquestioning confidence: the medicine man, the shaman, the

[276] In *Evangelium Vitae* 58, John Paul II alludes to the view that abortion is a form of "self-defense" against a fetus-intruder and rejects it as absurd: "The moral gravity of procured abortion is apparent in all its truth if we recognize that we are dealing with murder and, in particular, when we consider the specific elements involved. The one eliminated is a human being at the very beginning of life. No one more absolutely innocent could be imagined. In no way could this human being ever be considered an aggressor, much less an unjust aggressor! He or she is weak, defenceless, even to the point of lacking that minimal form of defence consisting in the poignant power of a newborn baby's cries and tears. The unborn child is totally entrusted to the protection and care of the woman carrying him or her in the womb."

[277] See Regis Martin, "Overcoming Hardness of Hearts on Abortion," *Crisis Magazine*, May 17, 2022, www.crisismagazine.com/2022/overcoming-hardness-of-hearts-on-abortion.

witch doctor. In her state of emotional uncertainty and turmoil, she is an easy victim for reassuring lies. The doctor — or nurse, or clinic adviser, or guidance counselor — has taken advantage of her vulnerability.

On a small British isle, there was a 1910 law defining abortion as homicide and stipulating life imprisonment as punishment. The law was rescinded late in the twentieth century, and now abortion is legal there up to twenty-four weeks. This incident, typical of too many others, deserves to be savored by everyone with a capacity for logic. How can something that was once held to be an act of homicide, punishable by life imprisonment, suddenly be owed to people as their legal right? Can one and the same act be murder and a health decision? And would it not be foolish for someone to say, as if to explain the reason for the change: "Today, we know *more* about the fetus than was known in 1910"?

Indeed, what we *now* know is how fully developed a child it is at a very early stage, with all his limbs in place, sleeping, moving around, sucking his thumb, dreaming, possessed of sensation, capable of feeling pain, influenced by moods and music. We also know more about genetics and the development of the embryo from the zygote, and the fetus from the embryo. That which defines human life at the material level is wholly present in the fertilized ovum; the full pattern of the human body coming to be is already there from the first moment. The remaining nine months are the unfolding of a preexistent plan. *Everything* that takes place after conception is a gradual organic development or unfolding, with no obvious breaking point. Puberty is in some ways a more radical developmental change than the almost imperceptible stages of embryonic growth.

If one makes "viability" the criterion, one is openly admitting the relativity — and willfulness — of one's position. Viability is largely a matter of what our technology can accomplish, and abortions are regularly performed long after the current threshold of viability. Thus, babies are routinely killed in spite of the fact that they could have survived outside the mother *and* that the killing of a baby of the same age which *had* been prematurely born would be prosecuted as murder.

Doesn't everyone know that a pregnant woman is "a woman with child"? Where does that chubby little boy or girl come from? Is it carried in by a stork on the day of delivery? What about each one of us: after a certain age, are we not aware of our own origins? Does a person in the twenty-first century know *more* about the basic *fact* of pregnancy, namely, that a woman is carrying a child, than a person on an island in 1910 knew — or for that matter, someone living in the Middle Ages or the Roman Empire or the Egypt of the Pharaohs?

Of course not. Everyone knows that when a woman becomes pregnant, she is carrying new life, a new human life, a child soon to be born. In the bigger picture, nine months is not a very long time. If gestation lasted nine *years*, it might be harder to make the connection between sexual intercourse, conception, and the birth of a child. In reality, everyone knows all about this, without the need for any books or experts. That so many have forgotten — or rather, choose to avert their gaze from — the truth that nature and experience unerringly teach is a sign of the dangerous unworld of unreality into which souls have drifted.

O Lord, awaken us Thy creatures before it is too late, lest we sleep through the one life Thou hast given us in which to know and love Thee! Help us to awaken our fellow men and to remain vigilant ourselves!

The trend toward dehumanization

The bond of mother and child has been mocked before. Thomas Hobbes (1588–1679), a materialist philosopher (if that is not a contradiction in terms), had this to say about mothers and infants existing in his fanciful state of nature:

> For in the condition of meer Nature, . . . the right of Dominion over the Child dependeth on her will, and is consequently hers. Again, seeing the Infant is first in the power of the Mother, so as she may either nourish, or expose it [to death], if she nourish it, it oweth its life to the Mother; and is therefore obliged to obey her, rather than any other, and by consequence the Dominion over it is hers.[278]

One cannot fail to see the parallel with modern pro-abortion arguments. Yet Hobbes maintains this position only for his hypothetical state of nature or state of war. In civil society, exposure of infants would never be allowed by the sovereign power (so he thinks). As we have seen, John Locke, Hobbes's more subtle follower, argues in his *Second Treatise* that parents have no power or right over the life and death of their children. For Locke, procreation is the "chief end" of marriage, and parents are accountable for their children. Even "Mr. Property," who defends an almost absolute right over one's property and one's body, can see that marriage is ordered to children!

There are *always* hardships involved in having children — indeed, more in the past than now, in spite of efforts by glossy magazines to convince people that they cannot possibly afford the price-tag of a human person. This makes the fundamental change in attitude or habit of thinking all the more ominous. It is the ebbtide of *Lebenslust,* love for life.

[278] Thomas Hobbes, *Leviathan,* ed. C. B. Macpherson (New York: Penguin, 1986), pt. II, chap. 20, p. 254.

What is the root of this fundamental change in attitude? It has a deep and complex root system, but surely, an important contributor is materialism, the philosophical driving force behind the abortion mentality. As applied to human beings, materialism amounts to a denial of the *human soul*, the form or actuality of the body that causes it to be alive and to serve as the instrument of the soul's many powers. For the materialist, there is nothing in a man other than physical springs and cogs. To commit suicide is to relegate oneself to the scrapheap. To commit euthanasia is to release a worn-out machine from its poor functioning condition. To kill a developing child is to remove some unwanted parts from a machine.[279]

How (one might object to a materialist) can a being that is organically growing toward some perfection be understood as a machine, when no machine in the world ever does anything of the sort? A child is *alive*, full of desire to grow, to mature. Abortion violently interferes with the most natural human process, the growth of a child from a fertilized cell to a baby and onward to adulthood.

This materialism that reduces the individual to his matter is akin to the collectivism that reduces the body politic to masses ready for manipulation. In his brilliant Gifford Lectures, Marcel observes:

> What is immediately obvious is that whenever circumstances prevailing here and now lead to men being not only regarded as masses but actually treated as such — treated, that is, as aggregates, whose elements are transferable according to the demands of temporal vicissitudes — it becomes more and more difficult to keep in mind the inalienable characteristics of uniqueness and dignity which have hitherto been considered as attributes of the human soul created in the image of God. To say that these characteristics are becoming more and more lost to view is not enough; they are being, if one may so put it, actively denied, they are being trodden upon. Man may end by imagining that he can prove by his very behavior that he is not such a being as the theologians have defined.
>
> If we look at the question carefully we shall see, also, that we have here a real vicious circle. The less men are thought of as beings [with

[279] Penetrating critiques of materialism are plentiful. For a succinct treatment, see James Matthew Wilson, *The Vision of the Soul: Truth, Goodness, and Beauty in the Western Tradition* (Washington, DC: Catholic University of America Press, 2017), 49–55 and 139–44, and for a more thorough refutation, see Gerard M. Verschuuren, *At the Dawn of Humanity: The First Humans* (Brooklyn: Angelico Press, 2020), 157–81.

> innate worth],... the stronger will be the temptation to use them as machines which are capable of a given output; this output being the only justification for their existence, they will end by having no other reality. There lies a road which runs straight to the forced labour camp and the cremation oven.[280]

In the same lectures, Marcel talks about the effort to create (or at least envision) a *soulless* world and modern man's tendency toward "de-creation." People have bought into the illusion that man is all exteriority and no interiority:

> In a world in which the arid influence of technique seems to prepare the radical disappearance of intersubjective relations, death would no longer be a mystery, it would become a raw fact like the dislocation of some piece of mechanism. In fact, however, this world deserted by love is not our world, it is not yet our world; and it depends on us whether it will ever be so, even though we may see the daily increase in strength of conscious and malignant forces — malignant because conscious — which seem to have set as their goal the creation of this soulless world. I may add, though it is in any case self-evident, that to the eye of any faith worthy of the name, this soulless world can appear only as the wholly sacrilegious experiment of a will for de-creation.[281]

In a similar way, Charles De Koninck spoke of the "lifeless world of biology." The suppositions and framework of the modern science of biology, which are thoroughly materialistic, paved the way for human reductionism.

Materialism and cruelty

Why was it such a big deal when "the Bloody 14" Catholic Senators voted *against* a ban on abortions performed after twenty weeks of gestation?[282] Why was

[280] Gabriel Marcel, *The Mystery of Being*, vol. 2: *Faith & Reality*, trans. René Hague (Chicago: Henry Regnery, 1960), 165.

[281] *Mystery of Being*, 2:169–70.

[282] See Ed Peters, "The Bloody 14 and the Question of Excommunication," *Catholic World Report*, January 31, 2018, https://www.catholicworldreport.com/2018/01/31/the-bloody-14-and-the-question-of-excommunication/; Lisa Bourne, "Priest Calls for Excommunication of 14 Catholic Senators Who Voted against Late-Term Abortion Ban," *LifeSiteNews*, February 5, 2018, https://www.lifesitenews.com/news/priest-calls-for-excommunication-of-14-catholic-senators-who-voted-against/.

Bishop Thomas Paprocki acting justly when he chastised one of them (Senator Durbin), stating publicly that until he repents of this crime, he may not receive Our Lord in Holy Communion?[283] Why are bishops who do nothing to confront recurring scandals — such as Georgetown University's cynical celebration of Durbin — personally guilty of complicity in grave sin?[284]

All of the inhumanity for which the twentieth century has gone down in history as the blackest of centuries is concentrated in each act whereby a developing child, quietly curled up within his mother's womb, awaiting delivery into the human world, is sliced apart or dissolved by poison. The dark spirits behind Hitler, Stalin, Pol Pot, Mao, and every other dictator who consigned the innocent to death are busily at work in the hands of the abortionist. And behind their hands are the devil and his angels, who are eager to snuff out the natural and supernatural lives of as many of God's rational creatures as they can.

Let us not be lulled into thinking that the evil carried out by Hitler and the Nazis is a thing of the past, "never again" to be repeated, as the naïve slogans say. The abortion industry has far exceeded in its toll of murders anything that Hitler or Stalin could have dreamed of. As Thomas J. Craughwell wrote:

> The Nazis' first victims were the weakest members of society: disabled children. Officially, they were known as "life unworthy of life"; a cruder term was *Ausschusskinder*, "garbage children." Physicians administered overdoses of sedatives which "put them to sleep," as one physician who participated in the euthanasia of children put it.[285]

[283] See "Statement from Bishop Thomas John Paprocki on Senate Failure to Pass Pain-Capable Unborn Children's Act," February 13, 2018, *Catholic Citizens of Illinois*, https://catholiccitizens.org/news/77774/statement-bishop-thomas-john-paprocki-senate-failure-pass-pain-capable-unborn-childrens-act/.

[284] See Claire Chretien, "Georgetown Honors Pro-Abortion Senator Whose Bishop Just Barred Him from Communion," *LifeSiteNews*, February 28, 2018, https://www.lifesitenews.com/news/georgetown-honors-pro-abortion-senator-whose-bishop-just-barred-him-from-co/.

[285] Thomas J. Craughwell, "The Gentile Holocaust," in *Sursum Corda!* (Summer 1998), 28; available online at *Catholic Culture*, https://www.catholicculture.org/culture/library/view.cfm?recnum=472. To this day, the remains of aborted children are denied burial or cremation and thrown out in plastic bags with "medical waste." See Catherine Glenn Foster, "How Abortionists Dispose of Their Victims," *First Things*, July 18, 2022, www.firstthings.com/web-exclusives/2022/07/how-abortionists-dispose-of-their-victims.

The human world becomes inhuman when it denies being, nourishment, and welcome to an innocent man or woman. Such an act turns man into an ugly inversion of "the Lord and Giver of life." Through it, man becomes a cruel and arbitrary dictator, exceeding the worst arrogance and megalomania that could ever be attributed to religious fanatics or political dictators.

How *dare* we deny to the unborn the right to live, as we ourselves live? To think that one may take another's life into one's power and do with it as one pleases is the root of tyranny.[286] When false arguments are swept away, only one thing remains: the violent exercise of brute force upon unprotected life, violence countenanced by law — by a law that is no law but an abuse, parody, and solvent of law. Abortion is really a question of audacious power: Who can commit murder and get away with it? Which bully is in charge? Feminist Camille Paglia had the honesty to stay outright:

> I have always frankly admitted that abortion is murder, the extermination of the powerless by the powerful. Liberals for the most part have shrunk from facing the ethical consequences of their embrace of

[286] A belief in one's absolute power over another's life seems to be consistently connected with anti-theism: rejecting the source and measure of oneself causes a diseased inflation of the ego and a blindness to the selfhood of others. See Marcel, *Mystery of Being*, vol. 2, 197 and 203; cf. Joseph Ratzinger, "Truth and Freedom," *Communio* 23, no. 1 (Spring 1996), republished in *Joseph Ratzinger in* Communio, vol. 2: *Anthropology and Culture*, ed. David L. Schindler and Nicholas J. Healy (Grand Rapids, MI: William B. Eerdmans, 2013), 147–67. Naomi Wolf stated in 1995: "War is legal; it is sometimes even necessary. Letting the dying die in peace is often legal and sometimes even necessary. Abortion should be legal; it is sometimes even necessary. Sometimes the mother must be able to decide that the foetus, in its full humanity, must die." Note the philosophically incoherent parallelism of war (presumably just war against aggression); allowing someone to die, as when extraordinary means of life support are withheld; and actively killing an innocent person. These three cases are ethically completely different. See Naomi Wolf, "Our Bodies, Our Souls: Rethinking Abortion Rhetoric," *New Republic*, October 16, 1995, 26–35. Similarly, Faye Wattleton of Planned Parenthood admitted: "I think we have deluded ourselves into believing that people don't know that abortion is killing. So any pretense that abortion is not killing is a signal of our ambivalence, a signal that we cannot say yes, it kills a fetus" (*Ms. Magazine*, 1997). Both quotations from Steve Skojec, "Why Are 'Pro-Choice' Advocates So Afraid of Choice?," *The Skojec File*, May 3, 2022, https://skojecfile.steveskojec.com/p/why-are-pro-choice-advocates-so-afraid.

> abortion, which results in the annihilation of concrete individuals and not just clumps of insensate tissue.[287]

As if responding to Paglia's implicit challenge, a pro-abortion mother released a video on TikTok that quickly made its way via Twitter to a much wider audience.

> In the video, the young mom cradles her sweet, vulnerable baby in her arms, looking into her innocent eyes as she softly croons: "I could have killed you, but I chose to let you live." It's a line straight out of a horror movie. At the very least, it's something only the most deranged, disturbed, and thoroughly self-centered mother would ever utter to her helpless child. The young woman in the video, who was apparently responding to a pro-lifer's message asking if this were how pro-aborts talk to their kids, goes on to defend her remarks, saying she's fully aware that she used the word "kill," and that she means it. You could use a different phrase, soften the reality a little, she suggests, but in the end it's the same thing. Get an abortion or don't, is her message. Kill your child or don't. Who cares? Do what you want. Getting an abortion is like using hand sanitizer, she says. Killing a baby is like killing germs. It's stunning how quickly the pro-abortion movement went from "it's a clump of cells" to "yes it's a baby and yes I will still kill him."[288]

This mentality of violence displays unmistakable parallels with the practices, so routinely contemptuous of human life, characteristic of twentieth-century mass political movements and tyrannies. The spread of such brutality infects a society and numbs its members, killing compassion no less than lives, killing consciences and deadening the awareness of evil, administering a moral poison that eventually makes it impossible to understand how human life itself can have intrinsic worth or value.[289]

[287] Camille Paglia, "Fresh Blood for the Vampire," *Salon*, September 10, 2008, www.salon.com/2008/09/10/palin_10.

[288] Ashley Sadler, "Abortion Is the Exertion of Power over the Vulnerable, and One Pro-Choice Mom Just Proved It," *LifeSiteNews*, May 26, 2022, www.lifesitenews.com/blogs/abortion-is-the-exertion-of-power-over-the-vulnerable-and-one-pro-choice-mom-just-proved-it. See Kelly Marcum, "The Self-Hate of Abortion Advocates," *American Conservative*, July 2, 2022, www.theamericanconservative.com/the-self-hate-of-abortion-advocates.

[289] Examples are plentiful nowadays. A group calling itself Jane's Revenge spray-painted "Abortion is liberation" across the doors and windows of a Minnesota pregnancy center, their behavior demonstrating an ingrained lack of respect

Materialism has always been an ideology, a theory that people have entertained more or less inconsistently with the actual practice of their lives. One would expect the last sanctuary against this absurd theory to be a mother's experience of bearing and loving her own children. An ivory-tower scientist might try to believe the theory that there is no such thing as reason or personhood or friendship, that we are all nothing but atoms and cells, elaborate heaps of stuff with no intrinsic worth, whereas one would think that a mother holding a helpless and trusting baby to her breast would be far too wise with the wisdom of reality to succumb to a theory so palpably false. Yet for a woman to let the child who is growing in her womb be dismembered and destroyed portends nothing less than the triumph of an absurd and heartless ideology.[290]

This materialism itself is radically inconsistent, as any falsehood must be. It excludes some human beings as "blobs of tissue" but wants to spread the message of humanitarianism, enforce animal rights, and protect rain forests. On what basis? When a pregnant woman is assaulted and her child perishes, the attacker can (in certain places where laws harmonize with common sense) be charged with homicide. If the same pregnant woman chooses to destroy her own child, however, she is permitted to do so, protected, even honored for it.

It is frightening to realize that the human soul can be so poisoned by falsehood that all arguments drawn from nature, from reason, from common sense become useless. One might as well be talking to a vegetable, as Aristotle said of those who deny the principle of noncontradiction (viz., a thing cannot both

---

for "the other," whether it be another's life or another's property — which is why such people cannot be good citizens of a regime. Attacking a center that exists only to help women who wish to keep their children indicates, moreover, that in their minds, motherhood itself is necessarily at odds with womanhood, which raises questions about the perpetrators' mental health in regard to self-love and love of their own mothers. One thinks of the motto emblazoned over the Nazi concentration camps: "*Arbeit macht frei*," which we could translate for our purposes as "Work is liberation." The descent into ideological slavery is most evident in the abuse of language. See Clare Marie Merkowsky, "Minnesota Pregnancy Center Vandalized by Jane's Revenge in Latest Act of Pro-Abortion Violence," *LifeSiteNews*, June 20, 2022, www.lifesitenews.com/news/minnesota-pregnancy-center-vandalized-by-janes-revenge-in-latest-act-of-pro-abortion-violence/.

[290] Identifying the guilty ideology as materialism could be challenged; for example, Marc Barnes ("Abortion Is Eugenics") makes a persuasive and eloquent case that it is a kind of cowardly voluntarism.

be and not be in the same respect at the same time).[291] Those who claim that a fetus is both a child and not a child, depending on how you look at it, are guilty of speaking nonsense. If it were a matter of speech alone, one might pity them. As it is, they have weapons and wealth, and they carry their nonsense into action, bringing sin, death, and nihilism into the world.

Materialism is the worldview that underlies cruelty. Yes, religious idealism can be a weapon in the hands of sinners, but it can also — and this is far more common throughout history — lead men and women to heights of self-sacrificial love. Materialism, on the contrary, is a system that can only be abused because it only leads downward, into the pit of utilitarian egoism. There is no possible room for human dignity and human rights in the worldview of a materialist; there are just atoms and void.

The enemy of human nature

Liberal Americans continue to work themselves into a frenzy about the decision by which a majority of judges on the U.S. Supreme Court finally concurred that it is not the role of the judiciary to eliminate the authority of fifty states to legislate in favor of protecting the lives of persons unborn. Liberal states are vying for the status of "abortion safe havens," and liberal companies are lavishing blood money on employees who "need" to travel out of state for abortions. We would do well to ask ourselves a question: What is driving this secular crusade against baby humans?

Once upon a time, a fearless worker in the pro-life movement returned from China to report to NARAL and NOW on the atrocity of forced abortions, thinking that "pro-choice" organizations would respond with passionate indignation to his countless stories of coercion. To Steven Mosher's (initial) surprise, they couldn't care less about what he had to say. Forced abortions were "unfortunate," they said, but then shrugged their shoulders: "There *is* overpopulation, after all." The scales fell from Mosher's eyes, and he saw the truth: the constant praise of "choice" is nothing more than lip service. What these organizations really want is to extend the abortion empire itself as far and wide as possible. They pretend that the cause for which they fight is "freedom of choice," when, in reality, their cause is to make what they call "safe abortion" available everywhere and for any reason.

The first piece of the explanation is crassly financial: it's big business. Money blinds people to reality, to other persons, to duties and obligations.

[291] See Aristotle, *Metaphysics* IV.4, 1006a12–15 and 1008b10–12.

The second piece can be teased out of the cruelty of the materialistic ideology espoused by abortion's promoters. They are more than pro-abortion: they are anti-child, anti-motherhood, anti-family. As Pope John Paul II and the Holy See during his reign emphasized, the abortion movement pursues as its global agenda "making the world safe for casual murder." As long as there are still loving mothers, loved children, and coherent families in the world, the monstrous aims of such organizations are threatened, and they feel it keenly. They will continue to fight until mothers become unloving, children are unloved, and traditional families are shattered.

Such a view cannot take root in people who are mentally healthy and live a normal life. This view suggests a profound misery, unhappiness, and self-loathing at the core of abortionism — a failure in having been loved or in returning love that is projecting itself outward as an insistence that no one should be "forced" to love another person. Deep inside, pro-abortionists are torn between an idolatrous self-love and a pathetic self-hatred. They exalt the militant "I," which always says "I want," and so they would deny existence to the vulnerable baby who is all want and cannot say "I" at all.

What reasons might they give? They are, so they feel, "sparing" the babies the misfortune of living, "sparing" their parents the misfortune of having to make sacrifices — sacrifices that can be sustained only by a love stronger than self-love. Beneath all of the propaganda is a nihilism that denies to human life inherent meaning, value, dignity, or beauty. And let's be honest about it: to the extent that modern men and women live without God, without grace, without love, nihilism is a self-fulfilling prophecy. Without God and His gifts, life will not seem worth living; it will be vapid and pointless. The system perpetuates itself, alienation breeding alienation. From lovelessness comes an attitude of contempt for others, and from this contempt comes still greater meaninglessness, until it becomes a "self-evident fact" that human life is, on the whole, a burden, a curse, instead of a blessing and a gift.

If people *knew* they were loved, they would love who and what they are. If they saw that their lives have a transcendent meaning, they would welcome every new life as a summons to love, a harbinger of hope, a presence of beauty. As it is, the dominant modes of technology, the dazzling media, and the secularized, hypersexualized world of education conspire to insulate men and women from fundamental truths or distort the truth past all recognition.[292]

[292] See, on these various points, Peter Kwasniewski, "Listening with an Attentive Ear to God's Poetry," in *The Glory of the Cosmos: A Catholic Approach to the Natural World*, ed. Thomas Storck (Waterloo, ON: Arouca Press, 2020), 139–50.

The third piece of the explanation, finally, is spiritual. St. Ignatius of Loyola called Satan "the enemy of our human nature."[293] There is no question that "pro-choice" organizations furnish evidence of diabolical activity at every level of their work.[294]

Hope or despair: Which will it be?

"The woman who is expecting a baby is literally inhabited by hope."[295]

What is it that we human beings hope for? We hope for the love of others, for fullness of life, for friendship, for joy. We hope, ultimately, for happiness — understood not as a warm fuzzy feeling but as the completion of all of our yearnings and strivings, the binding up of our wounds, the restoration of our strength, the revelation of the meaning of all we have been, done, and suffered.

Men would rather live without bread than without hope. With hope, it is possible to endure the most inhuman tortures, as we see in the lives of the martyrs. Without hope, even the good things of daily life turn sour and lose their appeal.

Christianity entered into a world that was drunkenly careening from superstition to esotericism, from world-weary despair to unappeasable hedonism, and introduced a way that was lofty, luminous, and liberating. It was truly experienced as a "breath of fresh air," as good news that gave a new meaning and purpose to

[293] See *The Spiritual Exercises of Saint Ignatius of Loyola*, nos. 325–27, where the saint three times refers to the devil as "the enemy of our human nature." I am consulting Thomas Corbishley's translation (Wheathampstead, Hertfordshire: Anthony Clarke, 1973).

[294] See, for two recent examples of connections between abortion and Satanism: Emily Mangiaracina, "Satanic Temple to Demand 'Religious Exemption' for 'Abortion Ritual' in Court if Roe Overturned," *LifeSiteNews*, May 13, 2022, www.lifesitenews.com/news/satanic-temple-plans-to-demand-religious-exemption-to-perform-abortion-ritual-if-roe-overturned; the video "Abortion Supporters Admit They're Motivated by Satan and That the Battle for Life Is 'Spiritual,'" *LifeSiteNews*, www.lifesitenews.com/episodes/abortion-supporters-admit-theyre-motivated-by-satan-and-that-the-battle-for-life-is-spiritual. There is historical precedent for this connection. In the Middle Ages, witches were known to be able to procure abortions; this was seen as one of their most hated crimes. This connection between abortion and witchcraft remains with us today, although many are ignorant of it. One need only surf the Internet to find "midwives" who proudly advertise their expertise in procuring abortions through "natural" means; not surprisingly, they often state their adherence to modern witchcraft and the New Age movement.

[295] Marcel, *Homo Viator*, 31.

life. Christians became known for their kindness and hospitality — and especially, as early documents indicate, for their custom of *not* exposing infants to death, as the pagans did. Christianity made life worth living again — so much so that it made giving life to others, to offspring, worthwhile too. Unlike the pagans, the Christians did not try to prevent pregnancies or end them, nor did they do away with the "unwanted." Those who knew that God had looked upon them with love, *wanting* them for Himself, gained the power to look upon others with love. Under the reign of Christianity, life came to be seen as inherently valuable; indeed, its value became quasi-infinite, because of the divinization of man offered in the sacraments, and the life eternal to which they lead. This is the power of love that the religion of Christ brings into the world. No other religion is like it; no other promises to do what it does; no other confirms its promises with so vast a number of heroic lovers and wonders (that is, saints and miracles).

Since grace builds on nature, however, we can also say that the goodness of life, of being alive, is an elementary truth. Mankind, as a whole, feels a fundamental and unquestioned attachment to life and, if asked, would declare that life is the first and most basic of all good things, without which any other good would be impossible. The hearts of true lovers, moreover, yearn for growth and life — so, too, does the human child who proceeds naturally from their love.

Thus, to sink to a point where life is avoided like the plague or thrown away as though it meant nothing or was worth nothing, as though we had the right to *decide* when or if a life should be lived, and not only our own life but *another's* life (!) — to reach this point is already to have been divorced from one's bond to the world, detached from the goodness of being, and deceived into thinking that life is something over which we have final say. We ourselves would *deny* a fictitious right over our own lives to anyone else, if we had committed no crime deserving of death. In a monstrous contradiction, we then allow ourselves to sit in a tyrannical court of judgment over the lives of unborn children, of future men and women like ourselves, who have done nothing to deserve being cut off from existence.

In the battle over marriage, procreation, and the defense of life, we must realize that we are up against a combination of metaphysical nihilism and spiritual egoism vastly more powerful than any human army or political system — a demonic corruption of mind and heart that cannot be driven out except by prayer, fasting, and martyrdom, as were the errors and crimes faced by the early Christians — and faced down by them. There is much we can do within our society to spread the truth and fight evil; there is counseling and picketing at clinics, lobbying and writing letters, distributing pamphlets, donating time, money, and clothes to pregnancy centers. Remaining silent on the evil of abortion, the evil of contraception, and the evil of divorce would make us complicit in the reduction of man to a machine, the replacement of sacrificial love with egotistical calculation, and the Luciferian effort to uncreate the world.

But there is one thing that every Christian can and must do every day: *pray*—pray for the mothers and the children, for the doctors and the nurses, for the lawmakers and the judges. *Thy kingdom come, Thy will be done, on earth, where now there is so much bloodshed, as it is in heaven, where peace reigns through the Blood of the Lamb, who gave His life for the little ones.* The Lord, who searches hearts, can see what is at work behind the scenes: contempt for the Creator, rejection of the Giver of Life. God, who is love, yearns to pour out His mercy, His precious blood, upon all sinners, especially the most desperate and wretched, if only they would turn to Him, acknowledge their guilt, and ask His forgiveness.

32

Four Surreal Scenes and a Radio Station

How is it that someone cannot see that abortion is wrong — wickedly wrong, horribly wrong, gruesomely wrong? How can there be anyone who does not know that a woman pregnant is a woman with child, and that abortion, by "terminating the pregnancy," has destroyed a human life, an innocent baby human? Yet modern men and women are so accustomed to wielding a perverse power over nature that they might merely shrug their shoulders and say: "Yeah, and so what? There are too many kids already."

The following fictional dialogues between a pregnant mother and a young daughter who asks the right questions take place in the waiting room of an abortion clinic.

Scene 1

JANE. Mama, why are we here?

MAMA. Jane, sweetie, Mama just has to have a little problem taken care of; it will only take a little while. You keep playing with the dolls.

JANE. What's the problem, Mama? Are you feeling sick? It looks like we're in a hospital.

MAMA. Jane, Mama has a little baby in her tummy, but we don't want the baby. So I am going to a doctor who will kill the little baby for me.

JANE (*raising her voice*). But, Mama, I want a little brother or sister!

MAMA. Shut up; I could have had you killed, too, but I chose not to, so remember that before you complain about how small our family is.

Scene 2

MAMA. Jane, Mama has a little baby in her tummy, but Daddy doesn't want the baby. So I am going to a doctor who will terminate the pregnancy.

JANE. Mama, why do you say it that way? You mean the doctor will kill the baby and throw it away, like the kitchen trash.

MAMA (*shocked*). Oh, no, dear, we don't speak like that. The state would never allow murder. It must be something else.

JANE. Mama ... how does the doctor ... "terminate" the baby?

MAMA. Oh, I don't know — I think he uses acid to scorch it to death, or he rips apart the limbs and the head, or he vacuums it out.

JANE. You mean, the way you vacuum up crumbs from the kitchen floor, and then empty the thingy into the trash?

Scene 3

MAMA. I need to have this little problem taken care of.

JANE. What little problem?

MAMA. Mama has a baby, but she can't take care of it. So the doctor will take it away.

JANE. But, Mama, didn't God give us this baby? Shouldn't we take care of it? I mean, love it, the way you love me?

MAMA. Hush, child — every child should be a *wanted* child.

JANE. Mama, does that mean that the difference between me living and me being killed is that you just decided to keep me? You could have seen me as a problem too. But you wanted me, and so you didn't kill me.

MAMA. Hush, child; *you* are not the problem; this new baby is.

JANE. But I could have been the problem, and you could have chosen to get rid of me.

MAMA. Sweetie, I love you, and I would never want to harm you.

JANE. Then why don't you love my little brother or sister? Why do you want the bad, bad doctor to harm the baby?

Scene 4

(*Jane picks up a doll in the clinic office and starts bashing its head against the floor.*)

MAMA (*embarrassed*). Jane, stop that!

JANE. Mama, why should I stop it?

MAMA. Because this doll doesn't belong to you!

JANE (*after a pause*). Mama, why are you here?

MAMA. To get ... a problem taken care of.

JANE. What kind of problem?

MAMA. A baby.

JANE. How does a baby get taken care of by a doctor? I thought a mother took care of a baby by nursing it and clothing it.

MAMA. No, here the doctor takes it ... away.

JANE. You mean — he destroys it?

MAMA. Uhhh ... yes, that's right.

JANE. So you mean the doctor does to the baby what I was doing to the dolly — but for real?

MAMA (*sighing*). Yes.

JANE. So then why do you grown-ups get to bash the baby, when we kids don't get to break our toys or hurt our pets?

MAMA (*getting annoyed*). Because the toys and the pets don't belong to you — but the baby is *mine,* and I can do what I want with it!

JANE. Mama, that doesn't make any sense. Isn't a baby worth more than a Barbie doll or a pet rat? And doesn't the baby belong to the family, to the world, to God?

The contradictions tearing apart our hearts, our families, our societies are so ubiquitous at this point that they have become nearly invisible, undetectable, like a lethal gas with no odor that seeps through the house and gradually poisons its inhabitants before they have an opportunity to identify and repair the leak. One may sometimes feel as if human beings have trained themselves — or been trained — to live under a perpetual cloud of illusion, unawareness, self-cancellation, forgetting what has been said from moment to moment, the ongoing connection between ideas and realities.

During a long car trip in October 2018, I turned on National Public Radio, which is always a good way to stay awake as the liberal news coverage raises one's heart rate and dilates the nostrils. Apart from noticing that, as usual, the news coverage was obviously biased in favor of Democrats, without even an attempt made to disguise it, I was struck by an enormous contradiction that kept me pondering all day long and days after.

The NPR news featured (not once but multiple times) statements from Planned Parenthood and NARAL. These were responding to "the fear of the reversal of *Roe v. Wade*" in the wake of Brett Kavanaugh's confirmation to the Supreme Court — a fear that was proved to be abundantly justified when the same court, thanks be to God, overturned that unconstitutional and iniquitous decision by means of *Dobbs v. Jackson Women's Health Organization.* Planned

Parenthood and NARAL made pledges to expand access to surgical and pharmaceutical abortion across the country, to ensure that state legislatures were as strongly "pro-choice" as possible (just in case the question were thrown by the court back to the state level), to promote heavily programs that would "destigmatize" abortion, and so on. It was demonic to hear the unwavering commitment of these organizations to the ongoing slaughter of unborn baby humans, which, of course, NPR reported on as neutrally as if they were talking about the weather or the stock market.

The banality of evil — has it ever been clearer?

The contradiction loomed when, a few moments later, a feature show began, in which a person from NPR conducted an extremely interesting interview with Nicole Chung, author of *All You Can Ever Know: A Memoir*. Chung speaks about her experience growing up as a Korean in a white family. She was born ten weeks premature, and her biological parents, being overwhelmed with other cares, gave her up for adoption. A Catholic family adopted her and lavished great love on her — a fact to which Chung returned again and again with obvious affection and gratitude. I found myself really impressed with Nicole Chung, with her respectfulness, eloquence, honesty, and radiance as she spoke about the life that her adoptive parents gave her.[296]

Did anyone at NPR think about the fact that this joyful woman of thirty-seven, with a family of her own, who has written a memoir that has already been immensely helpful for countless adoptive parents and adoptees, this woman who was being honored on national radio for her literary accomplishment — she would have been a prime victim of the abortionists of Planned Parenthood and NARAL? They would have counseled her biological parents to "terminate the fetus" on account of the difficult circumstances. They would have argued that it was only a "blob of tissue" with no human or personal value. They would have maintained that adoption is an emotionally draining and expensive process and that it is far simpler and "cleaner" to end the pregnancy (and leave the world better off, with one less hungry mouth to feed and one less source of environmental pollution). In short, they would have expunged Nicole Chung from the face of the earth.

[296] See Mariya Karimjee, "'All You Can Ever Know' Offers a Personal Account of Transracial Adoption," *National Public Radio*, October 4, 2018, www.npr.org/2018/10/04/654240953/all-you-can-ever-know-offers-a-personal-account-of-transracial-adoption.

In doing so, they would have deprived her of a life of her own and the experience of love; they would have deprived her adoptive parents of a child to lavish love upon. The world would have lost a great writer; above all, and most simply, the world would have lost a *person*, with the dignity and depth found in every human soul. Isn't Nicole Chung's story potentially the story of every aborted child? Of every child who could have been brought to term and offered up for adoption but whom the bloody hands of Planned Parenthood and kindred organizations have ripped prematurely from its mother's womb?

No one, short of God, could ever grasp the gaping wound that has been left in the human race due to so many hundreds of millions of persons missing from our world, our lives, our families, our communities. So much that has been lost and will never be found. May the Lord create soon the new heavens and the new earth, where righteousness will, at last, be at home (see 2 Pet. 3:13), and the murderer will no longer stalk outside the womb to seize the child (see Rev. 12:4). *Maranatha.*

33

Protecting the Innocent and the Weak

Stephen R. L. Clark, an expert in ancient Greek philosophy, animal rights and ethics, and the thought of G. K. Chesterton, found a way to bring these varied interests together in a work published in 2020, *Can We Believe in People? Human Significance in an Interconnected Cosmos.* The book is not one that I can endorse without qualification: certain poorly supported assumptions concerning the evolution of mankind deserve criticism, the author taking the Darwinian paradigm too much for granted without giving due credit to its now numerous and sophisticated opponents. He too readily attributes quasi-human intelligence and motivation to subrational animals and dismisses traditional accounts of human distinctiveness. Seemingly unaware of Marie George's substantial body of work on the extreme improbability of extraterrestrial life, Clark also appears to assume that there are other species of rational animals in the universe.[297]

It is in the book's defense of moral absolutism that Clark shines brightest. His third chapter, on moral realism, shreds atheism to pulp by arguing that atheists should have no absolute moral convictions whatsoever, should not indeed acknowledge justice, rights, fairness, conscience, freedom, or any other ethical concept that cannot be reduced to atoms and void. He argues that they cannot rationally object to God's existence on the basis of the evil in the world or the unfairness of life or whatever it might be that they consider somehow inexplicable if a God were to exist, since without a God — or, to put it more loosely, without an objective order of being that culminates in an absolute good — there could be no good to love or evil to hate at all.

His chapter 5, on human dignity, is valuable for its consistent and well-argued defense of human life at all stages. Clark probes and finds wanting the

[297] See Marie I. George, *Christianity and Extraterrestrials?: A Catholic Perspective* (Lincoln, NE: iUniverse, 2005).

assumption made by secular philosophers that adult-centered utilitarianism is the only form of reasoning possible:

> One of the oddest features of much secular moral philosophy, as well as more theologically inspired enquiry, is the assumption that our *primary* obligations can only be to actually "rational" people: that is, to those with whom we could be expected to have made bargains, and who can themselves acknowledge congruent obligations. This is explicit in most post-Kantian moralizing, drawing on ancient Stoic notions: we can be obliged to do only what all other rational beings can also be obliged to do. Even those who have adopted a more "consequentialist" outlook, for whom our primary duty is to do as much good as possible (sometimes interpreted as ensuring as much pleasure, for as little pain, as possible), think chiefly of their effect on adult, rational beings. Utilitarians may insist, in Bentham's familiar words, that creatures are morally significant because they can *suffer*, and that we should minimize their suffering — but even those who emphasize the "moral considerability" of animals will usually add that most biologically "animal" organisms have no conception of their own continued being, and that their pains and pleasures are therefore transient, and easily to be ignored in favor of the *conscious* enjoyments and torments of the adult human.[298]

When I read this, I thought with a groan: we can't even get fetal pain bills passed. The minimalist idea that we should at least not cause suffering has been thrown out; we have fallen below Bentham's utilitarianism. Modern Westerners would sooner give "rights" to pigs than protect unborn children from pain or distress or lethal violence.

In chapter 1, Clark had noted that the image and likeness of God in man does not concern *solely* man's rationality; after all, reason is also the power by which we subjugate, torment, and destroy in a manner and to a degree that no subrational being can equal. Reason is therefore ambivalent. It may be truer that we should search for man's likeness to God in the realm of moral qualities, and strive to live according to it:

> But what is the likeness that we lost? And what is it that we are required to seek again? The answer to both questions lies in the declaration that

[298] Stephen R. L. Clark, *Can We Believe in People?: Human Significance in an Interconnected Cosmos* (Brooklyn: Angelico Press, 2020), 110.

God is "holy," and that we are to seek that "holiness," *qadosh* (1 Pet 1:15). It is not wrong to see that the term has associations also with "purity": God's people are to separate themselves from iniquity, from all forms of self-indulgent greed and cruelty, and adopt strict dietary and other rules to help them (see Lev 11:44). But the principal association of the term *qadosh* in the Hebrew texts is with compassion: we are to seek to imitate and express God's generosity, to orphans, widows, strangers and the wild things in our country (that is, the country we are given to help guard and garden). We are not to seize all things for ourselves alone, but leave resources — or more actively provide resources — for all those in need (see Lev 19:9–10; 23:22; 25:6–7). Conversely, our failure to do this deserves deep condemnation. We are not to steal or cheat or keep back an employee's wages, nor deprive the poor and the stranger of the chance to glean the harvest, nor "treat the deaf with contempt nor put an obstruction in the way of the blind" (Lev 19:13–14). "This was the iniquity of your sister Sodom: she and her daughters had pride of wealth and food in plenty, comfort and ease, and yet she never helped the poor and wretched" (Ezek 16:49).[299]

We are to avoid greed and cruelty, and to imitate God's generosity. What does that say for our modern Western ethic (or anti-ethic), which is based on hoarding pleasure for oneself and destroying any beings that interfere with one's egoistic project, however dependent on us they may be, pleading for our mercy? Orphans, widows, strangers, and wild things do not fare well under cancer-phase capitalism. Contrast the sane attitude found in St. Benedict's *Rule*, wherein he says of the cellarer of the monastery: "Let him take the greatest care of the sick, of children, of guests, and of the poor, knowing without doubt that he will have to render an account for all these on the Day of Judgment,"[300] and wherein he writes the tender words:

> Before all things and above all things, care must be taken of the sick, so that they may be served in very deed as Christ himself; for he said: *I was sick and ye visited me*; and, *what ye did to one of these least ones, ye did unto me....* Although human nature of itself is drawn to pity towards these times of life, that is, towards old men and children, yet let them

[299] Clark, *Can We Believe in People?*, 7–8.

[300] *Rule*, chap. 31.

> be provided for also by the authority of the Rule. Let there be constant consideration for their weakness.[301]

It was on the basis of such humbly compassionate foundations that the entire edifice of Western Christian civilization was built.

Clark notes again the serious narrowing of vision required to think and to live as if the only worthy object of moral concern or virtuous behavior is another fully functional, reasoning, and speaking adult against whom one could stand as an equal:

> Infants, the very ill, the elderly may all be unable to *speak* or even "reason" (in the sense of calculating outcomes and possibilities), but they are all the proper objects of love and reverence. They are made "in the image of God," and so to be reckoned sacred: any disrespect or injury to them is to be taken as disrespect or injury to God (Mt 25:40; see also Mt 18:6).[302]

For this reason, Clark argues, an ethic of justice should place *greater* emphasis on care of infants and the elderly who cannot care for themselves, since the tiny and the frail call forth our mysterious gift of compassion and show that we are not merely sophisticated brutes, ready to hurl a rock at the next cousin who interferes with our bananas, but really "gods," as Jesus said (John 10:34; cf. Ps. 81:6), who can go out of ourselves in affection. The author notes that, in fact, we do not love our babies just because of their probability of someday being adults, or because they have a potency to be adults; we love them right now for who and what they are: little humans, dependent on us. It is part of our nature (yes, we do have a nature) that we long for our own offspring and we consider ourselves obliged and beholden to our elders. We feel the pull of care and the pull of reverence:

> It should be obvious that any moral theory which explains our concern for babies, infants, toddlers and so on solely because these creatures are *potentially* adult, rational beings, is missing the point. It should also be obvious that any obligation we may have to obey or to revere *authority* cannot depend either on our having *agreed* to such obedience, or to

301 *Rule,* chaps. 36–37.

302 Clark, *Can We Believe in People?,* 111. Cf. Carl R. Trueman, "Why Pro-Abortion Activists Desecrate Churches," *First Things,* May 12, 2022, www.firstthings.com/web-exclusives/2022/05/why-pro-abortion-activists-desecrate-churches.

> our current calculation of the eventual consequences of obedience or disobedience. There are, in short, at least two sources of obligation: the pull to care for the young and the defenseless, and the pull to revere those placed "above" us, by their age, experience or obvious virtue (even if they are no longer what they were).[303]

An ethical theory that fails to explain this dual pull or explains it away as a by-product of evolutionary biology is simply bad philosophy, Clark suggests — like sloppy chemistry or imprecise mathematics or rigged sociology.

The failure to take seriously the insights that come from a now many-thousand-year-old religious tradition is symptomatic of the self-inflicted blindness of modern ethics. Clark implies that the images of Christ in the bosom of His Mother and of Christ in agony on the Cross tell us more about what it means to be in the image and likeness of God than a legacy of Cartesian rationalism, Baconian mastery of nature, Benthamite utilitarianism, and self-interest magnified into the social contract:

> The most familiar pictures of Jesus, whom Christians identify as the very Word of God, are of his infancy in Mary's arms, or on the cross. And yet it is this Jesus who is exalted (Acts 2:22–36; Eph 1:20–23; Phil 2:9). There is a fairly easy reading of the story that has no metaphysical implications: whenever a clear innocent is condemned, especially to death, by the powers and principalities of this world, it is those powers and principalities which are themselves condemned, and lose the moral authority they abused. We owe, or feel we owe, a primary obedience to authority — but that authority is borrowed from a higher source, and can be lost. Those who observe the event can feel themselves released, if not from reasonable fear of what the abusers can do, at least from any sense that the abusers have a right to do it.
>
> But the more strongly metaphysical sense of the Christian gospel should not be simply ignored, or allegorized away. The serious claim is being made that it is in the defenceless, the overtly powerless, the pitiable whose only power lies in the love they somehow evoke, that we see what God is like. Deane-Drummond, while offering some support to the traditionally Thomist view that it is *only* human beings, in virtue of their intellectual potential, that can be considered "images of God," adds that "we might want to push the idea [that human image-bearing

[303] Clark, *Can We Believe in People?*, 111.

still applies in those who have, in different circumstances, lost their use of reasoning powers] even further than Aquinas does and suggest that it is when human beings are at their most vulnerable that the veiled grace of God in image-bearing becomes most visible."[304]

Is it true that we "see God" in the powerless who have only the power of evoking love? I do not know how to analyze or defend this claim philosophically, but it seems true to life, irrefutable, and strangely appealing. Throughout the frightful history of human evils, and in the life of most, if not all, human beings, there are moments when it is our own powerlessness or that of another that triumphs over the normal (fallen) self-interest that drives us to our misery and, for a blessed moment, or perhaps even for the rest of a lifetime, this awakening to the veiled grace of God renders us capable not only of eating and sleeping but also of communing with another and for the other's good.

The news cycle seems never to be lacking novel horrors in the battle against the sanctity of human life, as when we heard that Chairman Cuomo's regime had approved the rental of wombs and the sale of babies.[305] One insane idea after another is floated by people who have no moral or metaphysical bearings, in a relentless quest to inaugurate the "brave new world" of limitless possibilities — which proves to be a world of limitless exploitation.

Sound arguments in defense of moral absolutes and the fundamental right to life are always needed, and it is important that these arguments be given *philosophically*, not just on the basis of religious convictions, even where such convictions are a deeper and firmer foundation for the truth. The right to life includes the right to be born of the natural union of husband and wife — the context within which human beings are most fittingly welcomed and brought up in love, in accordance with their dignity. Children are the gift par excellence of marriage; they define it as the type of communion of persons it is, and they give it its inherent structure and duties.

Above we saw how Clark spells out why protecting the innocent and the weak is distinctive to our humanity and separates us from the beasts of the field, which, in many cases, care little or nothing for their offspring. I wish now

[304] Clark, *Can We Believe in People?*, 113.

[305] See Jennifer Lahl, "Babies for Sale," *First Things*, May 22, 2020, www.firstthings.com/web-exclusives/2020/05/babies-for-sale.

to look at Clark's exposé of the eugenicism of H. G. Wells, which he cites as an example of the evils to which so-called scientific reasoning will lead among those who are blindly led by it.

Clark notes that Wells and his circle thought that "living in accord with nature" meant imitating a "kill or be killed" mentality of the wild,[306] and that this, in turn, meant ridding the world of those they considered inferior or inconvenient or defective:

> The New Republicans [a term from Wells's *A Modern Utopia*] will have no pity for such "contemptible and silly creatures" and "to make life convenient for the breeding of such people will seem to them not the most virtuous and amiable thing in the world ... but an exceedingly abominable proceeding.... The procreation of children who by the circumstances of their parentage, *must* be diseased bodily or mentally ... is absolutely the most loathsome of all conceivable sins."[307]

Clark reminds us that the Scopes Trial in 1925, which is now remembered as a contest over evolution, concerned a textbook that expressed an extreme eugenicist point of view: George William Hunter's *A Civic Biology: Presented in Problems* (New York: American Book, 1914). In a section called "Parasitism and Its Cost to Society," this textbook stated:

> Hundreds of families such as those described above exist today, spreading disease, immorality, and crime to all parts of this country. The cost to society of such families is very severe. Just as certain animals or plants become parasitic on other plants or animals, these families have become parasitic on society. They not only do harm to others by corrupting, stealing, or spreading disease, but they are actually protected and cared for by the state out of public money. Largely for them the poorhouse and the asylum exist. They take from society, but they give nothing in return. They are true parasites. The Remedy.—If such people were lower animals, we would probably kill them off to prevent them from spreading. Humanity will not allow this, but we do have the remedy of separating the sexes in asylums or other places and in various ways preventing intermarriage and the possibilities of perpetuating such a low

[306] See above, in chapter 14, the related discussion of the view that men should imitate the animals by living "according to instinct."

[307] Clark, *Can We Believe in People?*, 50.

> and degenerate race. Remedies of this sort have been tried successfully in Europe and are now meeting with some success in this country.[308]

H. G. Wells gave consummate expression to this way of thinking:

> It has become apparent that whole masses of the human population are as a whole inferior in their claim upon the future to other masses, that they cannot be given opportunities or trusted with power as the superior peoples are trusted, that their characteristic weaknesses are contagious and detrimental in the civilizing fabric, and their range of incapacity tempts and demoralises the strong. To give them equality is to sink to their level, to protect and cherish them is to be swamped in their fecundity.... There is reason to believe that vaccination has preserved thousands, who from a weak constitution would formerly have succumbed to smallpox. Thus the weak members of civilized societies propagate their kind. No one who has attended to the breeding of domestic animals will doubt that this must be highly injurious to the race of man. It is surprising how soon a want of care, or care wrongly directed, leads to the degeneration of a domestic race; but excepting in the case of man himself, hardly anyone is so ignorant as to allow his worst animals to breed.[309]

This side of Wells is expounded in an article by Jerry Bergman[310] and in an illuminating book by Peter Kemp.[311]

How often do we hear people say they oppose racism, when, in fact, they support organizations such as Planned Parenthood that trace their origins directly to Wellsian eugenicism and continue to target the poor, the needy, the vulnerable, and the underprivileged, getting rich off of their woes and preventing "their kind" from reproducing? It is one of the most disgusting examples of hypocrisy and cynicism to be met with in human history.

[308] Cited in Clark, *Can We Believe in People?*, 50.

[309] Cited in Clark, *Can We Believe in People?*, 95–96.

[310] Jerry Bergman, "H. G. Wells: Darwin's Disciple and Eugenicist Extraordinaire," originally published in *Journal of Creation* 18, no. 3 (December 2004): 116–20; online at https://answersingenesis.org/sanctity-of-life/eugenics/hg-wells-darwins-disciple-and-eugenicist-extraordinaire.

[311] Peter Kemp, *H. G. Wells and the Culminating Ape: Biological Imperatives and Imaginative Obsessions* (New York: St. Martin's Press, 1996).

Clark cites approvingly John Paul II's formulation of the fundamental problem of a subjectivist equation of highly functional rationality with personhood:

> The theory of human rights is based precisely on the affirmation that the human person, unlike animals and things, cannot be subjected to domination by others. We must also mention the mentality which tends to equate personal dignity with the capacity for verbal and explicit, or at least perceptible, communication. It is clear that on the basis of these presuppositions there is no place in the world for anyone who, like the unborn or the dying, is a weak element in the social structure, or for anyone who appears completely at the mercy of others and radically dependent on them, and can only communicate through the silent language of a profound sharing of affection. In this case it is force which becomes the criterion for choice and action in interpersonal relations and in social life. But this is the exact opposite of what a State ruled by law, as a community in which the "reasons of force" are replaced by the "force of reason," historically intended to affirm.[312]

Clark reasonably objects to the word "cannot" in the first sentence, the use of which is factually untrue; probably the intention was to say "*may* not be subjected to domination by others," as in: no one has the right to do this. Those who choose to subject human persons to domination lose their own dignity and plummet into a sickly caricature of humanity. Force is not and can never be the "criterion for choice and action in interpersonal relations," as it was for H. G. Wells and Margaret Sanger, and as it remains for Planned Parenthood, Andrew Cuomo, Joe Biden, Nancy Pelosi, and many others like them who, day by day, undermine the "force of reason" by "reasons of force."

Liberals claim to be deeply concerned for the poor, the underprivileged, the oppressed, the disadvantaged. Drawing on seemingly endless supplies of taxpayer money and careless of ballooning debts, they summon into being enormous and lavishly expensive social-welfare programs and administer them through wasteful bureaucracies. Yet the social problems do not go away. In a sort of parody of Darwin's survival of the fittest, the problems of our time adapt to the changing environment and develop special resilience against official cures. No one, it seems, knows how to address poverty without multiplying poverty.

[312] *Evangelium Vitae* 19, cited in Clark, *Can We Believe in People?*, 100–101.

Nowhere is this more obvious than in the progressivists' habit of combating evils with evils, as when they respond to sexually transmitted diseases, teenage pregnancies, and domestic abuse by counseling sex education, abortion, and easy-access divorce.

As Clark helps us to see, there is a totally different approach that begins with *love* for the poor as persons, *love* for who and what they are. To those who are steeped in history and keep their eyes open to the life of the streets, nothing is clearer than that the Catholic Church has never been equaled in her care for the poor and the needy, the sick and the dying, the widow and the orphan, the prisoner and the refugee, the dispossessed and the abandoned. Her religious orders cover the globe, performing works of mercy not only for those to whom it may be fashionable to give aid, but also for those from whom the rest of society turns away in disgust.

The Church has never been in the business of "social work"; her devoted religious and laity simply love God's poor with the love of Christ and want to raise them out of their misery, so that they, too, can become aware of their dignity as children of God, called to be co-heirs of Christ. The devoted Catholic sees in every man, woman, and child the face of Christ, and this face calls forth one response: the gift of oneself, the offering of one's life on behalf of the lives of others — self-denying, self-emptying love. The most ambitious secular social programs are timid, their achievements infinitesimal, in comparison with the radical "program" proposed by the Gospel, the many saints who, kindled by the words of Christ, expended their lives in service to the poor, and the even more numerous throng inspired, in turn, by their example and walking in their footsteps.

In this respect, too, the Church has the advantage, showing herself to be far ahead of the social workers and their programs and far more successful at alleviating mankind's misery. For one thing, she is energetic with a perpetual youthfulness that comes from beyond this world; how else can one account for the awe-inspiring fact of so many who voluntarily embrace poverty in solidarity with Christ and the poor and who spend themselves with a dedication very few unbelievers have ever equaled?

But more than this, she recognizes that misery is not only *material* but *spiritual*; she never forgets that the human heart needs God even more desperately than the body needs bread. The whole of mankind, whether "rich" or "poor," is equally needy when it comes to the life that is worth living. The worst human poverty is a life without God, without hope, without meaning, and it is this poverty that seems to be the special affliction of the mighty and the monied.

The poor need something more than philanthropy, with its condescending airs; like all men, they need *love*, and that is something that only the supreme Lover, Jesus Christ, has given to us and continues to give through all who obey His commandment of love.[313]

The joy man's heart wants to feast upon is not something that can be gotten from worldly goods, amusements, or diversions. It comes from above and from deep within. It is a joy that springs up with the force of a gushing torrent from the love of God for us and our love of Him in return. There is no other source of abiding happiness.

One might as well admit from the start: either there is a God and in Him alone is bliss, or human life is bracketed on either end, hemmed in, with inescapable nothingness, a meaningless impersonal void that threw us onto the stage to speak our insignificant lines and will blindly consume us in the end. As Josef Pieper often says, you cannot have a "good time" unless there is something *really good* standing above and beyond you, something that will not give way like a mirage or burst like a balloon.

What is there, in the whole world, that does not eventually give way? Can anything here fully and perfectly satisfy man's heart? Modern man: if you are looking for true joy, for lasting happiness, then you must turn your gaze elsewhere. Turn it to the source of these good but perishing things, and you will find a good that is imperishable, the one good that *is* abundant life and never-ending joy. The Catholic Church promises you something that you cannot obtain elsewhere, try as you may; she promises the reality of which all the enjoyments of this world are feeble imitations. She invites you to believe her when she says, in all simplicity, that her faithful children already begin to live that immortal life here and now. They begin to savor the joy that never grows old, the peace that surpasses all understanding. This is the first, last, and best service to the poor — to all of us — that the Church renders.

[313] In *Deus Caritas Est*, part II, Benedict XVI offers a vigorous defense of what is unique to Christian charity for the needy as opposed to government-organized or private-initiative social work.

34

The Case against Communion for Pro-Abortion Politicians

The following is put forward as a "model letter" to any bishop. It began as a letter to the Most Reverend Donald Wuerl in May of 2009.[314]

Your Excellency,

I have been following in the news your statements concerning the controversial subject of administering or denying Holy Communion to politicians who assert they are Catholic and yet reject fundamental moral teachings of the Church. I can only begin to imagine the many difficulties you must face every day in ruling your flock in a time of such great intellectual and moral confusion. As a parent by vocation and as a teacher by profession, I know that questions of discipline are always fraught with difficulties. All the same, I am deeply troubled by certain assumptions that seem to be operative in your statements and your approach to these difficulties.

Laity often hear it said that to deny the Eucharist to a politician is to politicize the Eucharist. This is not so. The ones who are politicizing the Eucharist are the politicians who insist on receiving it even though they are manifestly at odds with the well-known teaching of the Church. They make this most Holy Sacrament a validation of their good standing, an instrument of their reputation. It is a way for them to proclaim: "Look, what I hold and do isn't problematic as far as the Church is concerned. If it were really problematic, then something would be done; but as you see, nothing is being done, so it must be okay, or at least within the realm of disputable opinion."

[314] This letter — also published, with additional related documentation, in chapter 16 of my book *The Holy Bread of Eternal Life* — is included here for the relevance it bears to the themes of the present book.

The Church has the solemn obligation to protect the Blessed Sacrament from profanation and to protect the faithful against scandal. Is it any wonder that such a large number of American Catholics appear to think that the morality of abortion is not something about which the Church has a definite, unchanging teaching, and that it is up to each individual to decide for himself? Many American Catholics will continue to be confused until each and every bishop fulfills his task of proclaiming the truth unambiguously *and* taking all necessary, if regrettable, steps to make sure that no one misses or manipulates that truth because of compromises and evasions. A politician who is repeatedly corrected and yet repeatedly signifies no intention of changing his or her public position is manifestly not in a position to receive a Sacrament whose very meaning is unity with the Catholic Church in her faith and morals. This is, after all, what the *Catechism* teaches us about the *res sacramenti* of the Eucharist — that it is the unity of, and unity with, the Mystical Body. To exist at all, this unity *requires* adherence to the *ecclesia docens*.

Can a Catholic who supports in any way the murder of baby humans be unified with the Mystical Body? We know that Jesus welcomes sinners to His table, for all of us are sinners. But among murderers, He welcomes the repentant, not the unrepentant. If we have mortal sin on our souls, we are obliged to go to Confession — and not just say we are sorry but have a true purpose of amendment. With Biden, Pelosi, and too many others, where is the evidence of their amendment? As long as that is wanting, they should refrain from going to Communion. And if they insist on going anyway, who, then, is "politicizing the Eucharist"? The priest or bishop who denies it or the politician who treats it like his or her personal right "regardless"? The priest who is doing his best to keep the injunction of Jesus Himself — "throw not pearls before swine" (Matt. 7:6) — or the politician who wants to be known as a faithful Catholic *in spite of* persistent public dissent?

Your position, as far as I can tell, does not do justice to the ever-growing problem, or rather scandal, of persistent dissent from Catholic teaching, a dissent that is rarely met with the obviously appropriate response of denial of Communion at some level. Contrary to what you implied in a recent statement, the history of the Church is filled with countless examples of popes and bishops reasonably using the power of the keys to restrict or exclude lay members of the Church (in the old days, it was kings and princes) when their behavior ran clearly and dangerously contrary to the Gospel. I am not saying that Church leaders were right to do this in every instance, but they were surely right to do it in many instances.

What would have happened if St. Ambrose of Milan had not been courageous enough to reprimand the emperor Theodosius for the slaughter of seven thousand people at Thessalonica in 390? Ambrose refused Communion to Theodosius for several months, urging him to imitate the penance of King David. Finally, the emperor humbled himself and was readmitted. Here was a great bishop, a Father and Doctor of the Church, who knew that in dealing with the most powerful earthly ruler, he had to use the most powerful spiritual sanction of the Church. Nothing less would suffice. Anything less would have been to capitulate to the powerful of this world, as if the Church is subordinate to the state. In essence, the situation we are facing today is no different; indeed, the stakes are higher, for we are talking about the killing not of seven thousand but of *millions* of unborn children each year in our own country alone.

Is there a time and a place for *public* confrontation? Yes, absolutely, if there are truths worth living and dying for. The Holy Eucharist is the Mystery of Faith par excellence. It symbolizes and effects the unity of the Church for those who, already baptized, adhere to the Church's teaching, which is the teaching of Christ. It therefore strikes at the very meaning of the mystery to allow those who proudly proclaim their dissenting ways to approach unchecked and to profane the Sacrament by their practical rejection of what it *means*. If the Eucharist is not worth defending at all costs from profanation, *nothing is worth anything*. The approach that allows politicians to hold whatever they want and act however they want with no public consequences in Church membership or sacramental access does not have the long-term effect of winning them over but of emboldening them in their dissent, and of confusing, scandalizing, and weakening the faithful who are trying to live according to the mind of the Church.

Even our merciful Savior and the "all things to all men" St. Paul recommended severe measures in especially bad situations, so that there might be the hope of a startled awakening followed by repentance and reconciliation (see Matt. 18:15–18; 1 Cor. 5:4–5). This would be what Sheldon Vanauken called a "severe mercy": a medicine that may make things worse for a time, in order that there might be healing in the end. As Plato and Aristotle argue, a truly just punishment does not have the purpose of satisfying a private desire for vengeance; its purpose is to restore the order of justice in the souls of the guilty, in the hope that having been objectively corrected, they might also be subjectively reformed.

In their social encyclicals, the popes call upon Catholics to proclaim and defend their Faith in society at large and in the halls of power, even when doing so may bring persecution upon their heads. If the Church does not defend her name, her confession of faith and morals, and her legitimate rights in the public sphere, we have no one but ourselves to blame for the increasing boldness of anti-Christian, inhuman secularism.

For a shepherd of the Church to lead his flock in these troubled times, it is not enough to *be* pro-life; it is not enough to support pro-life organizations and initiatives; it is not enough to preach and teach the right to life. It is also necessary to protect the flock from the wolves of error, deception, hypocrisy, and opportunism; it is necessary to have the courage to call a spade a spade, to warn people against losing their souls for the sake of Caesar's favor.

Sincerely yours in Christ,
A pro-life Catholic

35

The Anti-Sacrament of Satan's Counter-Church

> Abortion is the Antichrist's demonic parody of the Eucharist. That's why it uses the same holy words, "This is my body," with the blasphemously opposite meaning.
>
> — Peter Kreeft

Back in 1997, I was browsing a bookshop and came upon a book that shocked and horrified me. A feminist theologian had written a book in which she argued that the two greatest "crosses" Catholic women must bear are — you guessed it — the Catholic Church's opposition to women's ordination and her opposition to abortion. I could hardly believe that blasphemy had reached this level, but there was no denying my senses, as much as I might have wished myself caught in a nightmare.

Then, not long after that, someone told me of a woman in Canada who spoke of abortion as "sacramental." The abuse of language is nothing short of Luciferian. In reality, there is nothing sacred or sanctifying about sin, destruction of life, and self-destruction, just as there is nothing beautiful in the devil after his rebellion. Sacraments are about bringing life to man. Abortion, therefore, is the anti-sacrament par excellence, since it deprives the unborn human of his or her opportunity to be brought to life, naturally and supernaturally.

"The devil is the ape of God," runs an old saying. The devil really does have an organized religion — organized at least to the point of bringing the enemies of Christ into the most rigid and efficient political, psychological, and cultural structures he can manage to devise with his superhuman intelligence. Everything done by the Catholic Church is parodied by the "church" of the devil, and in this parody, we find an explanation of the blasphemies of the people mentioned above, whose use of the words "cross" and "sacrament" are nothing less than a frontal assault on the holiness and mercy of God.

The only way God's infinite mercy can be turned away is by a direct affront to it: "Amen I say to you, that all sins shall be forgiven unto the sons of men, and the blasphemies wherewith they shall blaspheme: but he that shall blaspheme against the Holy Ghost, shall never have forgiveness, but shall be guilty of an everlasting sin" (Mark 3:28–29). If people repent of their sins — *any* sins whatsoever! — and seek God's mercy, He will give it to them, though not without a just punishment, in this life or the next. But if people directly offend against the divine mercy exhibited or communicated in the order of creation and the higher order of redemption, and they go to their grave in this state of rebellion against the Holy Spirit, how can He help them? By showing them mercy? That is the very gift they have scorned.

It is the hard truth that people choose hell for themselves; and I would add further that this hell is always of the sinner's own making. His prison is his own mind, and his punishment is to be stuck with his dark, twisted ego for eternity. That is hell enough, before we even talk about flames or any of the imagined torments of Dante's *Inferno*. I often think of what C. S. Lewis says in *The Great Divorce*: hell is like a suburb where the houses keep getting farther and farther apart, their residents more and more isolated as time goes on. And could we not connect this image with Ratzinger's conviction that hell is already irrupting into our modern world, seeping in through the cracks, as it were? The child-free suburbs of earth, evacuated by contraception and abortion, are the precursors of the God-free suburbs of Hades, indwelt by vacuity.

Abortion is the crime of people who, at root, hate themselves and despair of life's meaning. If people loved who they are and saw their lives as having meaning, they would welcome every new life as a continuation of what they love, a further verification of that immense meaningfulness of life, a harbinger of hope, a down payment on the future. The crime of extinguishing and discarding the child is the absolute nadir, the complete ebb, of life and existence; it is the death of the social and family instinct, the suicide of the human heart, the brutal murder of compassion and mercy, a sick parody of love soured into self-love. Seen in this way, it is the most evil act possible, since it is like murdering innocence, life, God, and the future, all at once. Abortion is both literally and symbolically the final stage of metaphysical decadence and loss of meaning.

Hence, our fight against abortion and all that leads to it and flows from it must have not only a practical, political side but a speculative side as well.[315] Christians, now more than ever, must study and internalize the speculative roots

[315] See "Pro-Life, Pro-Liturgy, Pro-Tradition" in Peter Kwasniewski, *Reclaiming Our Roman Catholic Birthright: The Genius and Timeliness of the Traditional Latin Mass* (Brooklyn: Angelico Press, 2020), 289–95.

of their heritage as well as the multitude of modern errors that undermine this heritage, this "gospel of life." We would be naïve to think that philosophy, that abstract and rarefied discipline, has little or nothing to do with our present-day culture of death. On the contrary, it has *everything* to do with it. In the words of Thomas Molnar:

> The philosopher is able to engage in very dangerous games with reality, games played by his shadowy colleagues, gnostics, alchemists, and magi, verbal games in the main but which easily degenerate through pride and through the wrong combination into distortions of reality. And if ideologies are such arrogant and evil combinations, it is because they are prepared in the philosophical hell's kitchen.[316]

We know from moral theology that there are some sins worse in kind than abortion — for example, profaning the Holy Eucharist or committing suicide. But as St. Thomas often says, there is nothing to prevent a sin from being the worst in a certain respect, even if it is not the worst absolutely speaking. No crime can be more abominable than abortion at least in this way: it is so utterly contrary to the fundamental natural good of life and to the deep-seated affection that human beings feel toward fellow human beings, especially the innocent and helpless. There can be no satisfactory excuse for this crime; everyone knows that a pregnant woman is, as the old saying goes, "a woman with child," that her abdomen is rounded because a child is growing and squirming in the womb, that from the moment of conception there is a *new human being* in addition to the mother. It is impossible not to know this if one still enjoys the use of reason.

This leads to a frightening conclusion: the prevalence of abortion in the modern world is a sign that the utmost spiritual darkness has descended upon mankind, a darkness unlike any that history has ever witnessed. For abortion to be "accepted" (let alone chosen), a person's intellect, indeed his or her entire soul, must be drifting away from reality, from self-knowledge, love for life, basic humanity — even the principle of noncontradiction, and with it, the possibility of logical thought. Contentions of man against man are one thing: as long as human beings fall prey to avarice, *libido dominandi,* and exaggerated nationalism, wars will arise and be fought. But a technologically refined and lucrative warfare against unborn children? There is nothing more depraved, nothing more profoundly contrary to the very nature of man. Abortion undermines that

[316] Thomas Molnar, *The Decline of the Intellectual,* new ed. (New Rochelle, NY: Arlington House, 1973), ix.

love of offspring written by nature upon the human heart and puts in its place an empty negation, in fact a murderous negation, of being; it turns a heart of flesh into a heart of stone.

This is why Cardinal Pell could say: "Abortion corrupts everything it touches — law, medicine, and the whole concept of human rights."[317] This it does because it corrupts the human heart first. That is why those who perform, counsel, or undergo abortions desperately need our prayers and penance: there is nothing they need more than the sacraments and the life of grace, the pardon and peace of the Lord.

St. Augustine says that Our Lord Jesus Christ heals us both by what is *like* us and by what is *unlike* us. Christ is man, so that through His humanity He may heal man; but Christ is God, and it is by His *divinity* that He has the power to heal. He can heal with His human touch because His human touch is that of Almighty God.

In parody of this, the devil, the "ape of God," seeks to harm man both by like means and by unlike means. Although the devil is pure mind, operating far above the realm of images, he leads men into the mindless activities of modern entertainment — movies, video games, virtual reality, drowning souls in the unreality of flickering images. Although silent in his intellectual evil, he leads men into ever greater noise — the din of speakers and earbuds, the pounding rock and pop music, drowning out thought, choking noble aspirations, pushing souls ever downward into the thrusting rhythm of concupiscible passion or the hot hammering of irascibility, chasing away the silence in which God can begin to speak. Although bodiless, he leads men into a fixation with bodies and bodiliness, such that they cannot raise their minds to spiritual things.

As for likenesses, on the other hand, the devil is swift in thought and fleet in motion, and he goads modern man to become ever more seemingly swift, ever more fleeting. Demonic speed translates into our mad rushing round, our minds never at rest, our desires always on the prowl, seeking what we may devour. Demonic "mastery over nature" is reflected in our technological ambitions, which are still far inferior to what the least demon has always been able to do (when permitted by Divine Providence) and yet are approaching more and more that infernal power of distorting and maiming reality that the demons exercise in their hatred of material creation and especially of man, its pinnacle

[317] Cardinal George Pell, "Varieties of Intolerance: Religious and Secular," Oxford University Newman Society, March 6, 2009, *Catholic Culture*, https://www.catholicculture.org/culture/library/view.cfm?recnum=9024.

and lord. For the devil is, as St. Ignatius of Loyola reminds us, "the enemy of our human nature."[318]

The devil is, one might say, the limit case of a mentality focused on self-will, the cult of the ego, which is the anti-spirituality that informs modern America and the modern West. The "pro-choice" mentality echoes the demons' choice to reject the divine means to happiness: the demons want everyone to be trapped in the same egoism as they are. The existentialists Jean-Paul Sartre and Albert Camus merely translate into human language the constant experience of the damned. As a medieval gloss remarked, the demons "carry the fire of hell with them wherever they go."[319] And their hell is pushing its way into this world, as modernity welcomes the demonic into its bosom.

In contrast, the pro-life mentality echoes and imitates the good angels, who chose eternal life by the power of sanctifying grace, the divinely appointed means to a supernatural end. It sees in all life an image of the Life itself, the eternal life that is properly God's and streams forth into the joy of countless saints in glory. Let us pray that we may be always guarded and guided by the holy angels, since, as the Apostle tells us, "we are not contending with flesh and blood, but against the principalities, against the powers, against the world rulers of this present darkness, against the spiritual hosts of wickedness in the heavenly places" (Eph. 6:12).[320]

In the Sermon on the Mount, Our Lord says: "The light of the body is the eye: if therefore thine eye be single,[321] thy whole body shall be full of light. But if thine eye be evil, thy whole body shall be full of darkness. If therefore the light that is in thee be darkness, how great is that darkness!" (Matt. 6:22–23 KJV). How we look at reality, how we "size it up" and "take it in" — with the eyes of the body and with the "eyes" of the spirit — this gaze either becomes a lamp that lights us up in the truth, lighting a path *per crucem ad lucem*, or it becomes a closure, a self-enclosure, a weight pulling downward, diminishing

[318] *Spiritual Exercises*, nos. 325–27.

[319] *Glossa ordinaria* on James 3:6, cited in *ST* I, Q. 64, art. 4, ad 3.

[320] On the importance of the angels and of the guardian angels in particular, see Scott Randall Paine, *The Other World We Live In: A Catholic Vision of Angelic Reality* (Brooklyn: Angelico Press, 2021); cf. my article "Why We Should Consecrate Ourselves to Our Guardian Angels," *LifeSiteNews*, October 22, 2019, www.lifesitenews.com/blogs/why-we-should-consecrate-ourselves-to-our-guardian-angels.

[321] Other translations have "healthy, clear, sound." The word in the Greek New Testament is *haplous*, which can, in addition to the foregoing, also mean "sincere, whole, fulfilling its office"; the Latin Vulgate has *simplex*.

our whole selves and other selves that come into its gravitational field. This is the stark division of vision about which Jesus speaks. We find it not only "out there" in the world, but also "in here," in our own imperfect hearts, and we look to Him who healed the blind to heal us, to be the Light that sustains our light.

Epilogue

Where the Domestic Church Becomes the Family of God

Let me begin with a plain fact: the sacred liturgy is where most Catholics most of the time encounter the Church and her teaching.

"The Church" and "the Magisterium" might well seem like abstractions until they take on *concrete form* in the liturgical rites — the texts, music, ceremonies, and other elements of worship — by which the Faith is expressed. No one has better articulated this "commonsense" point of view than Pope Pius XI in his Encyclical *Quas Primas* of December 11, 1925, explaining why he is instituting a feast in honor of the Kingship of Christ:

> People are instructed in the truths of faith and brought to appreciate the inner joys of religion far more effectually by the annual celebration of our sacred mysteries than by any official pronouncement of the teaching of the Church. Such pronouncements usually reach only a few and the more learned among the faithful; feasts reach them all; the former speak but once, the latter speak every year — in fact, forever. The Church's teaching affects the mind primarily; her feasts affect both mind and heart, and have a salutary effect upon the whole of man's nature. Man is composed of body and soul, and he needs these external festivities so that the sacred rites, in all their beauty and variety, may stimulate him to drink more deeply of the fountain of God's teaching, that he may make it a part of himself, and use it with profit for his spiritual life. (no. 21)

Today most Catholics have never heard of Pius XI or *Quas Primas*, but if they go to church at all, they will have heard of Christ the King Sunday, thus proving his point.[322]

[322] That the feast was transmogrified by Paul VI is not my concern at this moment. See my article "Between Christ the King and 'We Have No King

The Church is embodied and represented in her liturgy, and the faithful absorb their ecclesiology largely from it. Her doctrinal and moral teaching, too, is carried and conveyed by her liturgy, even if there normally are (and certainly should be) other sources by which the faithful become acquainted with it. While we know that liturgy is not primarily didactic in purpose, it will, nonetheless, catechize and spiritually shape those who participate in it.

Now, the liturgy can embody a more or less adequate ecclesiology, convey a more or less complete summary of doctrine on faith and morals, nurture a more or less correct devotional stance. A catechist and pro-life advocate eloquently made a case for these claims back in the era of Benedict XVI, using the example of the "culture of life":

> The Holy Father knows well that if God is obscured within the sacred liturgy — the very place that is not only the source and summit of the Church, but also the heart, soul, and primary point of contact for the faithful — then it is likely to follow that God will be absent or obscured in the lives of the faithful as well. Consequently, this lack of a sense of the Divine can lead to living a humanistic or self-centered existence which further leads to a lost sense of the sacredness of man; without a Creator, man becomes a mere organism in the vast universe of organisms that can be manipulated and used for any kind of fantasy by anyone who is stronger or more powerful.[323]

The author then notes how this obscuration and loss of sacrality take place:

> It is well known that many parishes today have become more centered upon themselves as a community than being clearly centered upon God — what Ratzinger has called the "self-enclosed circle." Many parishes are not following the authorized liturgical texts and rubrics — often out of a misguided sense of "pastoral" creativity, or even simply out of ignorance. Nor do they sufficiently consider (let alone express) those elements which lend a sense of transcendence to the worship of God, particularly as expressed through the medium of beauty.

but Caesar,'" *OnePeterFive*, October 25, 2020, https://onepeterfive.com/christ-king-no-king-caesar/.

[323] This and the following two quotations are from Deborah Morlani, "The Sacred Liturgy: The Neglected Foundation to Building the Culture of Life," *New Liturgical Movement*, February 3, 2010, www.newliturgicalmovement.org/2010/02/sacred-liturgy-neglected-foundation-to.html.

To the almost universal reaction of shrugged shoulders and "So ... your point is?," she responds:

> To some, these might seem rather unimportant surface considerations, but they are not. The sacred liturgy and doctrine are intertwined and the experiential dimension of the liturgy is a profound moment for catechesis and conversion. Accordingly, when there is a problematic approach to the liturgy, and when unauthorized innovations are introduced, there can be a deficiency as well as a coinciding distortion of Catholic belief passed on to the faithful, as well as a loss in the power of the liturgy to move the human heart and mind towards God.

In this way, the moral and religious imagination can suffer atrophy, the awakening to higher truths and deeper demands of the Gospel be impeded. The peculiar combination of consolation and challenge found in age-old rites is dampened to an unthreatening banality that reassures mediocrity and silences the divine voice questioning our compromises with the world. To Morlani's gentle words, we may compare the more blunt remarks of Frederick D. Wilhelmsen:

> The empty womb stripped of its child by an abortionist is analogous to the empty altar stripped of its God by the theological abortionist — the man who either denies, or, what is more frequent, ignores or plays down the Real Presence of Our Lord Jesus Christ in the Sacrifice of the Mass and in the Blessed Sacrament of the Altar.[324]

The casting aside in the 1960s and 1970s of so much that was good, holy, beautiful, and meaningful in Catholic life, as if it were a worthless, tattered old garment of no value, remains to this day, and indeed for all time, an astonishing testimony to the intoxicating power of momentary ideological enthusiasms. The decades thereafter have been like an enormous hangover that no number of aspirins, cold showers, or cups of coffee can get rid of.

The huge fallacy behind this strip-down strategy, as we see more clearly in retrospect, consisted in thinking that the substance of the Faith could be separated from its accidents. A sound metaphysics would indicate that, apart from the miracle of the Holy Eucharist, there is *never* a situation where a substance can

[324] Quoted in Msgr. Ignacio Barreiro Carámbula, "Sacred Liturgy and the Defense of Human Life," in *Sacred Liturgy — The Source and Summit of the Life and Mission of the Church*, ed. Alcuin Reid (San Francisco: Ignatius Press, 2014), 371–88, at 377.

exist without its accidents — and when we do enough damage to the accidents, we destroy the substance. To put it simply, if you change the shape and quantity of a duck enough, you will not have a duck left — only some messy parts that once were the parts of a duck. That seems to me to be analogous to what the Roman Church — or, more accurately, her more "with-it" and therefore less thoughtful members — did to the great heritage of prayer, rubrics, music, architecture, vesture, and poetry, the grand and complex language of public worship.

In his Apostolic Exhortation *Familiaris Consortio*, Pope John Paul II stated: "The fruitfulness of the Christian family in its specific service to human advancement, which of itself cannot but lead to the transformation of the world, derives from its living union with Christ, *nourished by liturgy,* by self-oblation, and by prayer" (no. 62, emphasis added). For all its humble "ordinariness," the family is the first school in which children learn about transcendent things — about God, the saints, eternal truths, virtues, commitment, self-sacrifice, self-discipline. Christian marriage witnesses to the children that there is something permanent, abiding, rock-solid, resting on Christ and sustained by His Spirit.

The liturgy should be inspiring and sustaining parents' efforts within the family to proclaim these wonderful truths, but it is often doing little or nothing of the sort or is promoting the opposite. In an age of great intellectual and moral confusion, the shepherds have failed their flocks by not supporting them with the fullness of Gospel truth and of Christian tradition in the most obvious place we would think to encounter it: the public worship of the Catholic Church.[325]

Many factors have contributed to the precipitous decline of Catholics' knowledge of and adherence to the Church's Magisterium on marriage and the family — including powerful forces of liberalism, secularism, hedonistic materialism, and individualism, the failure of many clerics to expound and defend sexual ethics (or even to address them at all), dissenting but uncensured Catholic politicians and Church leaders, and the continuing deficiencies in religious education and school curricula. All this is undeniable. Yet there is a much deeper connection between our collective liturgical worship and the spiritual health of marriages and families than the Church's hierarchy has yet

[325] For an extended treatment of the immense value of the traditional liturgical heritage of the West for the education of children and for the strengthening of the family, see the chapters "Children Change Everything," "What Children Learn from the Traditional Mass," "Good and Bad Liturgical Parenting," and "Helping Children Enter into the Mass" in Kwasniewski, *Reclaiming Our Roman Catholic Birthright*, 235–95.

seen fit to acknowledge, because (it would seem) of a settled commitment to a policy of never admitting mistakes that could implicate a council's prudential advisements or a pope's disciplinary decisions.[326]

May the Lord awaken the rulers of Christ's faithful, as if by a violent rousing from sleep, to begin searching in earnest for *deeper* causes of the culture of death that surrounds us, the practical atheism and the silent apostasy that characterize our times. Meanwhile, may clergy who celebrate the traditional rites of East and West, and the laity who assist at them, be assured that they are engaged in a necessary and long-overdue rebuilding of "the heart, soul, and primary point of contact for the faithful." As Glenn Arbery says, in words that serve as one of the epigraphs of this book: "Up in the heights of the tradition, protected in grandeur and difficulty, are life-giving waters that descend with surprising force into a world thirsty for courage."

Communion for life derives from and leads to Communion with Life Itself—with the Bread of Life Himself. "I am come that they may have life, and may have it more abundantly" (John 10:9–10).

[326] See chapter 8.

Bibliography

The following list of works cited or mentioned in this book does not include articles of a more journalistic nature, such as news reports.

Church Documents

Benedict XVI. Encyclical Letter *Deus Caritas Est*. December 25, 2005.

———. Post-Synodal Apostolic Exhortation *Sacramentum Caritatis*. February 22, 2007.

Catechism of the Catholic Church. Second edition. English translation for the United States of America. Washington, DC: United States Catholic Conference/Vatican City: Libreria Editrice Vaticana, 1997.

Council of Trent. *The Canons and Decrees of the Council of Trent*. Translated by H. J. Schroeder. Rockford, IL: TAN Books, 1978.

———. *The Catechism of the Council of Trent*. Translated by John A. McHugh and Charles J. Callan. Rockford, IL: TAN Books, 1982.

John Paul II. *Catechesis on Consecrated Life*. General audiences held during 1994 and 1995.

———. Discorso di Giovanni Paolo II ai partecipanti ad un incontro di studio sulla procreazione responsabile. June 5, 1987.

———. Discorso di Giovanni Paolo II ai partecipanti al IV Congresso Internazionale per la Famiglia d'Africa e d'Europa. March 14, 1988.

———. Discorso di Giovanni Paolo II ai partecipanti al II Congresso Internazionale di Teologia Morale. November 12, 1988.

———. Encyclical Letter *Evangelium Vitae*. March 25, 1995.

———. Post-Synodal Apostolic Exhortation *Familiaris Consortio*. November 22, 1981.

———. Letter to Families *Gratissimam Sane*. February 2, 1994.

———. *Man and Woman He Created Them: A Theology of the Body.* Translated by Michael Waldstein. Boston: Pauline Books & Media, 2006.

———. Post-Synodal Apostolic Exhortation *Redemptionis Donum.* March 25, 1984.

———. Encyclical Letter *Veritatis Splendor.* August 6, 1993.

Leo XIII. Encyclical Letter *Sapientiae Christianae.* January 10, 1890.

———. Encyclical Letter *Diuturnum Illud.* June 29, 1881.

———. Encyclical Letter *Libertas Praestantissimum.* June 20, 1888.

———. *Tametsi Futura.* Encyclical Letter, November 1, 1900.

Paul VI. Address to General Chapters of Religious Orders and Congregations. May 23, 1964.

———. Encyclical Letter *Humanae Vitae.* July 25, 1968.

Pius X. Encyclical Letter *Pascendi Dominici Gregis.* September 8, 1907.

Pius XI. Encyclical Letter *Casti Connubii.* December 31, 1930.

———. Encyclical Letter *Quas Primas.* December 11, 1925.

———. Encyclical Letter *Vigilanti Cura.* June 29, 1936.

Pius XII. Address to Midwives on the Nature of Their Profession. October 29, 1951.

———. Encyclical Letter *Miranda Prorsus.* September 8, 1957.

———. Encyclical Letter *Sacra Virginitas.* March 25, 1954.

Vatican II. Constitution on the Sacred Liturgy *Sacrosanctum Concilium.* December 4, 1963.

———. Dogmatic Constitution on the Church *Lumen Gentium.* November 21, 1964.

———. Pastoral Constitution on the Church in the Modern World *Gaudium et Spes.* December 7, 1965.

———. Decree on the Adaptation and Renewal of Religious Life *Perfectae Caritatis.* October 28, 1965.

Weller, Philip T., trans. and ed. *The Roman Ritual.* Vol. 1, *The Sacraments and Processions.* Boonville, NY: Preserving Christian Publications, 2005.

Other Works

Ahlquist, Dale. "Believing in Anything." *Faith & Culture,* May 29, 2019. www.faithandculture.com/home/2019/5/29-believing-in-anything.

Arias, Jennaya. "On the Primary Purpose of Marriage." *Catholic Culture.* Originally published 2002. https://www.catholicculture.org/culture/library/view.cfm?recnum=5822.

Aristotle. *Metaphysics*. Translated by W. D. Ross. In *The Complete Works of Aristotle: The Revised Oxford Translation*, edited by Jonathan Barnes. 2 volumes. Princeton, NJ: Princeton University Press, 1984.

———. *Nicomachean Ethics*. Translated by Robert C. Bartlett and Susan D. Collins. Chicago: University of Chicago Press, 2011.

———. *De Anima, or About the Soul*. Translated by Glen Coughlin. South Bend, IN: St. Augustine's Press, 2022.

Arjakovsky, Antoine. *What Is Orthodoxy?: A Genealogy of Christian Understanding*. Translated by Jerry Ryan and Penelope Cavill. Brooklyn: Angelico Press, 2018.

Asci, Donald P. *The Conjugal Act as a Personal Act: A Study of the Catholic Concept of the Conjugal Act in the Light of Christian Anthropology*. San Francisco: Ignatius Press, 2002.

Augustine of Hippo. *Confessions*. Translated by F. J. Sheed. Edited by Michael P. Foley. Indianapolis: Hackett, 2006.

Barnes, Jonathan, trans. and ed. *Early Greek Philosophy*. New York: Penguin, 1987.

Barnes, Marc. "Abortion Is Eugenics." *New Polity*, May 11, 2022. https://newpolity.com/blog/abortion-is-eugenics.

Barreiro Carámbula, Ignacio. "Sacred Liturgy and the Defense of Human Life." In *Sacred Liturgy: The Source and Summit of the Life and Mission of the Church*, edited by Alcuin Reid, 371–88. San Francisco: Ignatius Press, 2014.

Basil of Caesarea. "Address to Young Men on the Right Use of Greek Literature." In Frederick Morgan Padelford, *Essays on the Study and Use of Poetry by Plutarch and Basil the Great*, 99–120. New York: Henry Holt, 1902. www.tertullian.org/fathers/basil_litterature01.htm.

Bell, Luke. *The Mystery of Identity*. Brooklyn: Angelico Press, 2022.

Bellarmine, St. Robert. *A Commentary on the Book of Psalms*. Translated by John O'Sullivan. Fitzwilliam, NH: Loreto Publications, 2003.

Belloc, Hilaire. *Letters*. Edited by Robert Speaight. London: Hollis & Carter, 1958.

Benedict of Nursia. *The Rule of Saint Benedict in English and Latin*. Translated and edited by Abbot Justin McCann, O.S.B. Fort Collins: Roman Catholic Books, n.d.

Benedict XVI and Robert Cardinal Sarah. *From the Depths of Our Hearts: Priesthood, Celibacy, and the Crisis of the Catholic Church*. Translated by Michael J. Miller. San Francisco: Ignatius Press, 2020.

Benson, Robert Hugh. *Paradoxes of Catholicism*. London: Longmans, Green, 1913. Reprint, Miami: HardPress Publishing, n.d.

Bergman, Jerry. "H. G. Wells: Darwin's Disciple and Eugenicist Extraordinaire." *Journal of Creation* 18, no. 3 (December 2004): 116–20. https://answersingenesis.org/sanctity-of-life/eugenics/hg-wells-darwins-disciple-and-eugenicist-extraordinaire.

Borella, Jean. *Love and Truth: The Christian Path of Charity*. Translated by G. John Champoux. Brooklyn: Angelico Press, 2020.

Bulgakov, Sergius. *Spiritual Diary*. Translated by Mark Roosien and Roberto J. De La Noval. Brooklyn: Angelico Press, 2022.

Burke, Raymond Leo. "Cardinal Burke's Sermon at the Fota Conference." *New Liturgical Movement*, July 11, 2015. https://www.newliturgicalmovement.org/2015/07/cardinal-burkes-sermon-at-fota.html.

———. "A Sermon by Cardinal Burke: On the Marriage of the Virgin Mary with St. Joseph." *New Liturgical Movement*, January 23, 2015. https://www.newliturgicalmovement.org/2015/01/a-sermon-by-cardinal-burke-on-marriage.html.

Bux, Nicola. *No Trifling Matter: Taking the Sacraments Seriously Again*. Brooklyn: Angelico Press, 2018.

Buzzard, Kelli. "Abortion's Bed of Lies." *Crisis Magazine*, May 24, 2022. www.crisismagazine.com/2022/abortions-bed-of-lies.

Campbell, Phillip. "There's Always a Priest Shortage in Missionary Areas." *Unam Sanctam Catholicam*, June 20, 2019. http://unamsanctamcatholicam.blogspot.com/2019/06/theres-always-priest-shortage-in.html.

———. "The Truth about Priestly Celibacy in the Early Church." *Unam Sanctam Catholicam*, July 5, 2014. http://unamsanctamcatholicam.com/the-truth-about-priestly-celibacy-in-the-early-church.

Chesterton, G. K. *Orthodoxy*. In *The Collected Works of G. K. Chesterton*. Vol. 1. Edited by David Dooley. San Francisco: Ignatius Press, 1986.

———. *What's Wrong with the World*. New York: Sheed & Ward, 1942.

Cholij, Roman. *Clerical Celibacy in East and West*. Leominster: Gracewing, 1989.

Clark, Stephen R. L. *Can We Believe in People?: Human Significance in an Interconnected Cosmos*. Brooklyn: Angelico Press, 2020.

———. *Cities and Thrones and Powers: Towards a Plotinian Politics*. Brooklyn: Angelico Press, 2022.

Clayton, David, and Leila Marie Lawler. *The Little Oratory: A Beginner's Guide to Praying in the Home*. Manchester, NH: Sophia Institute Press, 2014.

Craughwell, Thomas J. "The Gentile Holocaust." *Sursum Corda!* (Summer 1998): 28–30, 47–49. *Catholic Culture*. www.catholicculture.org/culture/library/view.cfm?recnum=472.

Crean, Thomas, and Alan Fimister. *Integralism: A Manual of Political Philosophy.* Neunkirchen-Seelscheid, Germany: editiones scholasticae, 2020.

Daniel, William. *Christ the Liturgy*. Brooklyn: Angelico Press, 2020.

de Lubac, Henri. *Catholicism: Christ and the Common Destiny of Man*. Translated by L. Sheppard and E. Englund. San Francisco: Ignatius Press, 1988.

DiPippo, Gregory. "The Feast of the Holy Maccabees." *New Liturgical Movement*, August 1, 2021. https://www.newliturgicalmovement.org/2021/08/the-feast-of-holy-maccabees.html.

Donne, John. "The Extasie," in *The Complete English Poems*. Edited by A. J. Smith, 56–57. Harmondsworth: Penguin, 1971.

Dubay, Thomas. *Faith and Certitude: Can We Be Sure of the Things That Matter Most to Us?* San Francisco: Ignatius Press, 1985.

Dyikuk, Justine John. "Towards a Theology of the Body." *La Croix International*, July 13, 2022. https://international.la-croix.com/news/religion/towards-a-theology-of-the-body/16387.

Eliot, T. S. *The Complete Poems and Plays, 1909–1950*. New York: Harcourt Brace Jovanovich, 1980.

Esolen, Anthony. "A Conciliar Church on a Path to Schism with the Council Itself." *Crisis Magazine*, July 20, 2022. www.crisismagazine.com/2022/a-conciliar-church-on-a-path-to-schism-with-the-council-itself.

———. "No Way Out." *The Catholic Thing*, March 22, 2018. www.thecatholicthing.org/2018/03/22/no-way-out.

Ferrara, Christopher A. *Liberty, the God That Failed: Policing the Sacred and Constructing the Myths of the Secular State, from Locke to Obama*. Tacoma, WA: Angelico Press, 2012.

Feser, Edward, and Joseph M. Bessette. *By Man Shall His Blood Be Shed: A Catholic Defense of Capital Punishment*. San Francisco: Ignatius Press, 2017.

Foster, Catherine Glenn. "How Abortionists Dispose of Their Victims," *First Things*, July 18, 2022. www.firstthings.com/web-exclusives/2022/07/how-abortionists-dispose-of-their-victims.

George, Marie I. *Christianity and Extraterrestrials?: A Catholic Perspective*. Lincoln, NE: iUniverse, 2005.

Gillespie, Michael Allen. *The Theological Origins of Modernity*. Chicago: University of Chicago Press, 2009.

Hajduk, David C. *Healing the Culture and the Family According to John Paul II*. Waterloo, ON: Arouca Press, 2022.

Hardon, John. "Contraception: Fatal to the Faith and to Eternal Life." *Real Presence Association*. www.therealpresence.org/archives/Chastity/Chastity_004.htm.

———. "Prayer and Chastity." *Real Presence Association*. www.therealpresence.org/archives/Chastity/Chastity_006.htm.

Hobbes, Thomas. *Leviathan*. Edited by C. B. Macpherson. New York: Penguin, 1986.

Holböck, Ferdinand. *Married Saints and Blesseds through the Centuries*. Translated by Michael J. Miller. San Francisco: Ignatius Press, 2002.

Horn, Trent, and Leila Miller. *Made This Way: How to Prepare Kids to Face Today's Tough Moral Issues*. El Cajon, CA: Catholic Answers, 2018.

Hume, David. *A Treatise of Human Nature*. Edited by David Fate Norton and Mary J. Norton. Oxford: Oxford University Press, 2000.

Ignatius of Loyola. *The Spiritual Exercises of Saint Ignatius of Loyola*. Translated by Thomas Corbishley. Wheathampstead, Hertfordshire: Anthony Clarke, 1973.

John Paul II. *Crossing the Threshold of Hope*. Edited by Vittorio Messori. Translated by Jenny McPhee and Martha McPhee. New York: Alfred A. Knopf, 1994.

Kabel, Sharon. "Rite of Betrothal." *Latin Mass Wedding*. www.latinmasswedding.com/rite-of-betrothal/.

Kalinowska, Anna. "The Art of Dress — Problems with Normalcy." *OnePeterFive*, July 12, 2022. https://onepeterfive.com/art-dress-problems-normalcy.

Kemp, Peter. *H. G. Wells and the Culminating Ape: Biological Imperatives and Imaginative Obsessions*. New York: St. Martin's Press, 1996.

Kozinski, Thaddeus. *The Political Problem of Religious Pluralism: And Why Philosophers Can't Solve It*. Lanham, MD: Lexington Books, 2010.

Kwasniewski, Peter. "Between Christ the King and 'We Have No King But Caesar.'" *OnePeterFive*, October 25, 2020. https://onepeterfive.com/christ-king-no-king-caesar/.

———. "Christian Militancy in the Prayer of the Church." *OnePeterFive*, March 16, 2022. https://onepeterfive.com/christian-militancy-in-the-prayer-of-the-church/.

———. *The Ecstasy of Love in the Thought of Thomas Aquinas*. Steubenville, OH: Emmaus Academic, 2021.

———. "God Made Us for Heaven." *OnePeterFive*, August 10, 2022. https://onepeterfive.com/god-made-us-for-heaven-2/.

———. *The Holy Bread of Eternal Life: Restoring Eucharistic Reverence in an Age of Impiety.* Manchester, NH: Sophia Institute Press, 2020.

———. "Hominization, or Man at the Moment of Conception." *OnePeterFive,* May 13, 2020. https://onepeterfive.com/hominization-conception.

———. "How to Talk to Children about Liturgical Evils." *OnePeterFive,* October 23, 2019. https://onepeterfive.com/talk-children-liturgical-evils/.

———. "Listening with an Attentive Ear to God's Poetry." In *The Glory of the Cosmos: A Catholic Approach to the Natural World,* edited by Thomas Storck, 139–50. Waterloo, ON: Arouca Press, 2020.

———. "May His Kingdom Come: Catholic Social Teaching, Part VI — Conversion of Culture." *Catholic Family News,* September 25, 2020. https://catholicfamilynews.com/blog/2020/09/25/may-his-kingdom-come-catholic-social-teaching-part-vi-conversion-of-culture.

———. *Ministers of Christ: Recovering the Roles of Clergy and Laity in an Age of Confusion.* Manchester, NH: Crisis Publications, 2021.

———. "The New Lectionary and the Catholic Wedding." *OnePeterFive,* May 22, 2019. https://onepeterfive.com/lectionary-wedding/.

———. *The Once and Future Roman Rite: Returning to the Traditional Latin Liturgy after Seventy Years of Exile.* Gastonia, NC: TAN Books, 2022.

———. "On Discerning Vocations: How to Think about 'States of Life.' " *OnePeterFive,* January 23, 2019. https://onepeterfive.com/vocations-better.

———. "On Hell: Clarity Is Mercy in an Age of 'Dare We Hope.' " *OnePeterFive,* August 7, 2019. https://onepeterfive.com/hell-clarity-mercy/.

———. "On Intellectualism and the Beatific Vision." *Aquinas Review* 23 (2019–2020): 189–203.

———. *Reclaiming Our Roman Catholic Birthright: The Genius and Timeliness of the Traditional Latin Mass.* Brooklyn: Angelico Press, 2020.

———. "The Return of the 'Care Cloth' at the Traditional Nuptial Mass." *New Liturgical Movement,* September 13, 2021. www.newliturgicalmovement.org/2021/09/the-return-of-care-cloth-at-traditional.html.

———. *The Road from Hyperpapalism to Catholicism: Rethinking the Papacy in a Time of Ecclesial Disintegration.* Vol. 1, *Theological Reflections on the Rock of the Church.* Vol. 2, *Chronological Responses to an Unfolding Pontificate.* Waterloo, ON: Arouca Press, 2022.

———. "St. Thomas on the Grandeur and Limitations of Marriage." *Nova et Vetera* (English ed.) vol. 10, no. 2 (2012): 415–36.

———. "Should We 'Despise Earthly Goods and Love Heavenly Ones'? A Liturgical Lesson for Lent." *OnePeterFive,* March 2, 2022. https://onepeterfive.com/despise-earthly-goods/.

———. "Tensions in the Catholic Tradition on Frequent Communion." *New Liturgical Movement,* September 5, 2022. https://www.newliturgicalmovement.org/2022/09/tensions-in-catholic-tradition-on.html.

———. *True Obedience in the Church: A Guide to Discernment in Challenging Times.* Manchester, NH: Sophia Institute Press, 2021.

———. "Why We Should Consecrate Ourselves to Our Guardian Angels." *LifeSiteNews,* October 22, 2019. www.lifesitenews.com/blogs/why-we-should-consecrate-ourselves-to-our-guardian-angels.

Kwasniewski, Peter, and Edmund Waldstein, eds. *Integralism and the Common Good: Selected Essays from* The Josias. Vol. 1, *Family, City, and State.* Brooklyn: Angelico Press, 2021.

Lahl, Jennifer. "Babies for Sale." *First Things,* May 22, 2020. www.firstthings.com/web-exclusives/2020/05/babies-for-sale.

Lamont, John R. T., and Claudio Pierantoni. *Defending the Faith against Present Heresies.* Waterloo, ON: Arouca Press, n.d. [2021].

Lawler, Leila Marie. *God Has No Grandchildren: A Guided Reading of Pius XI's Encyclical* Casti Connubii, *On Chaste Marriage.* 2nd ed. Waterloo, ON: Arouca Press, 2021.

———. *The Summa Domestica: Order and Wonder in Family Life.* 3 vols. Manchester, NH: Sophia Institute Press, 2021.

Lemna, Keith. *The Apocalypse of Wisdom: Louis Bouyer's Theological Recovery of the Cosmos.* Brooklyn: Angelico, 2019.

Locke, John. *Second Treatise of Civil Government.* Edited by C. B. Macpherson. Indianapolis: Hackett Publishing, 1980.

Malloy, Christopher J. *False Mercy: Recent Heresies Distorting Catholic Truth.* Manchester, NH: Sophia Institute Press, 2021.

Marcel, Gabriel. *Being and Having.* Translated by Katharine Farrer. Westminster: Dacre Press, 1949.

———. *Homo Viator: Introduction to a Metaphysic of Hope.* Translated by Emma Craufurd. Chicago: Henry Regnery, 1951.

———. *Metaphysical Journal.* Translated by Bernard Wall. Chicago: Henry Regnery, 1952.

———. *The Mystery of Being.* Vol. 1: *Reflection & Mystery.* Translated by G. S. Fraser. Chicago: Henry Regnery, 1960.

———. *The Mystery of Being.* Vol. 2: *Faith & Reality*. Translated by René Hague. Chicago: Henry Regnery Co., 1960.

Marcum, Kelly. "The Self-Hate of Abortion Advocates." *American Conservative,* July 2, 2022. www.theamericanconservative.com/the-self-hate-of-abortion-advocates.

Marmion, Columba. *Christ the Ideal of the Monk: Spiritual Conferences on the Monastic and Religious Life.* Translated by a nun of Tyburn Convent. Stamullen, Ireland: Cenacle Press, 2022.

Martin, Regis. "Overcoming Hardness of Hearts on Abortion." *Crisis Magazine,* May 17, 2022. www.crisismagazine.com/2022/overcoming-hardness-of-hearts-on-abortion.

Merton, Thomas. *New Seeds of Contemplation.* New York: New Directions, 1972.

Miller, Leila. *Primal Loss: The Now-Adult Children of Divorce Speak.* Phoenix: LCB Publishing, 2017.

Molnar, Thomas. *The Decline of the Intellectual.* New edition. New Rochelle, NY: Arlington House, 1973.

Morlani, Deborah. "The Sacred Liturgy: The Neglected Foundation to Building the Culture of Life." *New Liturgical Movement,* February 3, 2010. www.newliturgicalmovement.org/2010/02/sacred-liturgy-neglected-foundation-to.html.

Mullady, Brian. *St. Thomas Aquinas Rescues Modern Psychology.* Irondale, AL: EWTN Publishing, 2022.

Newland, Mary Reed. *We and Our Children: How to Make a Catholic Home.* Tacoma, WA: Angelico Press, 2012.

———. *The Year and Our Children: Planning the Family Activities for Christian Feasts and Seasons.* Manchester, NH: Sophia Institute Press, 2007.

Newman, John Henry. *An Essay on the Development of Christian Doctrine.* London: Longmans, Green, 1909.

———. *Certain Difficulties Felt by Anglicans in Catholic Teaching Considered.* London: Longmans, Green, 1901.

Nicholson, D. H. S., and A. H. E. Lee, eds. *The Oxford Book of English Mystical Verse.* Oxford: Clarendon Press, 1917.

Novák, Lukáš, and Marie Tejklová, eds. *Dispelling the Fog: Critical Essays on* Amoris Laetitia. Neunkirchen-Seelscheid: editiones scholasticae, 2022.

Nietzsche, Friedrich. *Thus Spake Zarathustra.* Translated by Thomas Common. Mineola, NY: Dover Publications, 1999.

Paglia, Camille. "Fresh Blood for the Vampire." *Salon*, September 10, 2008. www.salon.com/2008/09/10/palin_10.

Paine, Scott Randall. *The Other World We Live In: A Catholic Vision of Angelic Reality*. Brooklyn: Angelico Press, 2021.

Pascal, Blaise. *Pensées*. Translated by A. J. Krailsheimer. New York: Penguin, 1966.

Pell, George. "Varieties of Intolerance: Religious and Secular." Oxford University Newman Society, March 6, 2009. *Catholic Culture*. www.catholicculture.org/culture/library/view.cfm?recnum=9024.

Perrin, Xavier. *The Radiance of Her Face: A Triptych in Honor of Mary Immaculate*. Translated by Sr. Laetitia Payne and Sr. Deirdre Michael Clarke. Kettering, OH: Angelico Press, 2017.

Peters, Edward N. "The Bloody 14 and the Question of Excommunication." *Catholic World Report*, January 31, 2018. https://www.catholicworldreport.com/2018/01/31/the-bloody-14-and-the-question-of-excommunication/.

———. "Sure, Celibacy Is 'Disciplinary,' but Then, So Is ..." *In the Light of the Law*, April 10, 2014. https://canonlawblog.wordpress.com/2014/04/10/sure-celibacy-is-disciplinary-but-then-so-is/.

Pieper, Josef. *Faith, Hope, Love*. Translated by Richard and Clara Winston and Sr. Mary Frances McCarthy. San Francisco: Ignatius Press, 1997.

Plotinus. *The Enneads*. Translated by A. H. Armstrong. Loeb Classical Library. Cambridge, Massachusetts: Harvard University Press, 1966–1988.

Ratzinger, Joseph. *Collected Works*. Vol. 11: *Theology of the Liturgy: The Sacramental Foundation of Christian Existence*. Edited by Michael J. Miller. San Francisco: Ignatius Press, 2014.

———. *Salt of the Earth: Christianity and the Catholic Church at the End of the Millennium*. Translated by A. Walker. San Francisco: Ignatius Press, 1997.

———. *The Spirit of the Liturgy*. Translated by John Saward. San Francisco: Ignatius Press, 2000.

———. "Truth and Freedom." In *Joseph Ratzinger in* Communio. Vol. 2, *Anthropology and Culture*, edited by David L. Schindler and Nicholas J. Healy, 147–67. Grand Rapids, MI: William B. Eerdmans, 2013.

Reid, Alcuin. *The Organic Development of the Liturgy: The Principles of Liturgical Reform and Their Relation to the Twentieth-Century Liturgical Movement prior to the Second Vatican Council*. San Francisco: Ignatius Press, 2005.

Reno, R. R. "Liberal Tradition, Yes; Liberal Ideology, No." *First Things*, December 2017. www.firstthings.com/article/2017/12/liberal-tradition-yes-liberal-ideology-no.

Rowland, Tracey. *Portraits of Spiritual Nobility*. Brooklyn: Angelico Press, 2019.

Ryland, Ray. "The Gift: A Married Priest Looks at Celibacy." *Crisis Magazine*, October 1, 2006. www.crisismagazine.com/2006/the-gift-a-married-priest-looks-at-celibacy.

Scruton, Roger. "'Cows Too … Can Easily Be Made into Ideas': An Interview with Roger Scruton." *Clarion Review*, October 9, 2009. www.clarionreview.org/2009/10/interview-roger-scruton.

Selin, Gary. *Priestly Celibacy: Theological Foundations*. Washington, DC: Catholic University of America Press, 2016.

Sertillanges, A. G. *The Intellectual Life: Its Spirit, Conditions, Methods*. Translated by Mary Ryan. Washington, DC: Catholic University of America Press, 1992.

Scheeben, Matthias. *The Mysteries of Christianity*. Translated by Cyril Vollert. St. Louis: B. Herder, 1946.

Skojec, Steve. "Modernists Are Tricky. That's Kind of the Point." *Steve Skojec*, July 12, 2014. https://steveskojec.com/2014/07/modernists-are-tricky-thats-kind-of-the-point.

———. "Why Are 'Pro-Choice' Advocates So Afraid of Choice?" *The Skojec File*, May 3, 2022. https://skojecfile.steveskojec.com/p/why-are-pro-choice-advocates-so-afraid.

Sola, Francis A. P., and Joseph F. Sagüés. *Sacrae Theologiae Summa IVB: On Holy Orders and Matrimony; On the Last Things*. Translated by Kenneth Baker. N.p.: Keep the Faith, 2016.

Spinoza, Baruch. *On the Improvement of the Understanding; The Ethics; Correspondence*. Translated by R. H. M. Elwes. New York: Dover Publications, 1955.

Storck, Thomas. *Foundations of a Catholic Political Order*. 2nd ed. Waterloo, ON: Arouca Press, 2022.

———. *From Christendom to Americanism and Beyond: The Long, Jagged Trail to a Postmodern Void*. Kettering, OH: Angelico Press, 2015.

Thomas Aquinas. *Catena Aurea: Commentary on the Four Gospels, Collected out of the Works of the Fathers*. Edited by John Henry Newman. Southampton: Saint Austin Press, 1997.

———. *Commentary on the Gospel of Matthew*. Translated by Jeremy Holmes and Beth Mortensen. Latin/English Edition of the Works of St. Thomas Aquinas, volumes 33–34. Green Bay, WI: Aquinas Institute/Steubenville, OH: Emmaus Academic, 2018.

———. *Commentary on the Letters of Saint Paul to the Galatians and Ephesians*. Translated by Fabian R. Larcher and Matthew Lamb. Latin/English Edition of the Works of St. Thomas Aquinas, volume 39. Green Bay, WI: Aquinas Institute/Steubenville, OH: Emmaus Academic, 2018.

———. *Commentary on the* Nicomachean Ethics. Translated by C. I. Litzinger. Chicago: Henry Regnery, 1964.

———. *Commentary on the "Sentences," Book IV.* Translated by Beth Mortensen, Peter Kwasniewski, and Dylan Schrader. Latin/English Edition of the Works of St. Thomas Aquinas, volumes 7–10. Green Bay, WI: Aquinas Institute/Steubenville, OH: Emmaus Academic, 2018.

———. *On the Perfection of the Spiritual Life*. Latin text at www.corpusthomisticum.org/oap.html. English translation at www.pathsoflove.com/aquinas/perfection-of-the-spiritual-life.html.

———. *Summa contra Gentiles.* Translated by Fr. Laurence Shapcote. Latin/English Edition of the Works of St. Thomas Aquinas, volumes 11–12. Green Bay, WI: Aquinas Institute/Steubenville, OH: Emmaus Academic, 2018.

———. *Summa Theologiae.* Translated by Fr. Laurence Shapcote. Latin/English Edition of the Works of St. Thomas Aquinas, volumes 13–22. Green Bay, WI: Aquinas Institute/Steubenville, OH: Emmaus Academic, 2018.

Trueman, Carl R. *The Rise and Triumph of the Modern Self: Cultural Amnesia, Expressive Individualism, and the Road to Sexual Revolution*. Wheaton, IL: Crossway, 2020.

———. *Strange New World: How Thinkers and Activists Redefined Identity and Sparked the Sexual Revolution*. Wheaton, IL: Crossway, 2022.

———. "Why Pro-Abortion Activists Desecrate Churches." *First Things*, May 12, 2022. www.firstthings.com/web-exclusives/2022/05/why-pro-abortion-activists-desecrate-churches.

Verschuuren, Gerard M. *At the Dawn of Humanity: The First Humans*. Brooklyn: Angelico Press, 2020.

Vianney, St. John. *Eucharistic Meditations: Extracts from the Writings and Instructions of St. John Vianney*. Edited by Abbé H. Convert. Translated by Sr. Mary Benvenuta. Wheathampstead, Hertfordshire: Anthony Clarke Books, 1923; repr. 1964.

von Trapp, Maria Augusta. *Around the Year with the Von Trapp Family*. Manchester, NH: Sophia Institute Press, 2018.

Waldstein, Edmund, ed. *Integralism and the Common Good: Selected Essays from* The Josias. Vol. 2, *The Two Powers*. Brooklyn: Angelico Press, 2022.

Waldstein, Michael. *Glory of the Logos in the Flesh: Saint John Paul's Theology of the Body*. Ave Maria, FL: Sapientia Press, 2021.

Weber, Samuel. *The Proper of the Mass for Sundays and Solemnities: Chants for the Roman Missal in English*. San Francisco: Ignatius Press, 2015.

Wilson, James Matthew. *The Vision of the Soul: Truth, Goodness, and Beauty in the Western Tradition*. Washington, DC: Catholic University of America Press, 2017.

Wolf, Naomi. "Our Bodies, Our Souls: Rethinking Abortion Rhetoric." *New Republic*, October 16, 1995: 26–35.

Wojtyła, Karol. *Sources of Renewal: The Implementation of the Second Vatican Council*. Translated by Paul Stephen Falla. San Francisco: Harper and Row, 1980.

Wrzaszczak, Chester. "Engagements — In Church." *American Ecclesiastical Review* (October 1962): 243–54. Online at *Catholic Culture*. www.catholicculture.org/culture/library/view.cfm?recnum=2978.

Additional Recommended Works

Anderson, Ryan T., and Alexandra DeSanctis. *Tearing Us Apart: How Abortion Harms Everything and Solves Nothing*. Washington, DC: Regnery Publishing, 2022.

Arminjon, Blaise. *The Cantata of Love: A Verse by Verse Reading of the Song of Songs*. San Francisco: Ignatius Press, 1988.

Bereit, David, with Shawn Carney. *40 Days for Life: Discover What God Has Done … Imagine What He Can Do*. Expanded ed. Nashville: Cappella Books, 2017.

Carney, Shawn D. *The Beginning of the End of Abortion: 40 Inspiring Stories of God Changing Hearts and Saving Lives*. Nashville: Cappella Books, 2018.

———. *To the Heart of the Matter: The 40 Day Companion to Live a Culture of Life*. Nashville: Cappella Books, 2020.

Carney, Shawn D., and Steve Karlen. *What to Say When: The Complete New Guide to Discussing Abortion*. Bryan, TX: Kolbe & Anthony Publishing, 2021.

Chesterton, G. K. *Brave New Family: G. K. Chesterton on Men and Women, Children, Sex, Divorce, Marriage, and the Family*. Edited by Alvaro de Silva. San Francisco: Ignatius Press, 1990.

Cochini, Christian. *The Apostolic Origins of Priestly Celibacy*. San Francisco: Ignatius Press, 1990.

Cole, Basil. *The Hidden Enemies of the Priesthood: The Contributions of St. Thomas Aquinas*. Staten Island, NY: Alba House, 2007.

Cooper, Adam G. *Holy Eros: A Liturgical Theology of the Body*. Kettering, OH: Angelico Press, 2014.

Delany, Selden P. *Married Saints.* Providence, RI: Cluny Media, 2020.

Derrick, Christopher. *Sex and Sacredness: A Catholic Homage to Venus.* San Francisco: Ignatius Press, 1982.

Dubay, Thomas. *"… And You Are Christ's": The Charism of Virginity and the Celibate Life.* San Francisco: Ignatius Press, 1987.

Eberstadt, Mary. *Adam and Eve after the Pill: Paradoxes of the Sexual Revolution.* San Francisco: Ignatius Press, 2013.

Elliott, Peter J. *What God Has Joined …: The Sacramentality of Marriage.* New York: Alba House, 1990.

Esolen, Anthony. *Defending Marriage: Twelve Arguments for Sanity.* Charlotte, NC: Saint Benedict Press, 2014.

———. *Out of the Ashes: Rebuilding American Culture.* Washington, DC: Regnery Publishing, 2017.

———. *Sex and the Unreal City: The Demolition of the Western Mind.* San Francisco: Ignatius Press, 2020.

Fagerberg, David W. *Consecrating the World: On Mundane Liturgical Theology.* Kettering, OH: Angelico Press, 2016.

Favale, Abigail. *The Genesis of Gender: A Christian Theory.* San Francisco: Ignatius Press, 2022.

Finley, John DeSilva, ed. *Sexual Identity: The Harmony of Philosophy, Science, and Revelation.* Steubenville, OH: Emmaus Road Publishing, 2022.

Grabowski, John S. *Unraveling Gender: The Battle Over Sexual Difference.* Gastonia, NC: TAN Books, 2022.

Griffin, Carter. *Why Celibacy?: Reclaiming the Fatherhood of the Priest.* Steubenville, OH: Emmaus Road, 2019.

Guitton, Jean. *Feminine Fulfillment.* Translated by Paul J. Oligny. Chicago: Franciscan Herald Press, 1965.

Heid, Stefan. *Celibacy in the Early Church: The Beginnings of Obligatory Continence for Clerics in East and West.* San Francisco: Ignatius Press, 2001.

Heris, Charles V. *Spirituality of Love.* Translated by David Martin. St. Louis: B. Herder, 1965.

Houghton, Bryan. *Judith's Marriage.* Brooklyn, NY: Angelico Press, 2020.

Jeffery, Peter. *The Mystery of Christian Marriage.* Mahwah, NJ: Paulist Press, 2006.

Kelly, Christine M., ed. *The Enemy Within: Radical Feminism in the Christian Churches.* Milton Keynes, UK: Family Publications, 1992.

Kreeft, Peter. *Three Approaches to Abortion: A Thoughtful and Compassionate Guide to Today's Most Controversial Issue.* San Francisco: Ignatius Press, 2002.

———. *The Unaborted Socrates: A Dramatic Debate on the Issues Surrounding Abortion*. Downers Grove, IL: InterVarsity Press, 1983.

Kwasniewski, Peter, ed. *A Reader in Catholic Social Teaching from* Syllabus Errorum *to* Deus Caritas Est. Tacoma, WA: Cluny Media, 2017.

Lanzetta, Serafino M. *The Symphony of Truth: Theological Essays*. Waterloo, ON: Arouca Press, 2021.

Lawler, Leila Marie. *The Summa Domestica: Order and Wonder in Family Life*. 3 vols. Manchester, NH: Sophia Institute Press, 2021.

Leone, Don Pietro. *The Family Under Attack: A Philosophical and Theological Defense of Human Society*. Fitzwilliam, NH: Loreto Publications, 2015.

McAleer, G. J. *Ecstatic Morality and Sexual Politics: A Catholic and Antitotalitarian Theory of the Body*. New York: Fordham University Press, 2005.

Nichols, Aidan. *Christendom Awake: On Reenergizing the Church in Culture*. Grand Rapids: William B. Eerdmans, 1999.

Peter Damian. *The Book of Gomorrah and St. Peter Damian's Struggle against Ecclesiastical Corruption*. Translation and introduction by Matthew Cullinan Hoffman. New Braunfels, TX: Ite ad Thomam Books and Media, 2015.

Pitre, Brant. *Jesus the Bridegroom: The Greatest Love Story Ever Told*. New York: Image, 2014.

Quay, Paul M. *The Christian Meaning of Human Sexuality*. Expanded ed. San Francisco: Ignatius Press, 2017.

Robinson, Carol Jackson. *This Perverse Generation*. Waterloo, ON: Arouca Press, 2020.

Smith, Janet. Humanae Vitae, *a Generation Later*. Washington, DC: Catholic University of America Press, 1991.

Smith, Janet, ed. *Why* Humanae Vitae *Is Still Right*. San Francisco: Ignatius Press, 2018.

———. *Why* Humanae Vitae *Was Right: A Reader*. San Francisco: Ignatius Press, 1993.

Stabińska, Jadwiga. *For Their Sake I Consecrate Myself: Sister Maria Bernadette of the Cross, Benedictine Nun of Perpetual Adoration, 1927–1963*. Translated by Justyna Krukowska. Waterloo, ON: Arouca Press, 2022.

Steichen, Donna. *Ungodly Rage: The Hidden Face of Catholic Feminism*. San Francisco: Ignatius Press, 1991.

Stickler, Alfons Maria. *The Case for Clerical Celibacy: Its Historical Development and Theological Foundations*. San Francisco: Ignatius Press, 1995.

Storck, Thomas. *Foundations of a Catholic Political Order*. 2nd ed. Waterloo, ON: Arouca Press, 2022.

Thibon, Gustave. *What God Has Joined Together: An Essay on Love*. Translated by A. Gordon Smith. London: Hollis & Carter, 1952.

Vitz, Paul C., ed. *The Complementarity of Women and Men: Philosophy, Theology, Psychology & Art*. Washington, DC: Catholic University of America, 2021.

———. *Faith of the Fatherless: The Psychology of Atheism*. 2nd ed. San Francisco: Ignatius Press, 2013.

van Zeller, Hubert. *Letters to a Soul*. Stamullen, Ireland: Cenacle Press, 2022.

———. *We Work While the Light Lasts*. Stamullen, Ireland: Cenacle Press, 2022.

von Hildebrand, Alice. *The Dark Night of the Body: Why Reverence Comes First in Intimate Relations*. Fort Collins, CO: Roman Catholic Books, 2013.

———. *Man and Woman: A Divine Invention*. Ave Maria, FL: Sapientia Press, 2002.

von Hildebrand, Dietrich. *Liturgy and Personality*. Steubenville, OH: The Hildebrand Project, 2016.

Walshe, Sebastian. *Understanding Marriage and Family: A Catholic Perspective*. Waterloo, ON: Arouca Press, 2020.

Williams, Thomas D. *Who Is My Neighbor? Personalism and the Foundations of Human Rights*. Washington, DC: Catholic University of America Press, 2005.

Wojtyła, Karol. *Love and Responsibility*. Translated by Grzegorz Ignatik. Boston: Pauline Books & Media, 2013.

Wyszyński, Stefan. *Love and Social Justice: Reflections on Society*. Translated by Filip Mazurczak. Waterloo, ON: Arouca Press, 2021.

Index

Index

About the Author

Peter A. Kwasniewski holds a B.A. in liberal arts from Thomas Aquinas College and an M.A. and Ph.D. in philosophy from the Catholic University of America, with a specialization in the thought of St. Thomas Aquinas. After teaching at the International Theological Institute in Austria, he joined the founding team of Wyoming Catholic College, where he taught theology, philosophy, music, and art history and directed the choir and schola until 2018. Today, he is a full-time writer and public speaker whose work is seen on websites and in periodicals such as *New Liturgical Movement, OnePeterFive, Rorate Caeli, Catholic Family News,* and *Latin Mass Magazine.* Dr. Kwasniewski has published extensively in academic and popular venues on sacramental and liturgical theology, the history and aesthetics of music, Catholic social teaching, and issues in the contemporary Church. He has written or edited more than twenty books, and his work has been translated into at least eighteen languages. For more information, visit his website: www.peterkwasniewski.com.

Sophia Institute

Sophia Institute is a nonprofit institution that seeks to nurture the spiritual, moral, and cultural life of souls and to spread the gospel of Christ in conformity with the authentic teachings of the Roman Catholic Church.

Sophia Institute Press fulfills this mission by offering translations, reprints, and new publications that afford readers a rich source of the enduring wisdom of mankind.

Sophia Institute also operates the popular online resource CatholicExchange.com. *Catholic Exchange* provides world news from a Catholic perspective as well as daily devotionals and articles that will help readers to grow in holiness and live a life consistent with the teachings of the Church.

In 2013, Sophia Institute launched Sophia Institute for Teachers to renew and rebuild Catholic culture through service to Catholic education. With the goal of nurturing the spiritual, moral, and cultural life of souls, and an abiding respect for the role and work of teachers, we strive to provide materials and programs that are at once enlightening to the mind and ennobling to the heart; faithful and complete, as well as useful and practical.

Sophia Institute gratefully recognizes the Solidarity Association for preserving and encouraging the growth of our apostolate over the course of many years. Without their generous and timely support, this book would not be in your hands.

www.SophiaInstitute.com
www.CatholicExchange.com
www.SophiaInstituteforTeachers.org

Sophia Institute Press® is a registered trademark of Sophia Institute.
Sophia Institute is a tax-exempt institution as defined by the Internal Revenue Code, Section 501(c)(3). Tax ID 22-2548708.